IMAGES
of America

LAWRENCE TOWNSHIP REVISITED

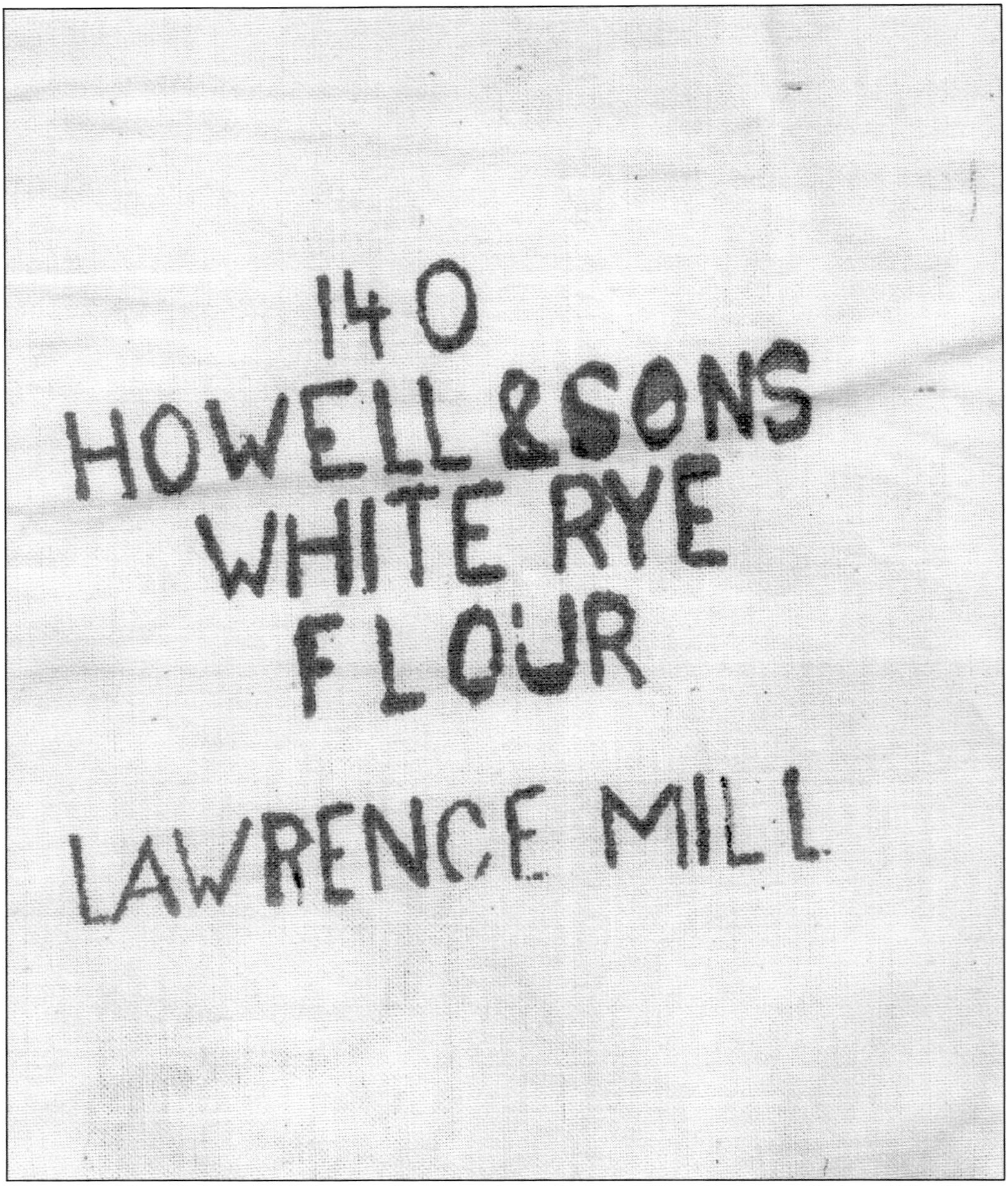

This small flour bag, pictured around 1900, is from the Howell and Sons Mill. A mill had been in operation, under various owners, at what is now the intersection of Youngs and Bakers Basin Roads since the 1700s. This area was likely chosen due to its location on the Assunpink Creek, as water was a necessity for millwork. The Howells were the last owners of the mill, from 1905 until it was shut down in 1920. (Courtesy of Lawrence Township Archives.)

On the Cover: The Lawrence Volunteer Fire Association is seen in front of their first firehouse, around 1914. The company was founded in 1914 and built the original firehouse, a wooden-framed garage, that same year. A new brick building was constructed in the 1920s. The company is now known as the Lawrence Road Fire Company. (Courtesy of Lawrence Township Archives.)

IMAGES
of America

LAWRENCE TOWNSHIP REVISITED

Lawrence Historical Society

ARCADIA
PUBLISHING

ISBN 978-0-7385-9814-7

Published by Arcadia Publishing
Charleston, South Carolina

Printed in the United States of America

Library of Congress Control Number: 2012945087

For all general information, please contact Arcadia Publishing:
Telephone 843-853-2070
Fax 843-853-0044
E-mail sales@arcadiapublishing.com
For customer service and orders:
Toll-Free 1-888-313-2665

Visit us on the Internet at www.arcadiapublishing.com

In memory of Winona Nash and Robert Immordino for their tireless dedication to the preservation of Lawrence Township history

Contents

Acknowledgments		6
Introduction		7
1.	Business	9
2.	Community and Military Service	27
3.	Emergency Services	39
4.	Houses and Neighborhoods	53
5.	Houses of Worship	73
6.	Parks and Recreation	81
7.	People and Families	87
8.	Schools	95
9.	Transportation	109
10.	Weather, Etc.	117
Bibliography		126
About the Organization		127

Acknowledgments

The Lawrence Historical Society would like to thank Laura Nawrocik and Ashley Morris for selecting these photographs, as well as researching and writing this volume. Thanks also go to Janet Bickel for photograph selection and editing, and to Lorraine Nawrocik for editing, layout, and typesetting.

The bulk of the photographs are from the Lawrence Township Archives, and we are very thankful to have a township dedicated to keeping such an archive. Unless otherwise noted, all images are courtesy of the Lawrence Township Archives.

We are very grateful to Fred Vereen, Kathleen Topley, and the Mershon Family Association for sharing their photograph collections as well as their recollections about the history of Lawrence. *The Lawrence Ledger*, Laurin McCracken, and Rider University's Moore Library Special Collections and University Archives were also generous to allow us to print their photographs.

We would also like to thank the following individuals for lending a hand as consultants on content: Vicki Chirco from the Delaware and Raritan State Park, Lea Kahn from *The Lawrence Ledger*, Jacqueline Haun from The Lawrenceville School, Julia Telonidis from Rider University, Jane Fetter, and Dennis Waters.

INTRODUCTION

The earliest recorded sale of land in what would become the village of Maidenhead occurred in 1690, when John Brearley purchased a plot of land that became Spring Grove Farm on Lewisville Road. The earliest settlers bore surnames that would remain common among the influential figures of township history, such as Brearley, Phillips, Smith, Mershon, and Hunt. By 1697, the village was large enough to incorporate as a town, and on February 20th of that year, Maidenhead Township was created in Burlington County. In 1700, the township was split in two, with the western half becoming Hopewell Township. By 1714, Burlington County also had become large enough to split, and the northern section, including Maidenhead, became Hunterdon County.

The town changed its name in 1816 after citizens, led by Maidenhead Academy (The Lawrenceville School) founder Rev. Isaac Brown, petitioned the State Legislature to reconsider what some deemed to be an inappropriate and morally offensive name for a town. On January 24, 1816, the Legislature responded by officially changing the name to Lawrence Township, in honor of Capt. James Lawrence, a naval hero from the War of 1812. Lawrence died in battle, and his dying words, "Don't give up the ship," became the motto of the US Navy.

The final two changes to the town's governmental affiliations and borders occurred in the 19th century. One came in 1838, when Mercer County was created out of parts of surrounding counties, including the southern part of Hunterdon that included Lawrence Township. Fifty years later, the township's current borders were set after the Millham portion in the southern part of town seceded. Millham lasted six years as an independent entity before being annexed by the City of Trenton in 1888.

The most significant event to take place in the township's early history was the delaying action of Col. Edward Hand at the Shabakunk Creek on January 2, 1777. Hand's troops skirmished with British reinforcements marching toward Trenton and successfully delayed the British long enough to prevent them from crossing the Shabakunk. This allowed the American army to leave Trenton at night and surprise the British troops at the Battle of Princeton on January 3, 1777.

Following the Revolutionary War, the township settled into a relatively quiet time; while it was slowly growing in terms of population, it remained primarily a farming community with an active village in the center of town. Two key events did take place in town during the century; these were the founding of Maidenhead Academy and the building of the Delaware and Raritan Canal.

Maidenhead Academy was opened by Rev. Isaac Brown in 1810. Brown was the minister at the Presbyterian Church of Maidenhead and sought to accomplish two main goals with the founding of the school: to address a need for a classical education facility in the area and to earn a steady income to support his family. Brown incorporated the school in 1808 and, after heavy advertising in regional newspapers, the school had an enrollment of 25 students by 1820. The name of the school was changed to The Lawrenceville School to match the change that was made in the township's appellation. Following the death of his wife and son, Brown sold the school to Alexander Phillips in 1834.

The Delaware and Raritan Canal was completed in 1834, connecting the Delaware River at Trenton with the Raritan River in New Brunswick. The canal was a major transportation route for both shipping goods and travelers, particularly in the 1860s and 1870s. The village of Port Mercer developed along the canal, near the Port Mercer bridge tender's house. Warehouses, an inn, taverns, a post office and a general store were among the businesses that called Port Mercer home, all serving both travelers and workers who lived in the area.

The canal represented the first major transportation route through the township, but it was not the last. Railroads, trolley lines, and major highways would also be built over the next 150 years, bringing new neighborhoods with them.

The railroad was the next form of transportation to come to Lawrence, with Lawrence Station near the Hamilton Township border being the hub of rail activity. The Camden and Amboy rail line was opened in September 1833, followed by the Pennsylvania Railroad in 1863. The latter is still used today by Amtrak and New Jersey Transit as part of the Northeast Corridor Line. Like Port Mercer, Lawrence Station developed with the railroads, and rail workers joined farmers in calling the area home. A mill, a store, and an ice plant were among the businesses that operated in the area.

Trolleys were key to the development of the suburbs in the southern part of the township at the turn of the century. Two lines, the Trenton and Mercer Traction Company and the Princeton-Trenton Traction Company, operated lines that ran along Route 206 and through the village of Lawrenceville to connect Trenton and Princeton. The main impact for Lawrence was the ease of access to the trolleys from the Eggerts Crossing, Slackwood, Colonial Lakelands, and Eldridge Park neighborhoods, as well as along Route 206 on both the Lawrence Road and Main Street ends. Not surprisingly, the areas became popular for new-home construction and business development.

Finally, the automobiles and highways helped complete Lawrence's transformation into a suburban center, with the opening of the Lincoln Highway (Route 206) in 1913, the expansion of Brunswick Pike (Route 1) into a superhighway in 1930, the building of the Trenton Freeway in 1955, and the construction of Interstates 95 and 295 in 1973. All of these roads made Lawrence an attractive location for homeownership, as it was now easy to commute to work in another town, particularly the city of Trenton. It is worth noting that the largest subdivision in the town's history was completed in an area with easy access to both Routes 1 and 206. The Norgate, Nassau, and Pine Knoll Estates almost doubled the township's population between 1950 and 1970. Businesses also flourished, specifically along Brunswick Pike, as roadside locations gave customers easy access to their stores and offices.

Predictably, as more people moved into parts of town with the addition of new transportation options, new social organizations, schools, religious centers, and community centers developed along with the new subdivisions. The photographs that follow illustrate the journey Lawrence Township has taken from an agricultural to a suburban community during the 19th and 20th centuries.

One

Business

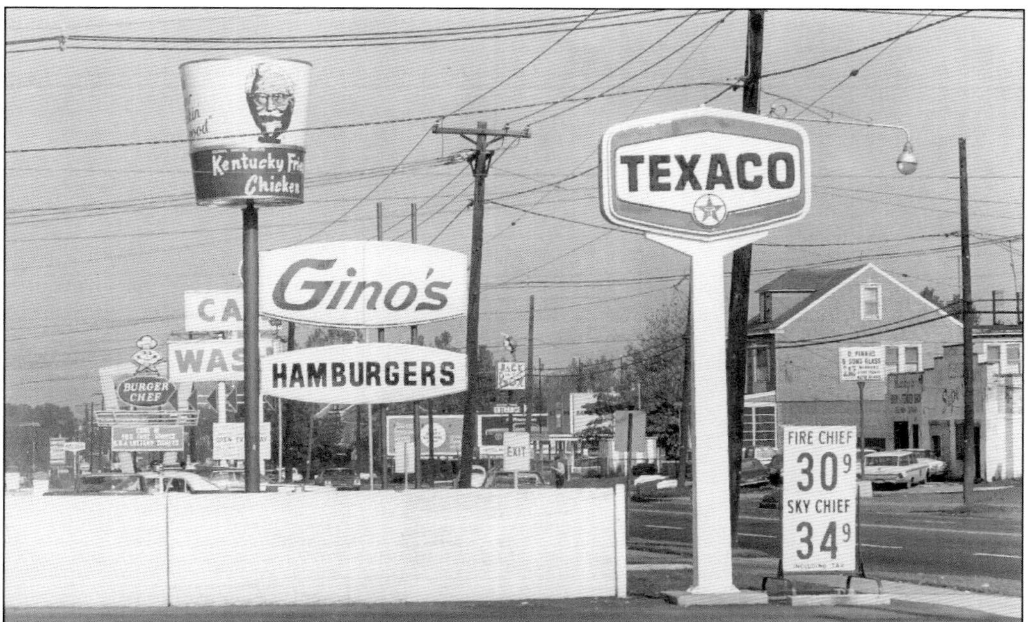

A view of Princeton Avenue in 1972 shows one of Lawrence's main business areas in the southern part of the township. The neighborhood near the Trenton border has been densely populated since the 1800s, and a variety of businesses developed to serve the residents. The Capitol Car Wash is one of the oldest businesses in the township, having opened in the early 1960s. (Courtesy of Laurin McCracken.)

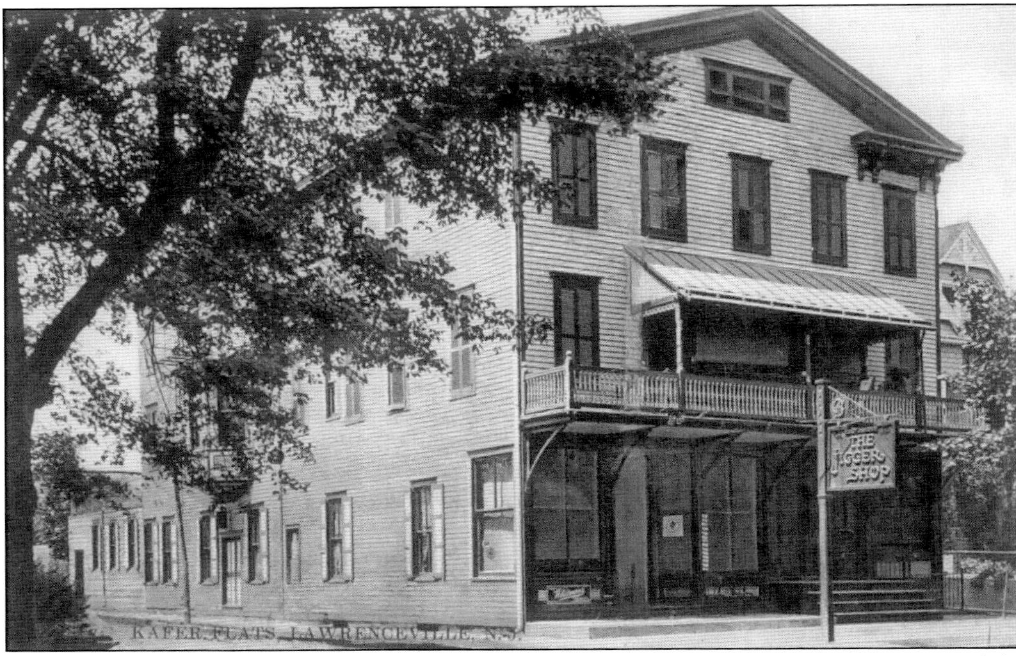

A c. 1907 postcard shows the Jigger Shop, which was located in the Kafer Flats section of the village of Lawrenceville, where T.J.'s Pizza and Pasta now stands. The shop was originally located on the corner of Phillips Avenue and Main Street. The shop moved to a new location near Craven Lane sometime around 1915.

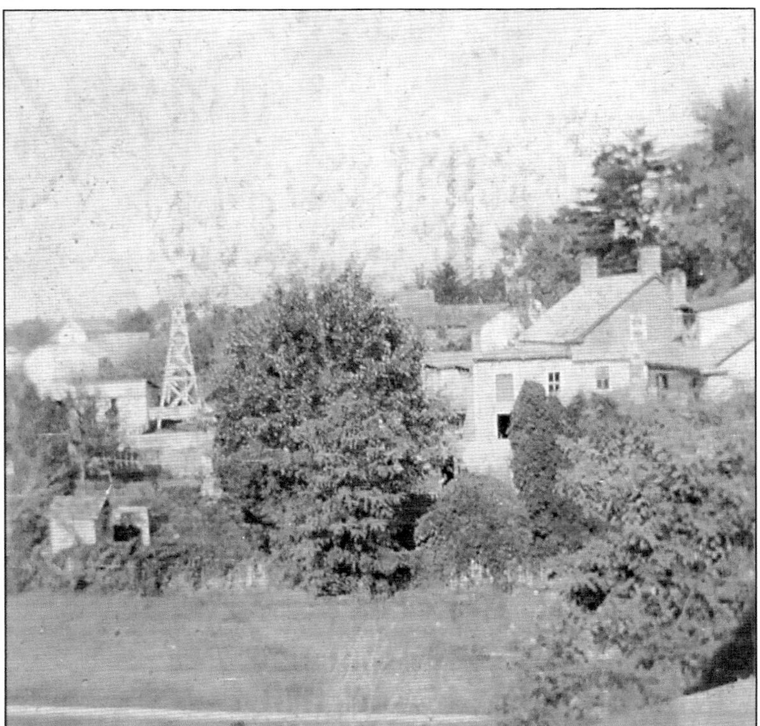

Applegate's Livery, shown here around 1880, included barns, grazing fields, and stables for the horses and wagons used by the business. The livery was a critical business, as Applegate's would have been used to deliver coal, food crops, and other farm and household supplies to the residents and businesses in town. In addition to the delivery service, the livery made drivers and wagons available for hire for out of town travel. (Courtesy of Kathleen Topley.)

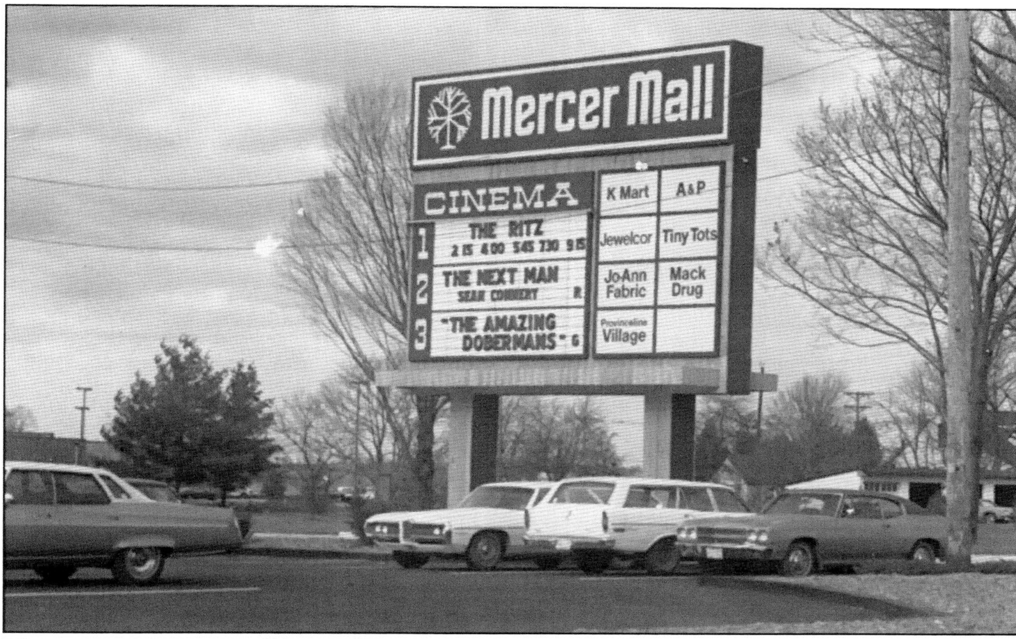

The year 1976 saw a mall boom for Lawrence Township, with the opening of the first stores in both the Mercer Mall and Quaker Bridge Mall. The Mercer Mall highway sign from the fall of 1976 shows one long-gone feature of the centers: each had a movie theater. The Eric Theatre operated at Lawrence Shopping Center, the General Cinema Theatre was at the Mercer Mall, and the AMC was at Quaker Bridge Mall.

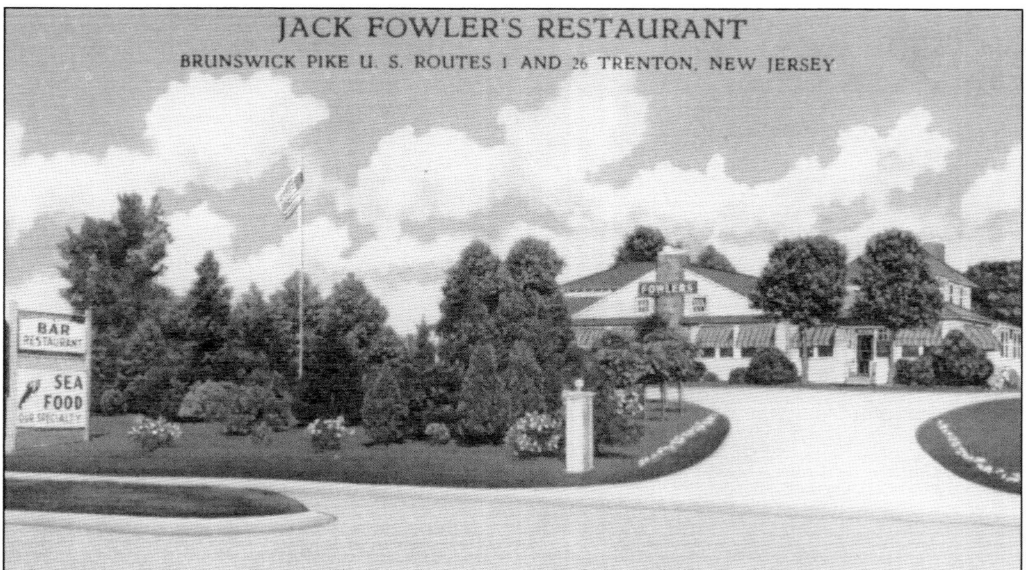

A 1948 postcard shows Jack Fowler's Restaurant, which was later torn down to make way for the Mercer Mall. The entrance to the restaurant was approximately where the sign for the mall is today. The postcard notes the location as Brunswick Pike, Routes 1 and 26. In addition to having two route numbers and the local name of Brunswick Pike, the road was also known to the post office as R.D. 4.

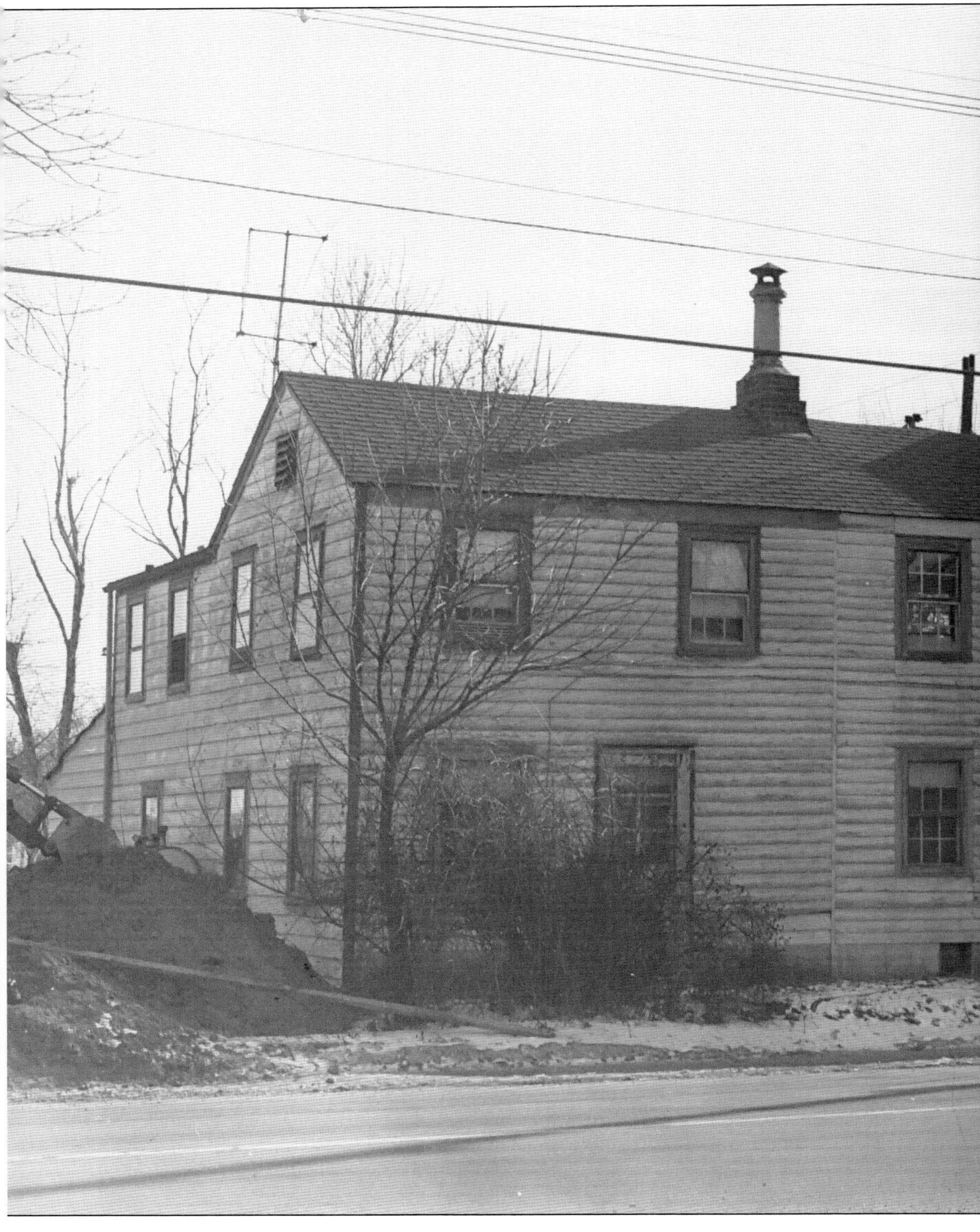

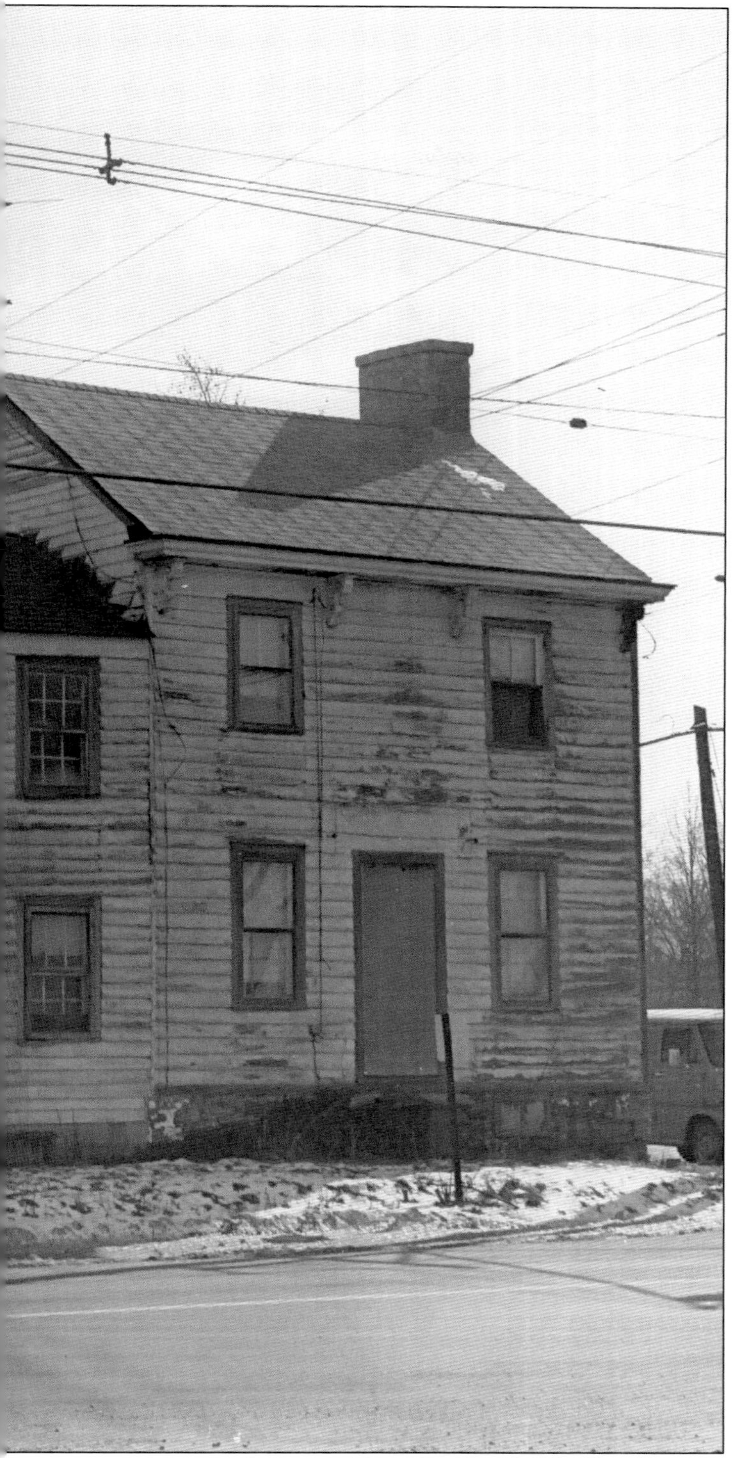

Drew House was once owned by the Brearley family and operated as a tavern by Jonathan Brearley. Taverns and inns were plentiful along Princeton Pike, which operated as a branch toll road from Trenton to New Brunswick from the early 1800s. The road served as a parallel branch of Brunswick Pike for local traffic. The house was a private residence before National State Bank purchased the property at the corner of Princeton Pike and Franklin Corner Road and tore the structure down shortly after this 1972 photograph was taken. Despite several name changes, the location is still occupied by a bank.

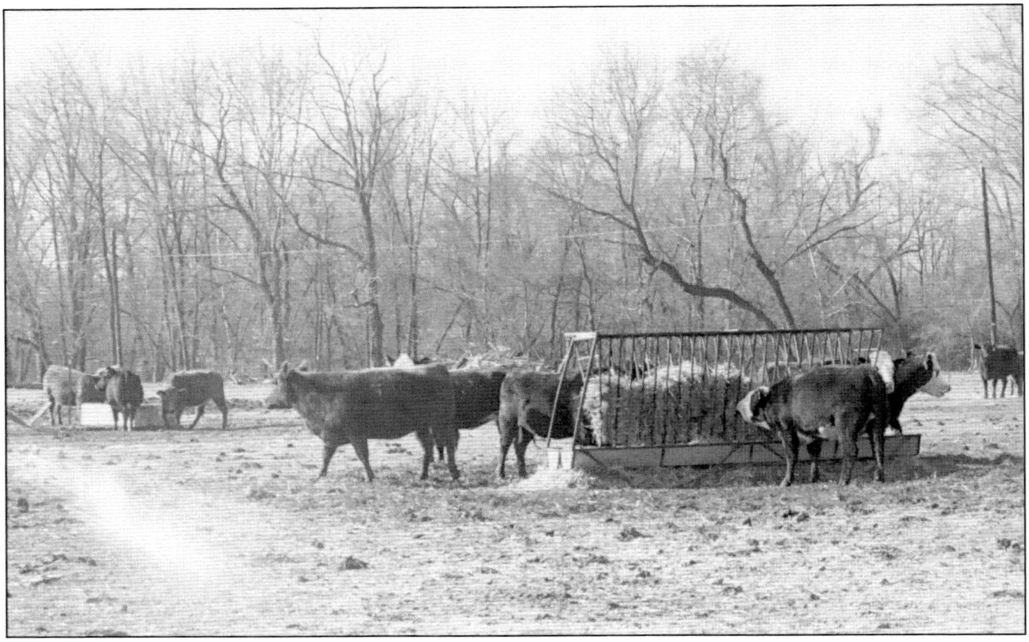

One of the more uncommon businesses to call Lawrence Township home was the Vacarro Beefalo Farm, which operated on the corner of Province Line and Quakerbridge Roads near the Port Mercer Canal House in the 1970s and early 1980s. A beefalo is a hybrid of domestic cattle and bison that was intended as a lower-fat, lower-cholesterol alternative to beef.

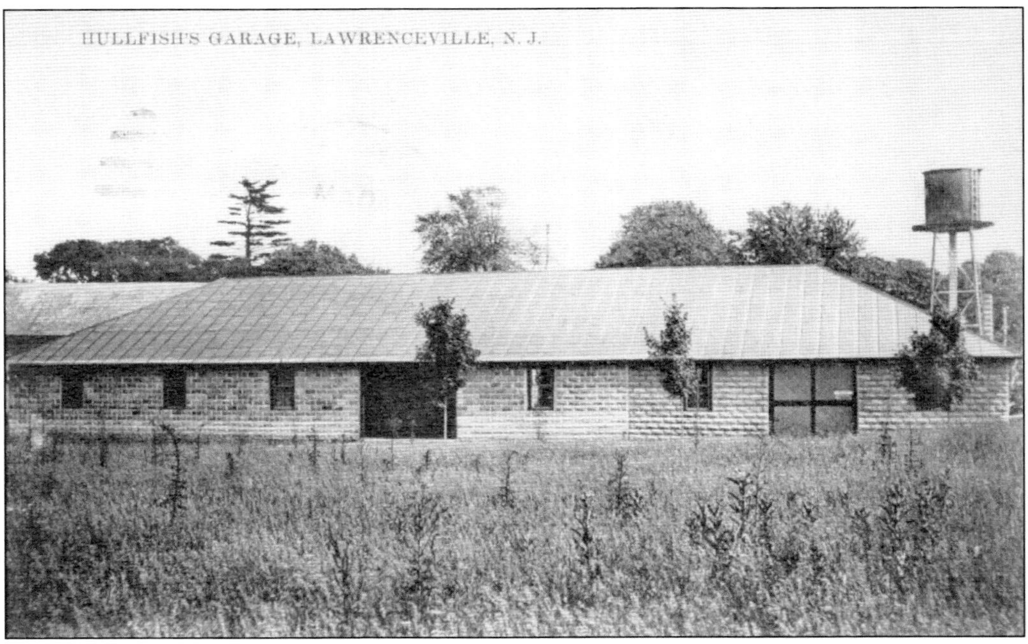

A postcard shows Hullfish's Garage, around 1912. The garage was located at the rear of Bailey's Market and the post office, both of which faced Main Street. The garage, built by James Hullfish, was in the vicinity of an apartment complex that currently fronts on George Street. After the post office was built on the Bentley property, the garage was no longer visible from Main Street.

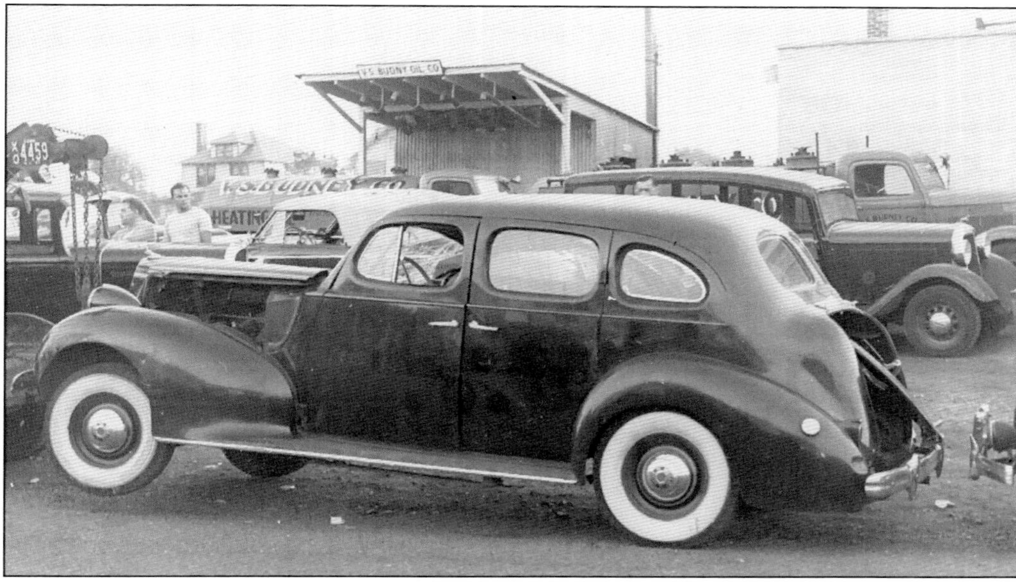

Vincent Budny opened a gas station on the corner of Cherry Tree Lane and Brunswick Pike in the 1930s. V.S. Budny Oil Co. also delivered home heating oil and had a large garage for repairing vehicles. Following an accident in 1941, this Packard was towed to the shop for some necessary bodywork. The Budnys changed the name to Budny Tire by the 1950s and had closed the shop by the mid-1980s.

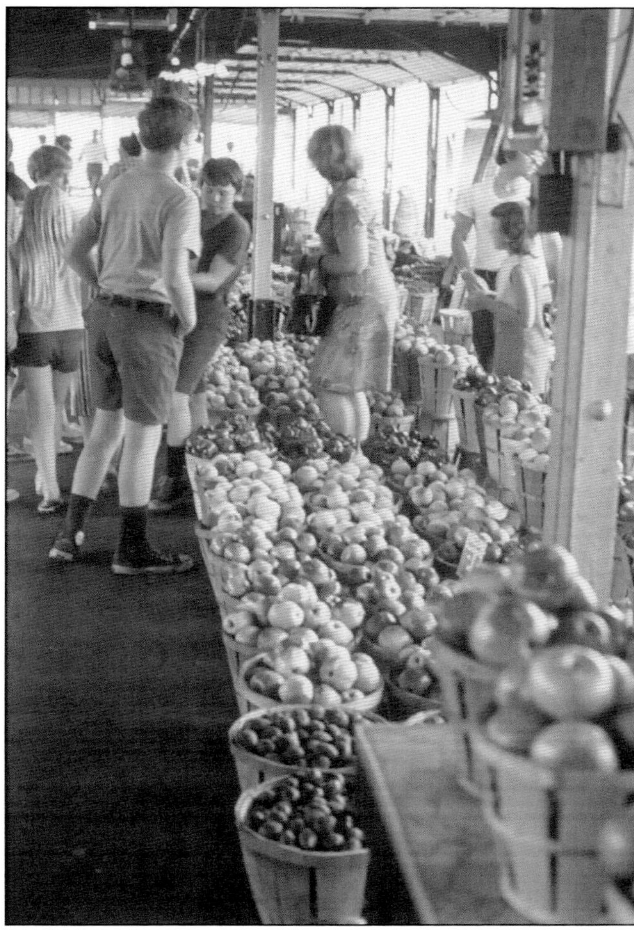

Shoppers look over produce at the Trenton Farmers' Market, around 1970. The market at the corner of Spruce Street and Princeton Avenue was originally located on Warren Street in the city, moving to Lawrence Township in the late 1940s. The market was founded to provide space for rural farmers to bring their products into the city and has operated under the Trenton Market Growers' Cooperative since 1939.

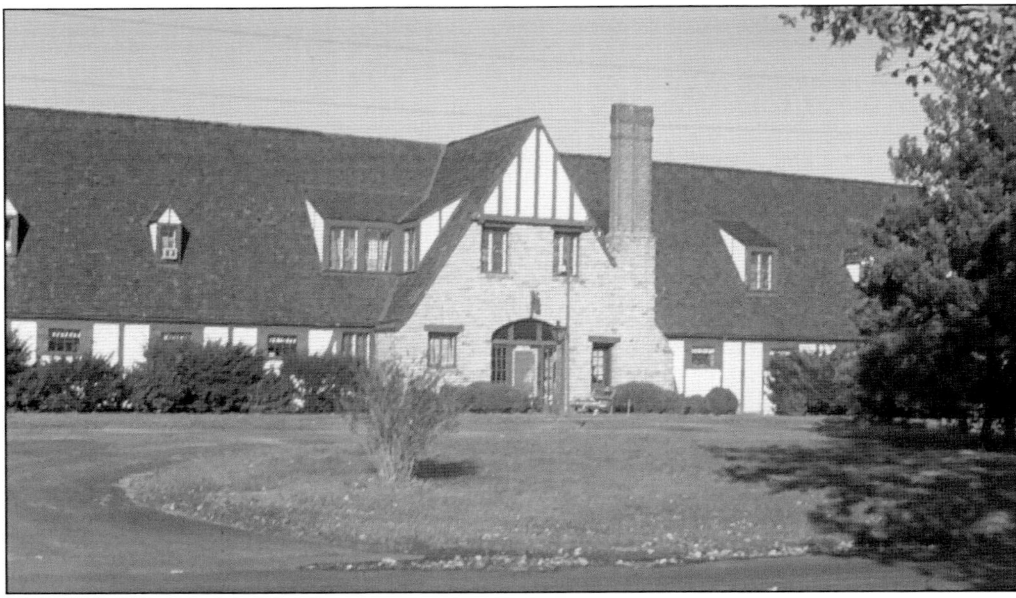

Manning Wayside Furniture Shop was located on the southbound side of Lawrence Road (Route 206), between the Lawrence Township Municipal Building and Morris Hall. The shop was demolished in 1972 to make way for the construction on Interstate 295. Below, the shop can be seen in the background with the stone wall that used to be in front of the Municipal Building in the foreground. Behind the sign for the furniture shop, to the right of the tree, are some houses that were also demolished as part of the highway construction. The store was known for its distinctive Tudor style.

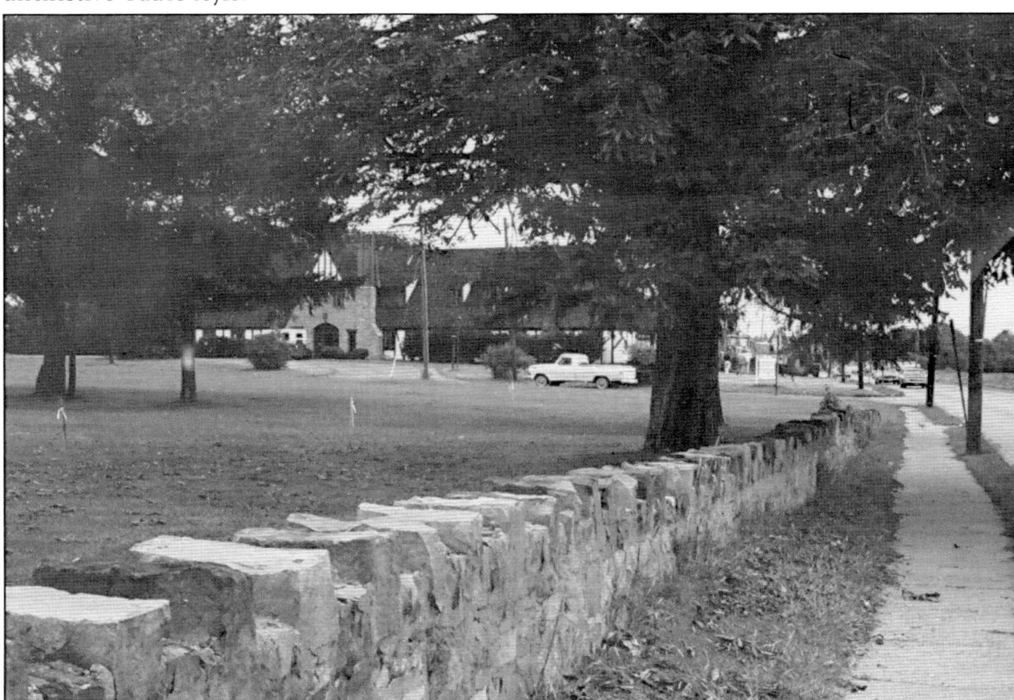

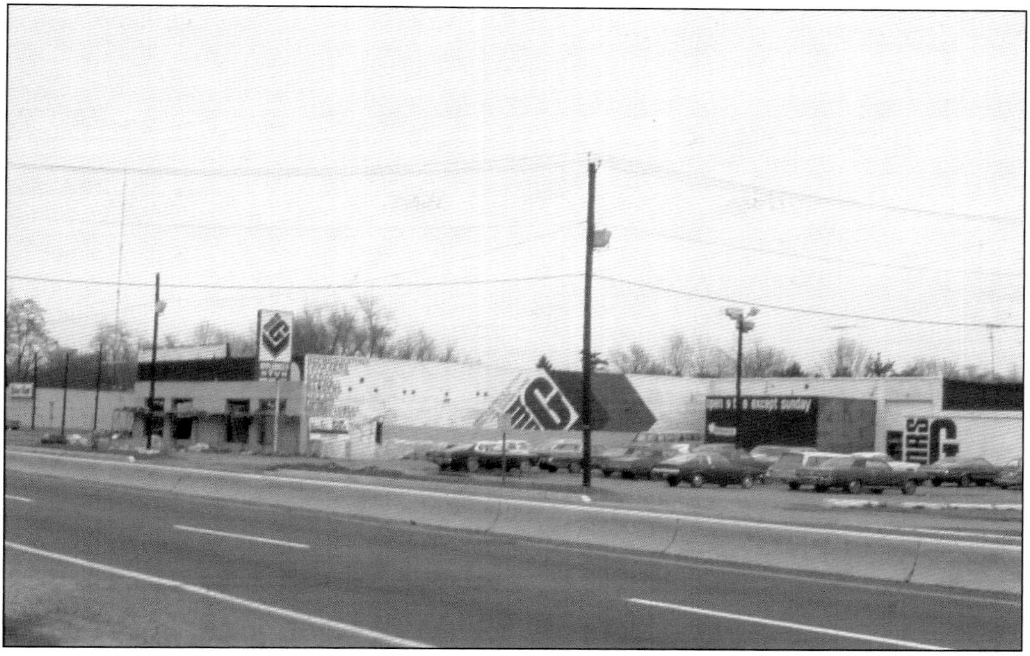

Mrs. G's appliance store has called the corner of Route 1 and Bakers Basin Road home for almost 40 years, making it one of Lawrence's oldest businesses. Originally a plumbing supply store when it opened on East State Street in Trenton in 1935, Mrs. G's moved to Olden Avenue in Ewing, and then to Lawrence after the Ewing location was leveled in a gas-pipe explosion.

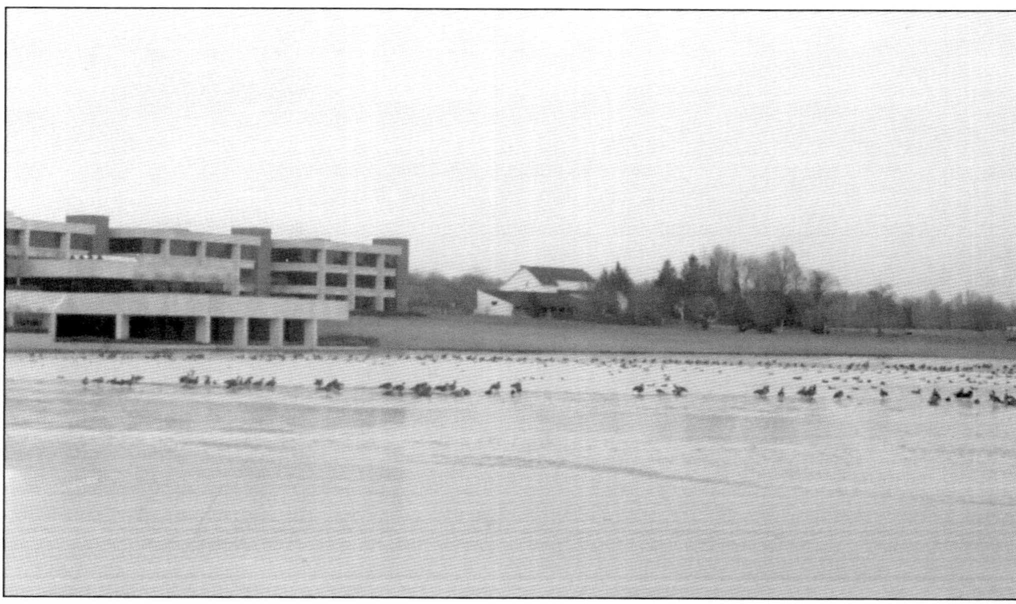

Bristol-Myers Squibb, known then as E.R. Squibb, moved its headquarters to Lawrence in 1971. A view of the campus in December 1976 shows the office and lab buildings to the left and an old farmhouse to the right. A lake in front was built as part of the construction. The land was formerly a 200-plus-acre farm.

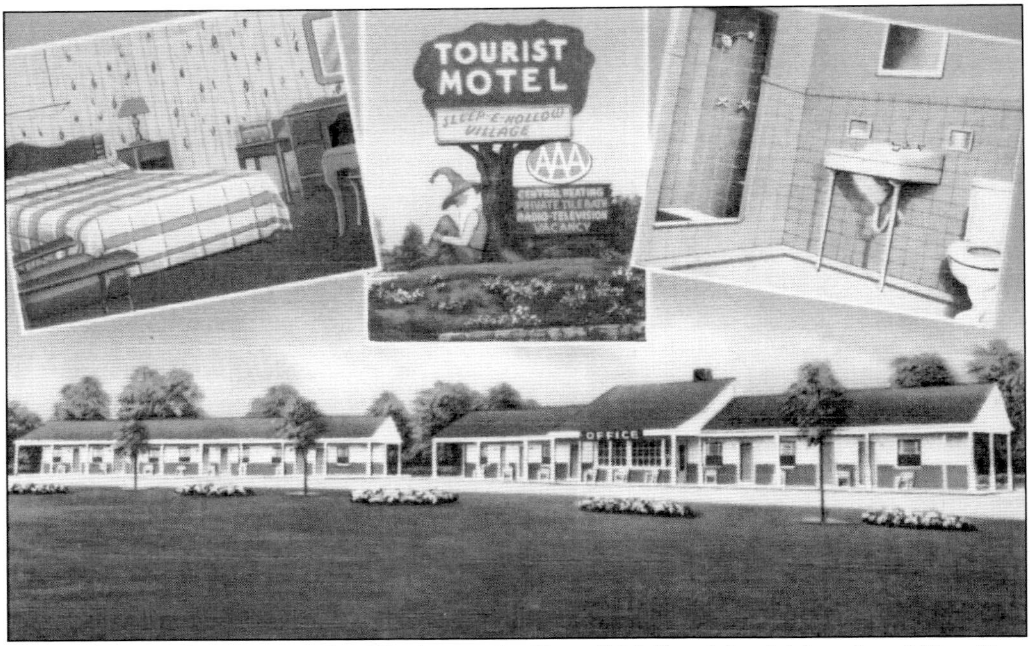

Postcards from the 1940s and 1950s depict the Sleep-E-Hollow Motel (above) and Pine Tree Cottages (below). Along with the Trent and Mount Motels, the motels were popular places to stay for visitors to Mercer County. All four were conveniently located on Route 1 and boasted of modern amenities, such as tiled bathrooms and in-room radios. Business travelers, tourists, and the families of students at area colleges and boarding schools were all frequent guests. Pine Tree Cottages offered spacious accommodations for larger families or long-term stays. By the end of the 20th century, only the Sleep-E-Hollow remained in operation, Pine Tree Cottages having been demolished in favor of new construction.

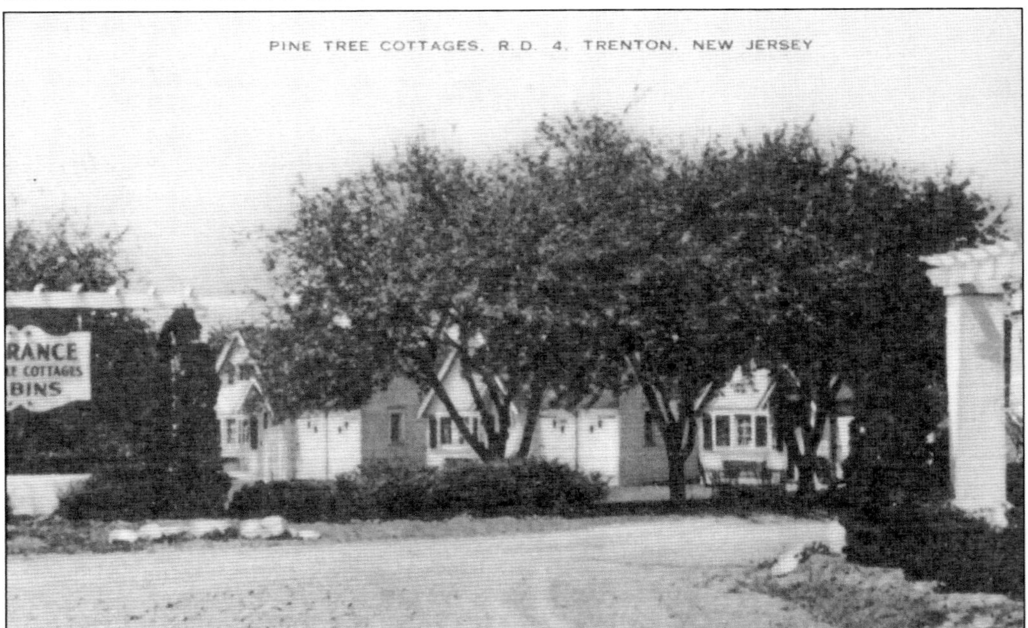

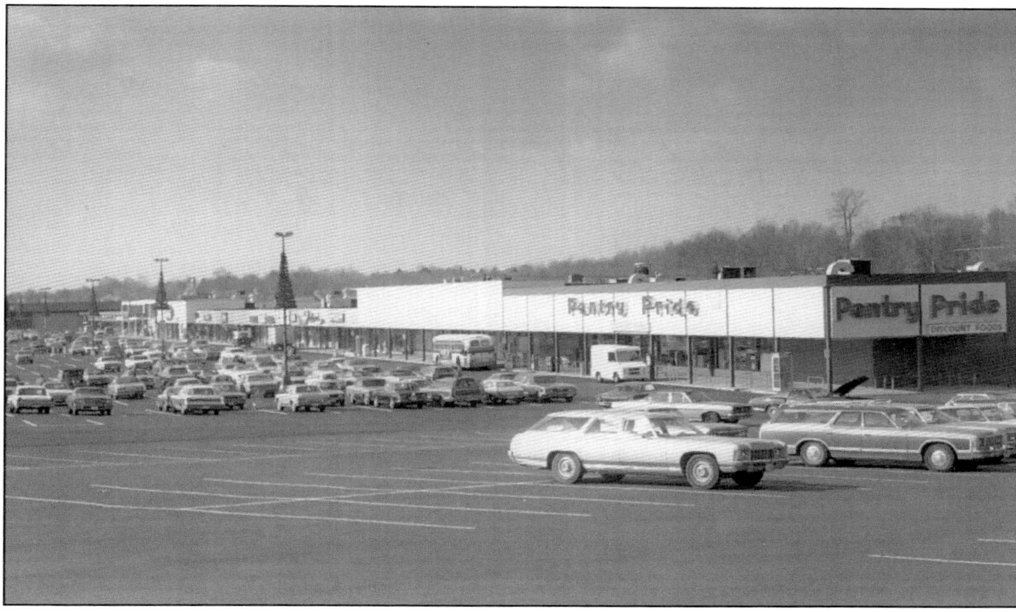

An expansion to the Lawrence Shopping Center was completed in late 1975, bringing more store space to the Princeton Pike end of the center. The initial set of stores was opened in the fall of 1960. The Pantry Pride grocery store (seen here around 1976) was an original tenant, having been known as Food Fair in the 1960s. The center underwent more expansion in the late 1970s, adding stores near Brunswick Pike.

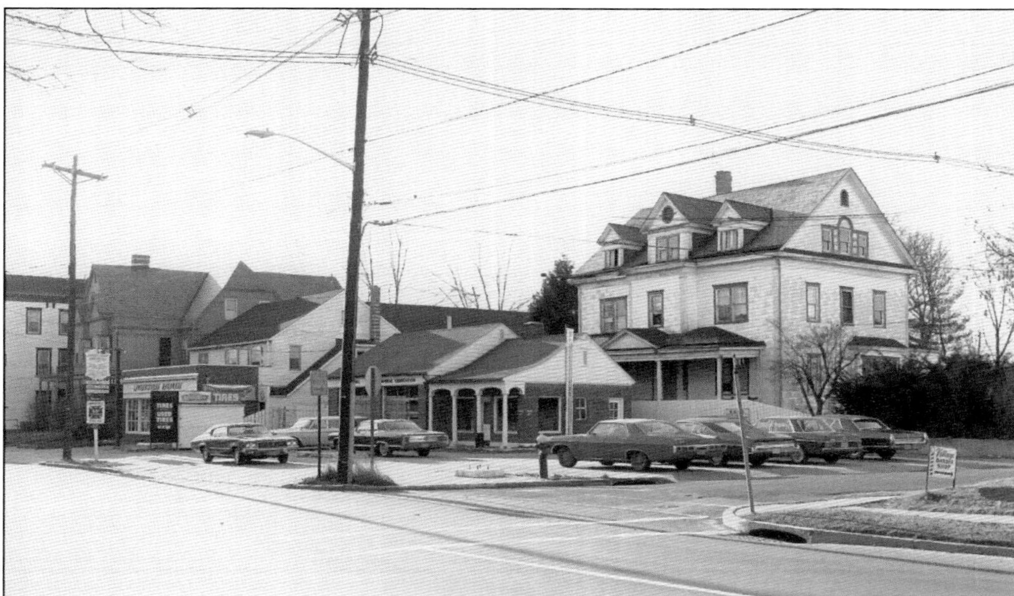
The village of Lawrenceville was still the main center of town in 1972. Despite being part of the larger Township of Lawrence, the village has maintained its unique identity along Main Street, where businesses are within walking distance of The Lawrenceville School and residential areas. A barbershop, bank, and several restaurants still call the business strip home. (Courtesy of Laurin McCracken.)

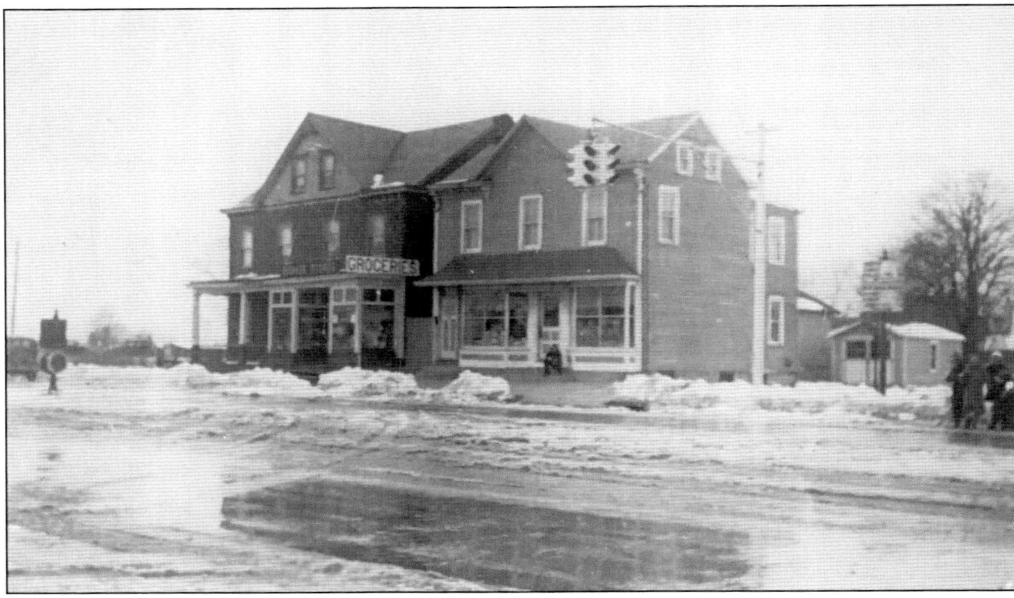

The Slackwood area, seen in November 1939, was once one of the busiest areas of town. The neighborhood was home to several industries and was one of the first concentrated suburbs of Trenton. Above, the intersection of Slack Avenue and Brunswick Pike shows William Jones's general store (left) and Benson's feed-and-hardware store (right). Both stores faced Brunswick Pike. Below, Bailey's Lumber and Millwork on Slack Avenue, next to the Slackwood firehouse, was one of the larger employers in the neighborhood. The area is named for Joseph Slack and William Wood, two real estate investors who owned most of the neighborhood land in the late 1800s. They developed the area and were the original owners of many of the businesses, including the general and feed stores.

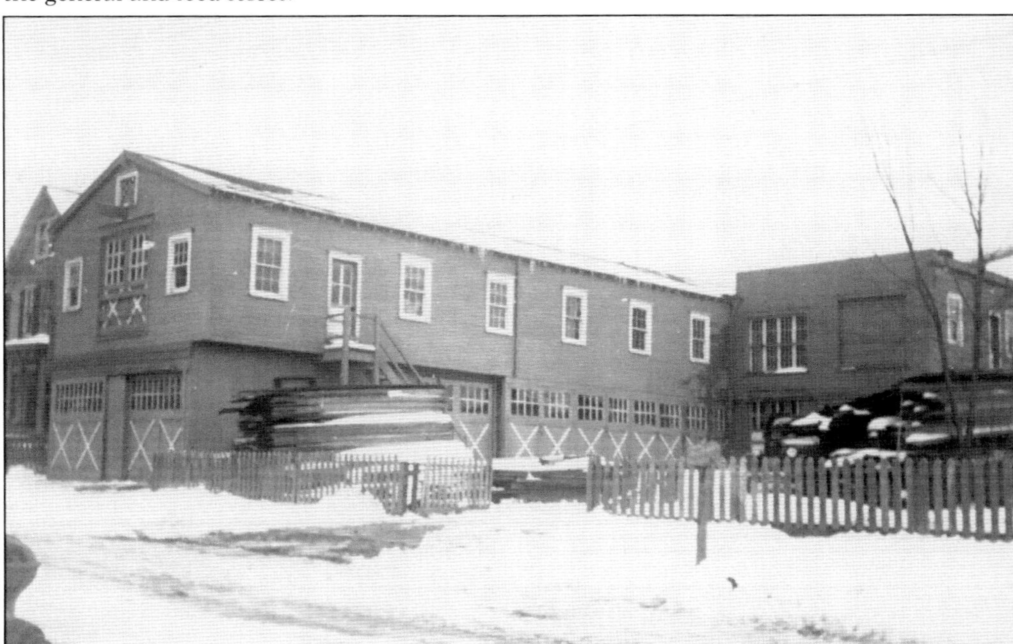

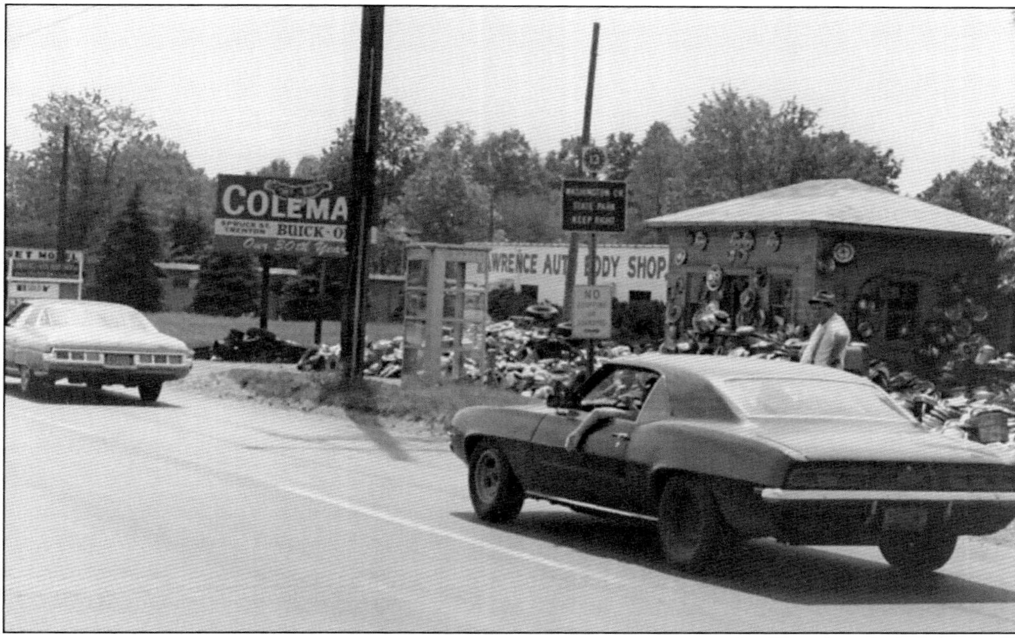

Travelers along Route 1 would often see the "Hub Cap Man" (right, in the hat) sitting by the road, across from the New Jersey DMV complex, waiting for new inventory. A public phone booth was also on the property and a motel and body shop can be seen in the background. The area has been redeveloped and now includes restaurants, a hotel, and car rental shop.

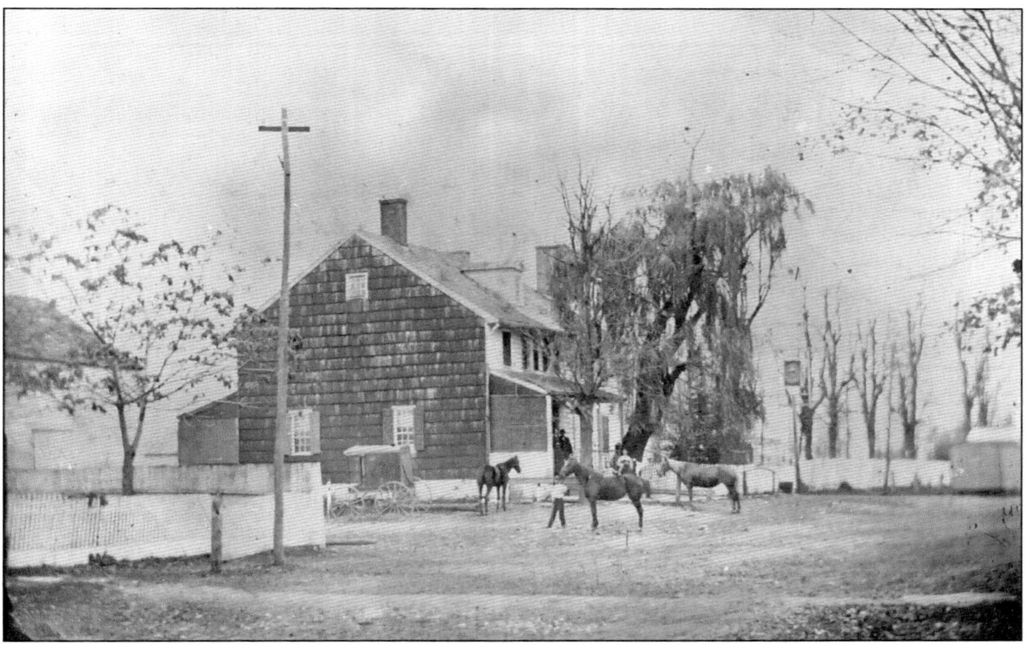

John Moore's Tavern on Main Street, photographed around 1865, was where township meetings were held for many years. It was not until the 20th century that the township rented a building on Phillips Avenue in which to conduct their business. The tavern, also known as "The Cock and Bull Tavern," was built around 1804.

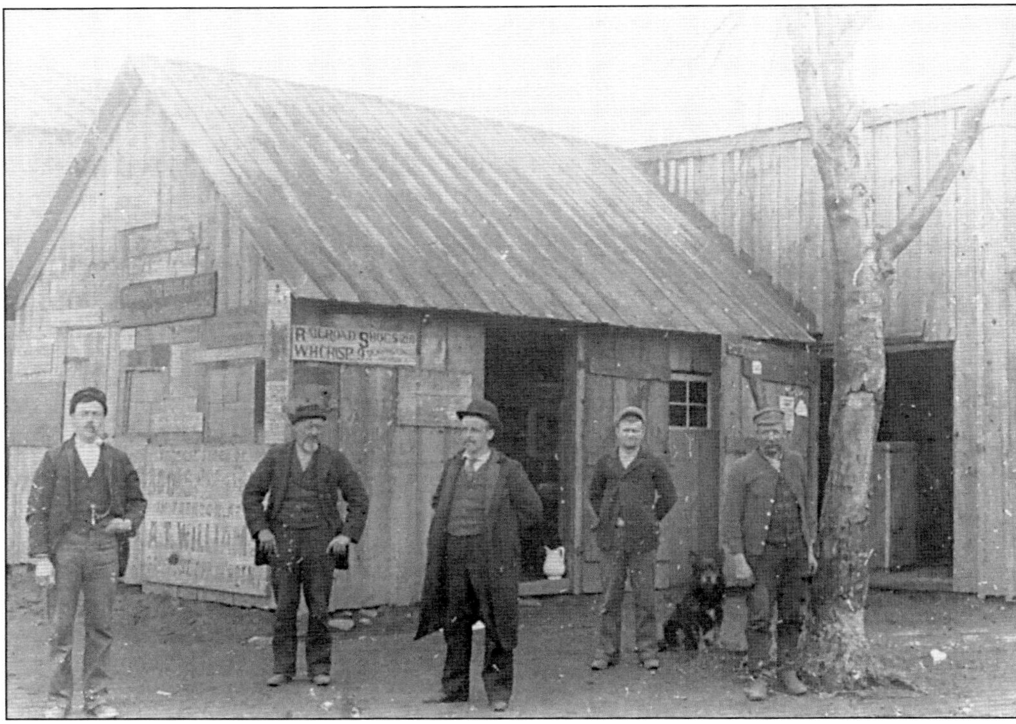

Mason's Blacksmith Shop was located at the corner of Brunswick Avenue and Cherry Tree Lane. This c. 1900 image shows workers at the shop, from left to right, Herbert Nash, William Walton, James Nash, Paul Grant, and Charles J. Carr. By November 1939 (below), the shop had progressed with the times and was out of the horseshoe business. The original wooden barn was replaced with a concrete service station and garage for automobiles. The Mason Brothers Garage serviced cars from the time of the Model T until the end of the century. The garage was torn down in the early 2000s to make way for an apartment complex.

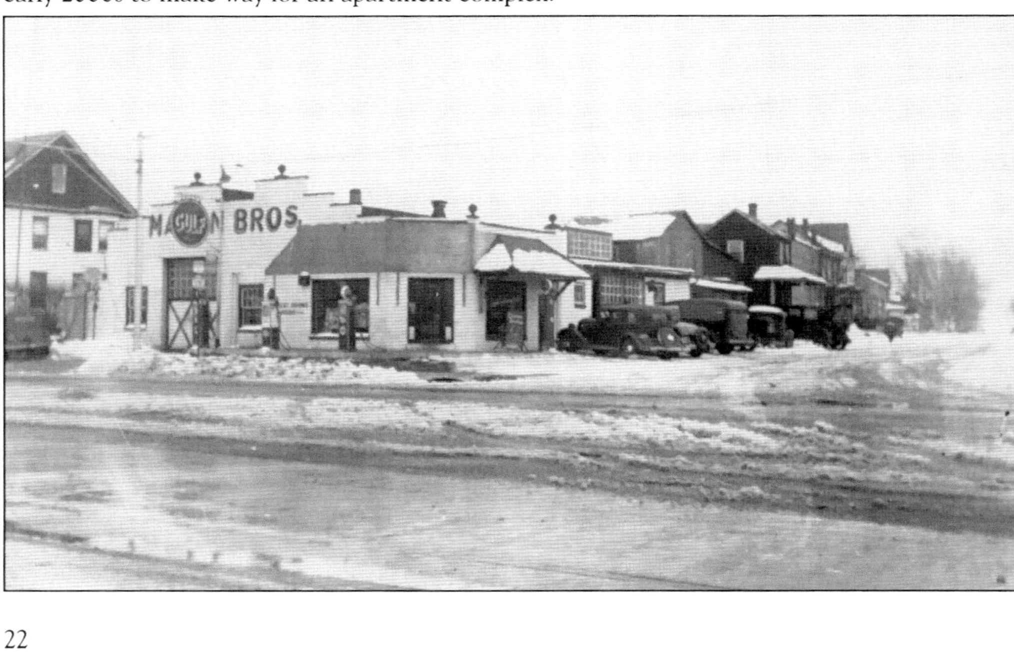

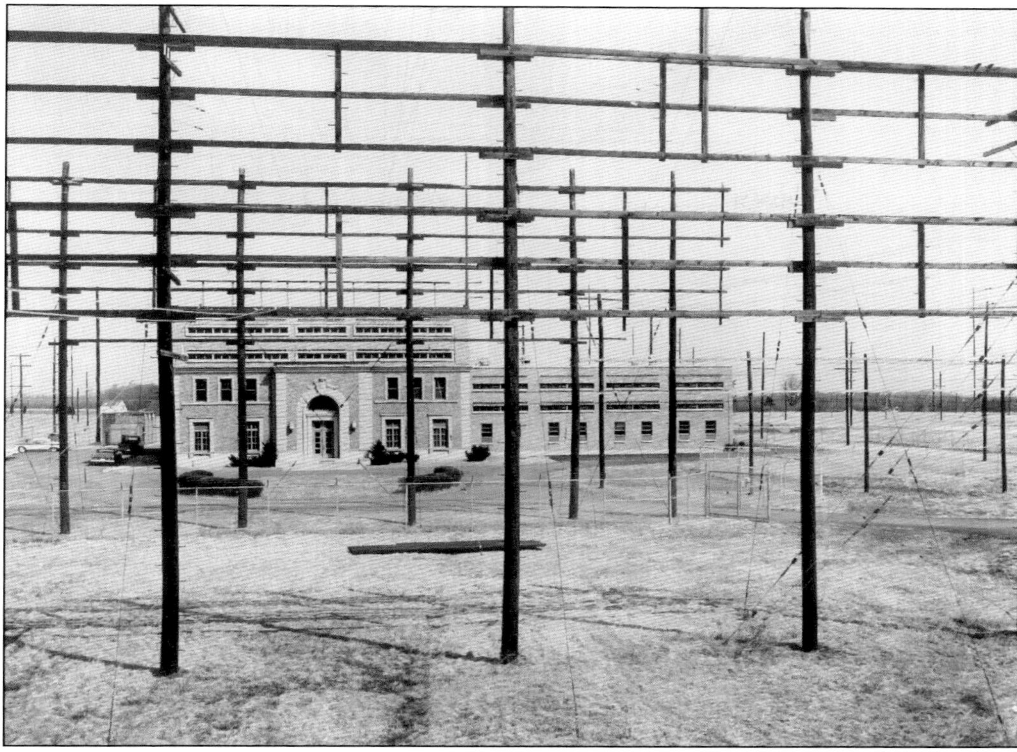

AT&T Overseas Transmission Facility is shown in 1958. AT&T opened a permanent transatlantic shortwave radio station on Cold Soil and Keefe Roads in 1929 to transmit all Europe-bound telephone calls from the United States. Because the facility used a large number of telephone poles for the transmissions, the station became known as the "Pole Farm." Today, at least one pole remains on the land, which is now a county park, Mercer Meadows. As the transatlantic cables were installed for a direct connection to Europe, the need for radio transmission diminished, and the center was shut down on December 31, 1975.

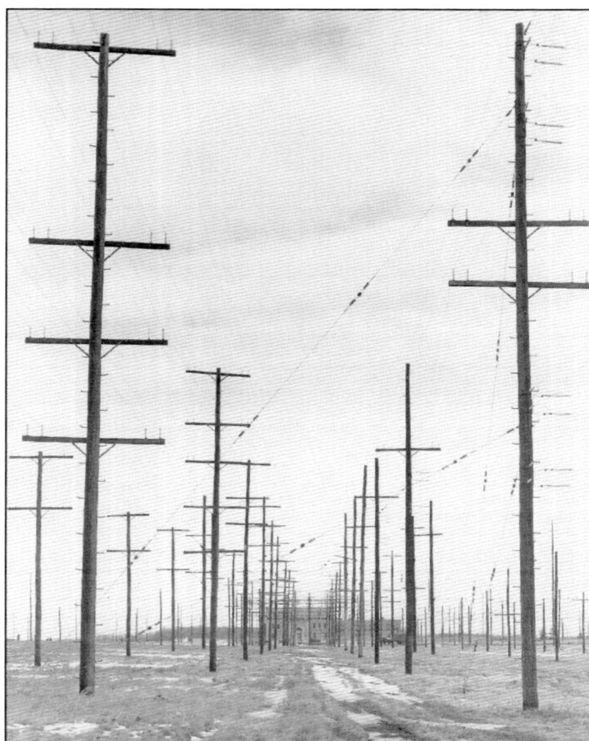

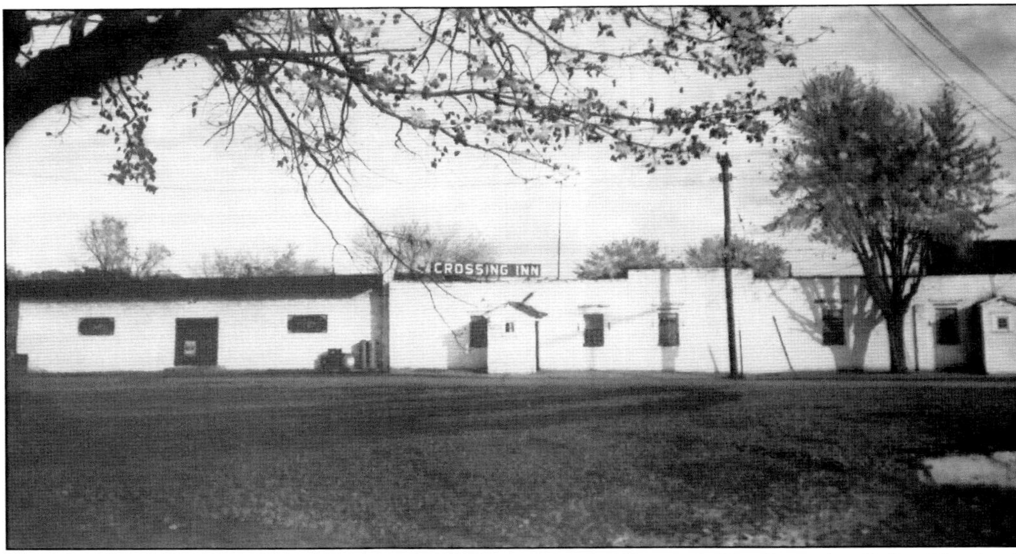

The Crossing Inn was built at the corner of Cheverly and Albemarle Roads in the 1940s. The Inn's second owner, Frank Vereen, expanded the building into a nightclub that could accommodate 850 people. The jazz club featured live performances from such well-known acts as Count Basie, Ray Charles, Ella Fitzgerald (who played there twice), Tina Turner, Lou Rawls, and Little Richard. Unfortunately, a fire destroyed the inn on August 7, 1980. (Courtesy of Fred Vereen.)

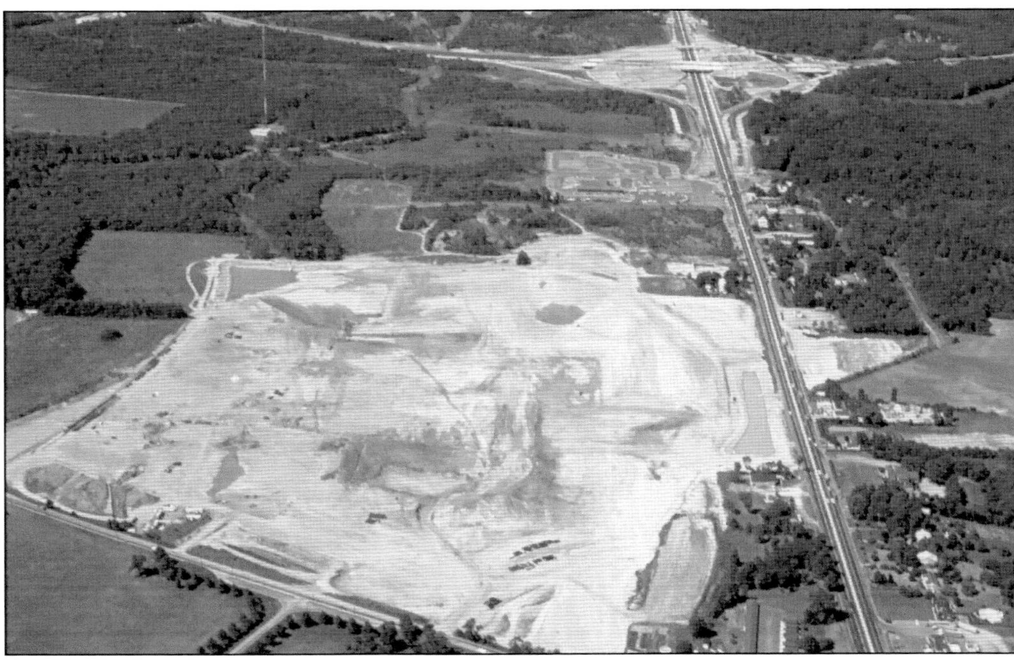

An aerial view of Route 1 in July 1974 shows the construction site of Quaker Bridge Mall on the northbound side of the highway. Interstate 295 was also being built at the same time, as is evident by the work being done on the cloverleaf in the background. Mercer Mall would later be built across from Quaker Bridge Mall but was not yet under construction.

This c. 1990 image shows a black oak, known as the Brearley Oak, at the entrance of Union Camp on Princeton Pike. The oak is believed to date to at least 1730 and sits on land once owned by the Brearley family. Union Camp was a paper-manufacturing company that took pride in protecting the tree until closing in 1999. Bristol-Myers Squibb now owns the land and tends to the tree.

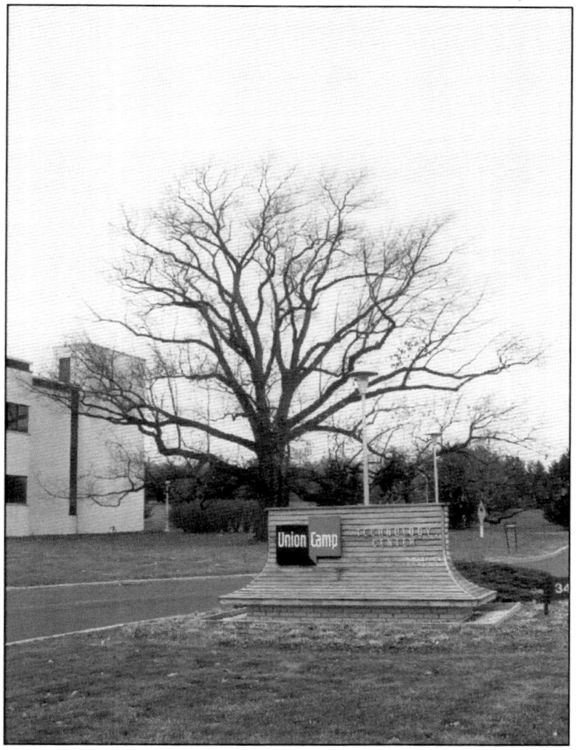

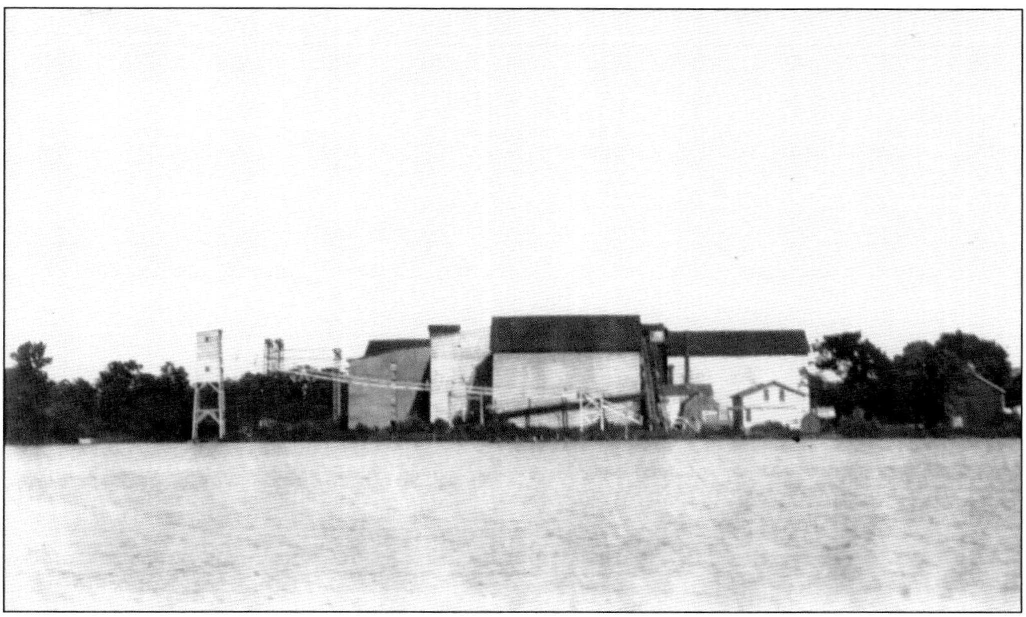

The John H. Bahrenburg's Natural Ice Plant, photographed around 1925, stood near Lawrence Station. There was an industrial area near the Baker's Basin and Youngs Road split that was home to several businesses, including the Howell and Sons' Flour Mill, a general store, a blacksmith shop and a coal distributor. The large pond in front of the mill was filled each fall and ice was harvested and stored during the winter. The insulated storage barns held ice all year.

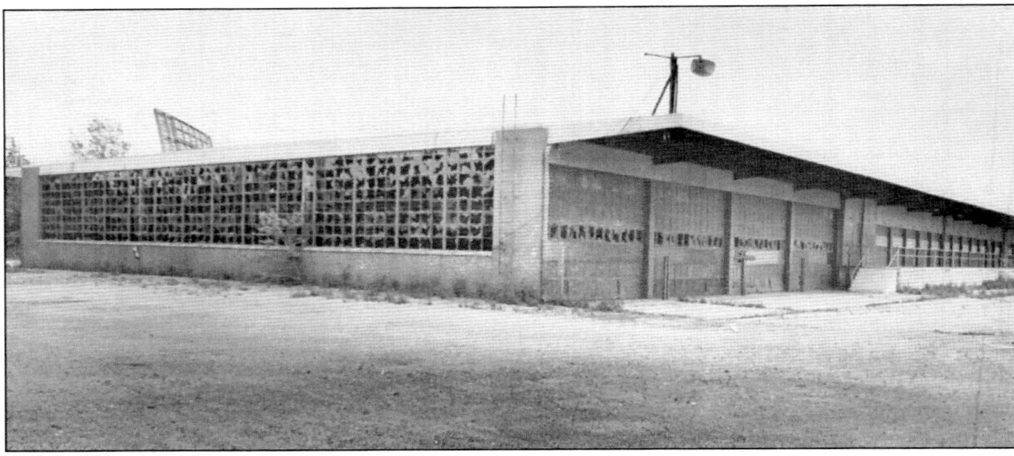

This image shows Riis Trucking Terminal at the corner of Darrah Lane and Brunswick Pike in June 1981. When the terminal was built in the 1950s, it was one of the largest warehouse terminals in the country. As shippers required more storage space, the terminal lost business and was eventually abandoned. It sat unused for at least a decade before being converted into the Lawrence Headquarters Branch of the Mercer County Library System in 1984. (Courtesy of the Lawrence Ledger.)

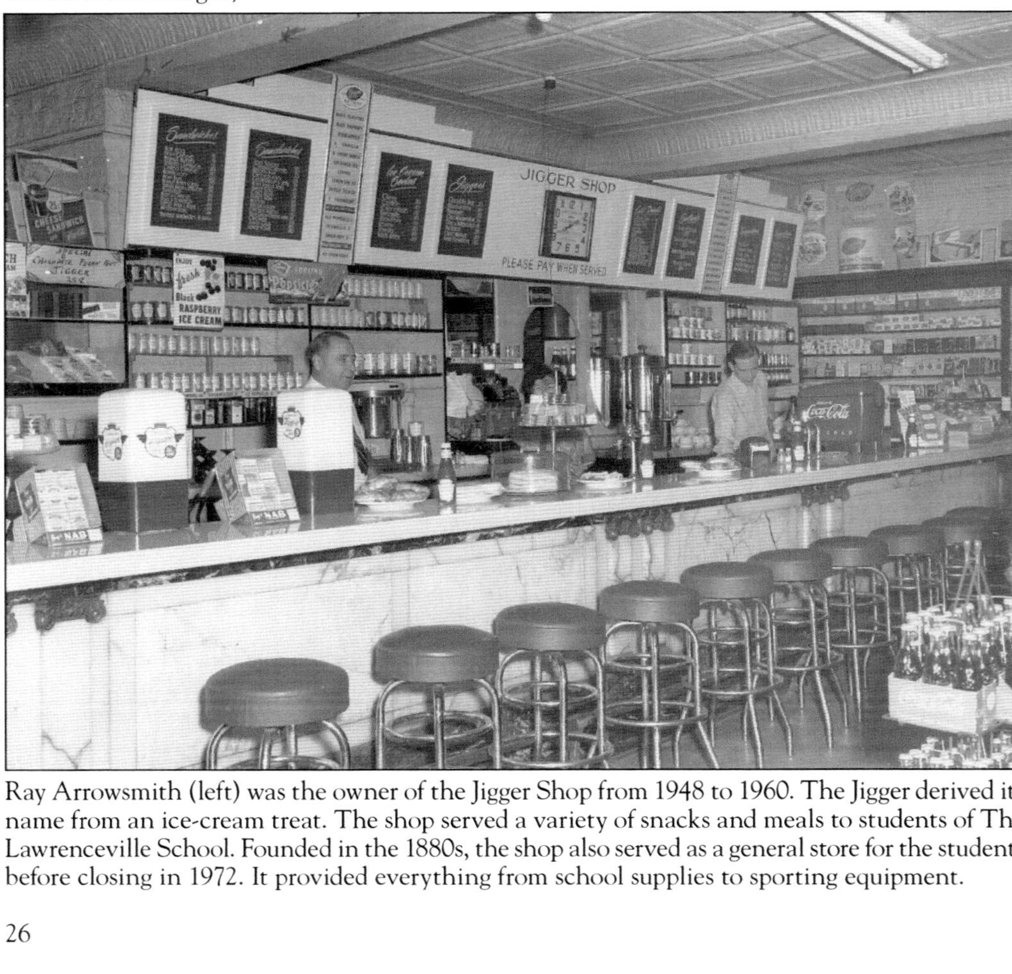

Ray Arrowsmith (left) was the owner of the Jigger Shop from 1948 to 1960. The Jigger derived its name from an ice-cream treat. The shop served a variety of snacks and meals to students of The Lawrenceville School. Founded in the 1880s, the shop also served as a general store for the students before closing in 1972. It provided everything from school supplies to sporting equipment.

Two

Community and Military Service

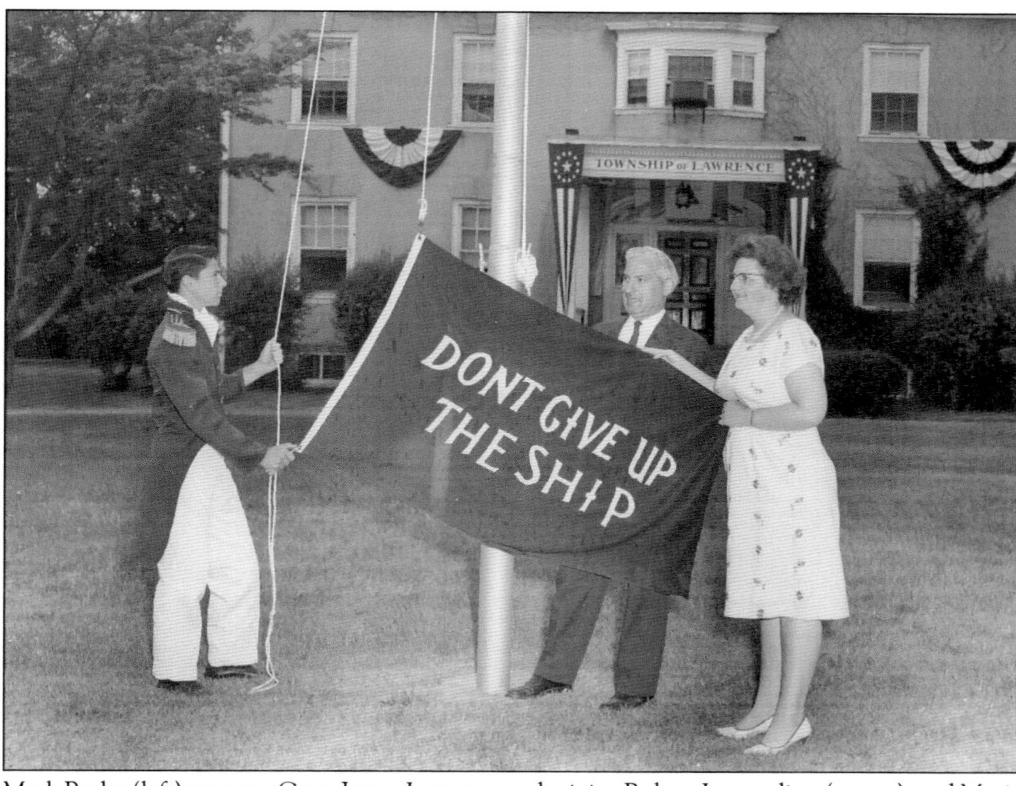

Mark Rader (left) portrays Capt. James Lawrence as he joins Robert Immordino (center), and Marie Loveless (right) in raising the *Don't Give Up the Ship* flag at a 1963 ceremony at the municipal building, commemorating the 150th anniversary of the mortal wounding of Captain Lawrence during the War of 1812. Captain Lawrence uttered the words as his last command.

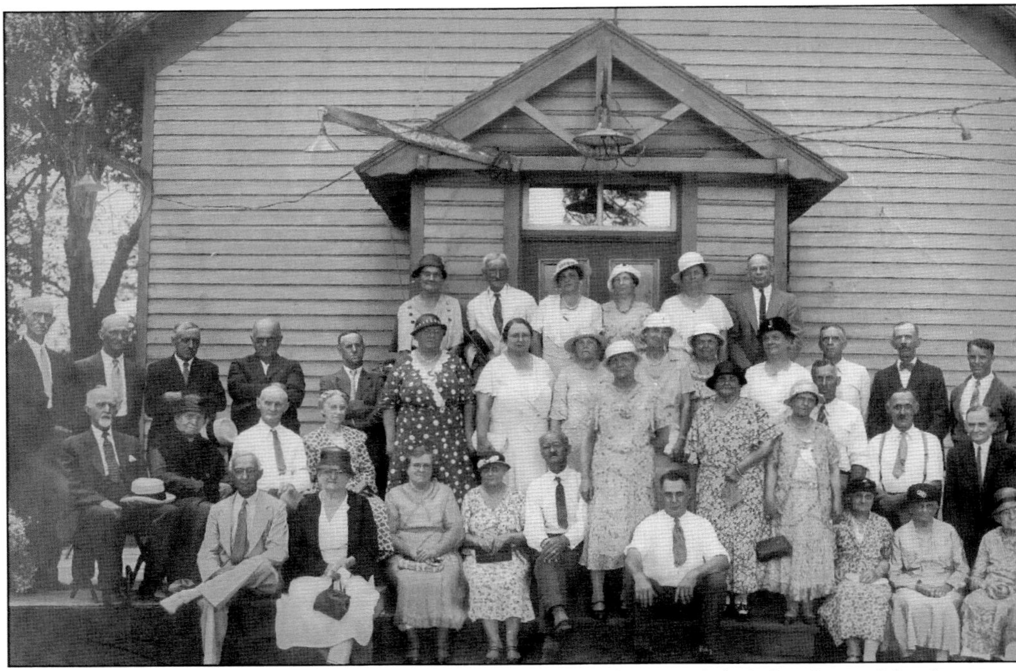

Attendees at a neighborhood covered-dish supper held at the Rosedale School posed for this group picture in August 1933. The school was located on Cold Soil Road opposite Terhune Orchard and was often used by the community for meetings or events, even after the school was closed in 1937.

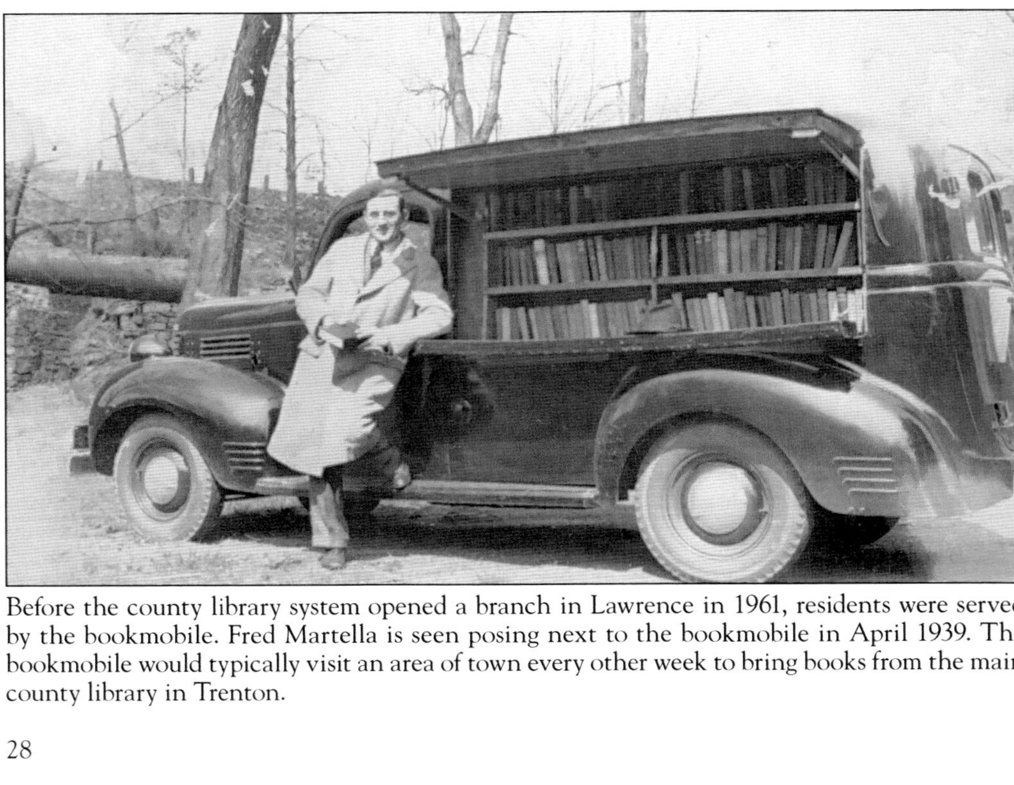

Before the county library system opened a branch in Lawrence in 1961, residents were served by the bookmobile. Fred Martella is seen posing next to the bookmobile in April 1939. The bookmobile would typically visit an area of town every other week to bring books from the main county library in Trenton.

Ruth Bills cuts the township birthday cake at the annual birthday celebration, around 1970. Bills was a beloved history teacher for many years in the Lawrence School system. The township's founding has been celebrated at an annual birthday party each February since the mid-1960s. The party was initially a separate event, but was later incorporated into the February Township Council meeting and is now held at the historical society's annual meeting.

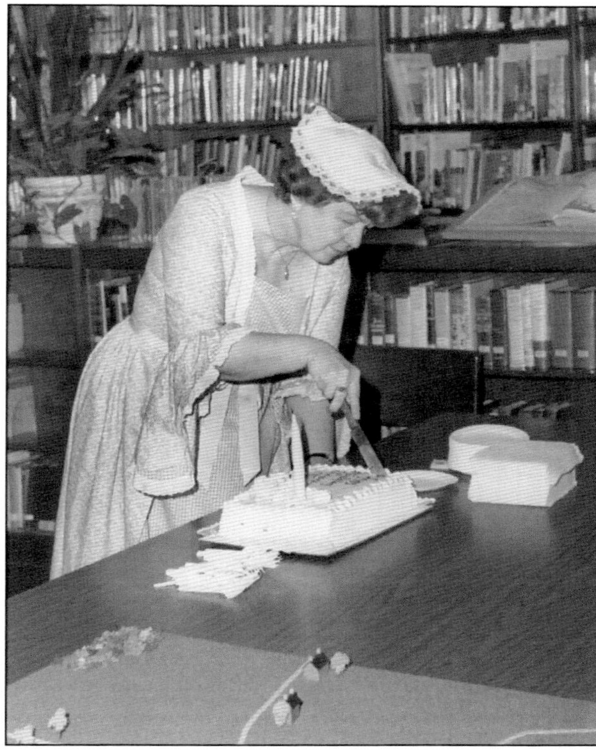

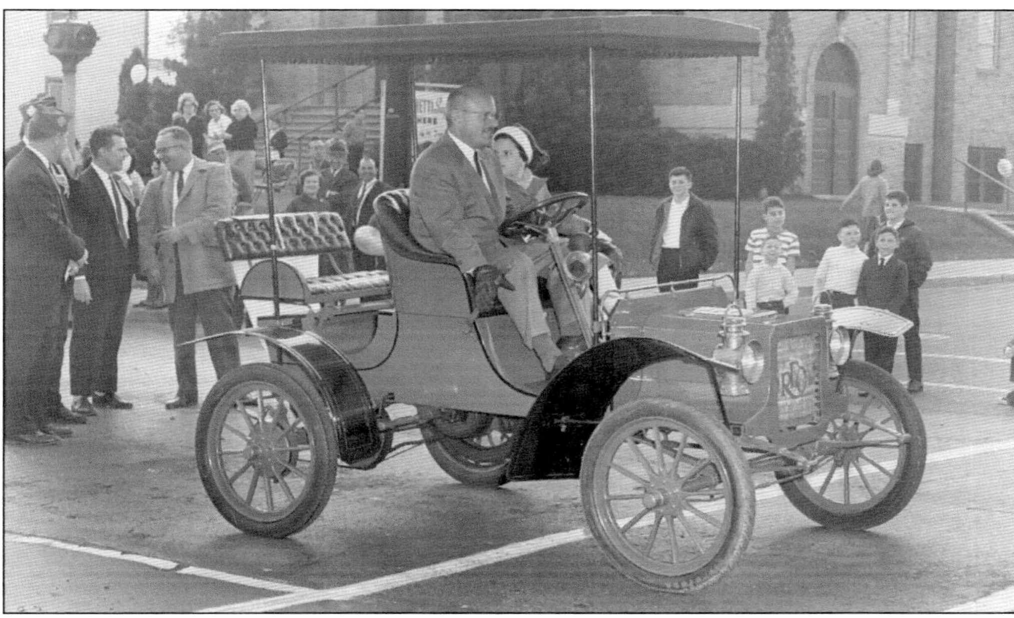

The township held a combination Veterans' Day/New Jersey Tercentenary parade on November 8, 1964, which drew over 10,000 spectators. The parade took 90 minutes to complete and followed a route along Lawrence Road (Route 206) to Veterans Park on Oaklyn Terrace. An antique car is seen passing in front of the original St. Ann's Church, which hosted the reviewing stand on their property at the corner of Lawrence Road and Lawrence Avenue.

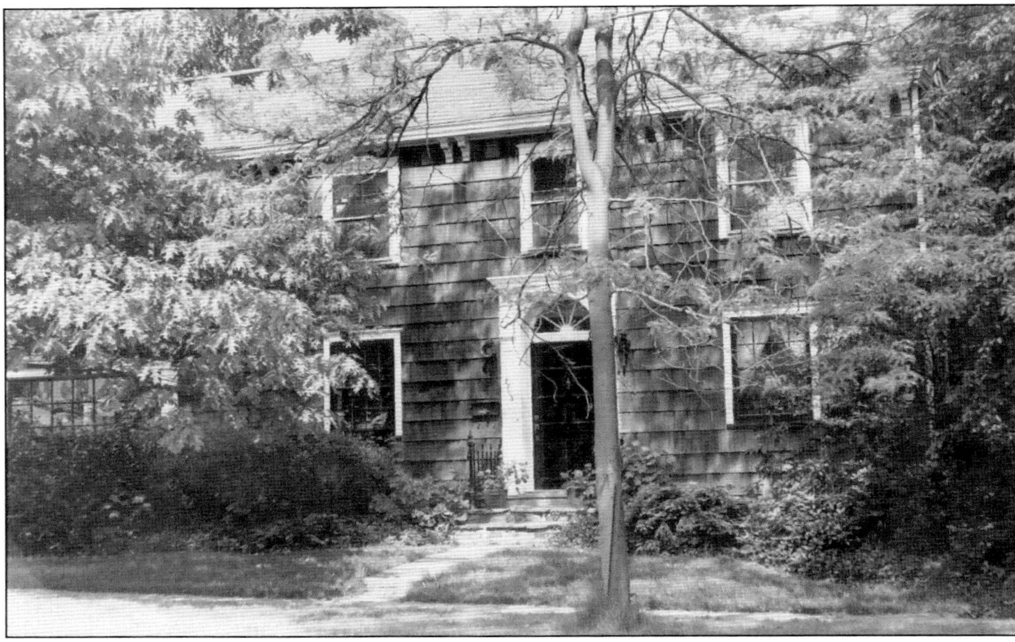

The first town hall was housed in the Conover/Scudder House on Main Street, which the township purchased in 1931. The township had previously rented space for the police department and court, and all other officials had conducted business out of their homes. Before serving as town hall, the building was an eatery. The house still exists and is used as a private residence.

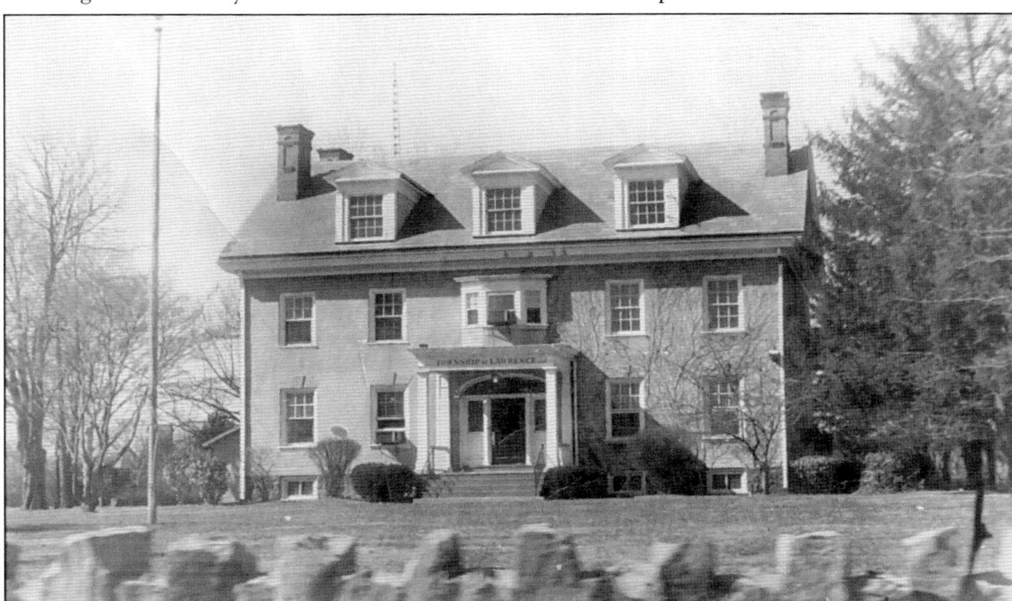

The second Lawrence Township Municipal Building was a converted house on the Parsonage Farm on Lawrence Road (Route 206). The township bought four acres and the home in 1944; the first floor was used for offices, and the second floor was maintained as rental apartments. The apartments were converted to additional office space in 1958. The house and its distinctive stone fence were demolished in 1965.

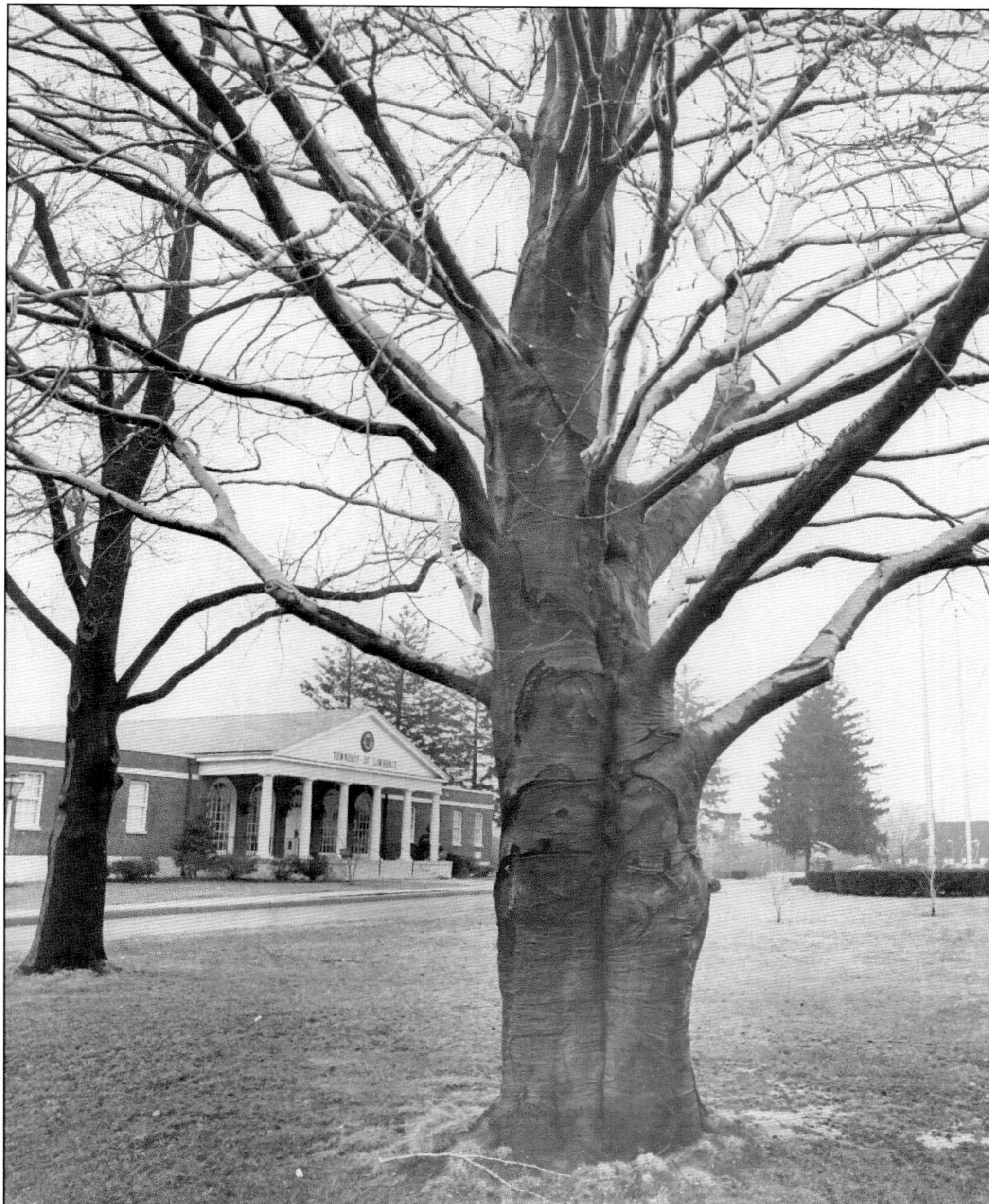

In 1961, the township was once again faced with a shortage of space in the converted house that served as the municipal building. Government officials decided it would be easier to construct a new building than to renovate the old house. For this purpose, the town purchased two plots of land that sat behind the second municipal building. Construction on the current municipal building began in 1963, and the building was ready for occupancy by 1965. The land it sits on was once known as Twin Oaks Farm because of the intertwined twin oaks that grew near the front of the property, seen in this 1966 view of front of the building. The twin oak has a long history as a symbol for the township. It appears on the municipal seal, and the old telephone exchange for the area was *TW*, or *twinoak*.

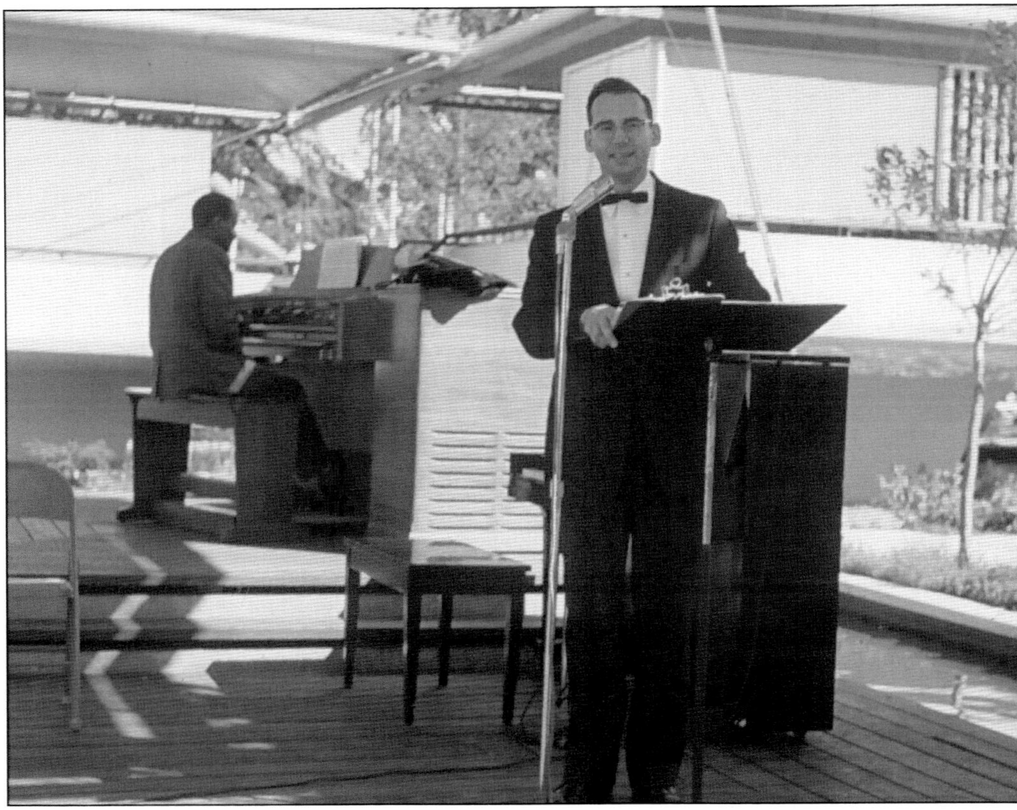

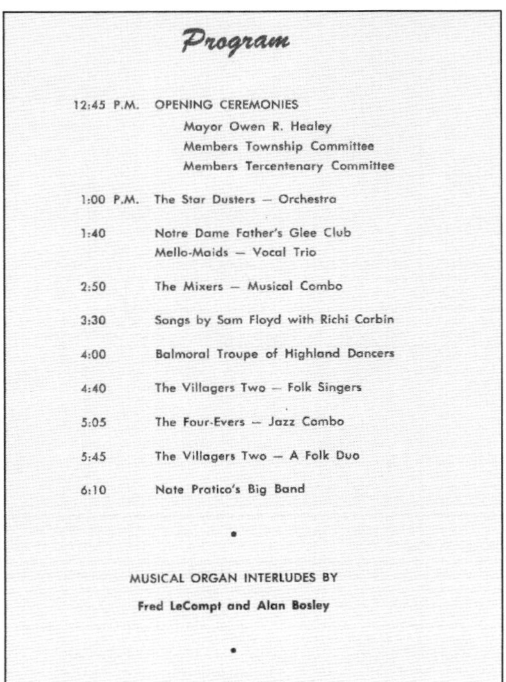

Program

12:45 P.M.	OPENING CEREMONIES Mayor Owen R. Healey Members Township Committee Members Tercentenary Committee
1:00 P.M.	The Star Dusters — Orchestra
1:40	Notre Dame Father's Glee Club Mello-Maids — Vocal Trio
2:50	The Mixers — Musical Combo
3:30	Songs by Sam Floyd with Richi Corbin
4:00	Balmoral Troupe of Highland Dancers
4:40	The Villagers Two — Folk Singers
5:05	The Four-Evers — Jazz Combo
5:45	The Villagers Two — A Folk Duo
6:10	Nate Pratico's Big Band

•

MUSICAL ORGAN INTERLUDES BY

Fred LeCompt and Alan Bosley

•

MASTER OF CEREMONIES

The Lawrence Tercentenary Committee sponsored a Lawrence Township Day in the New Jersey Pavilion at the New York World's Fair on October 3, 1964. Above, Robert C. Marince serves as the master of ceremonies, with Sam Floyd performing in the background. Floyd was part of the entertainment program during the six-hour event, which included musical and dance performances by Lawrence residents and Lawrence-based groups. Left, a program lists the acts set to perform during the day. More than 700 residents travelled to the event on bus trips organized by several non-profit organizations. Over all, about 5,000 people visited the New Jersey Pavilion during the program. (Bottom, Courtesy of Kathleen Topley.)

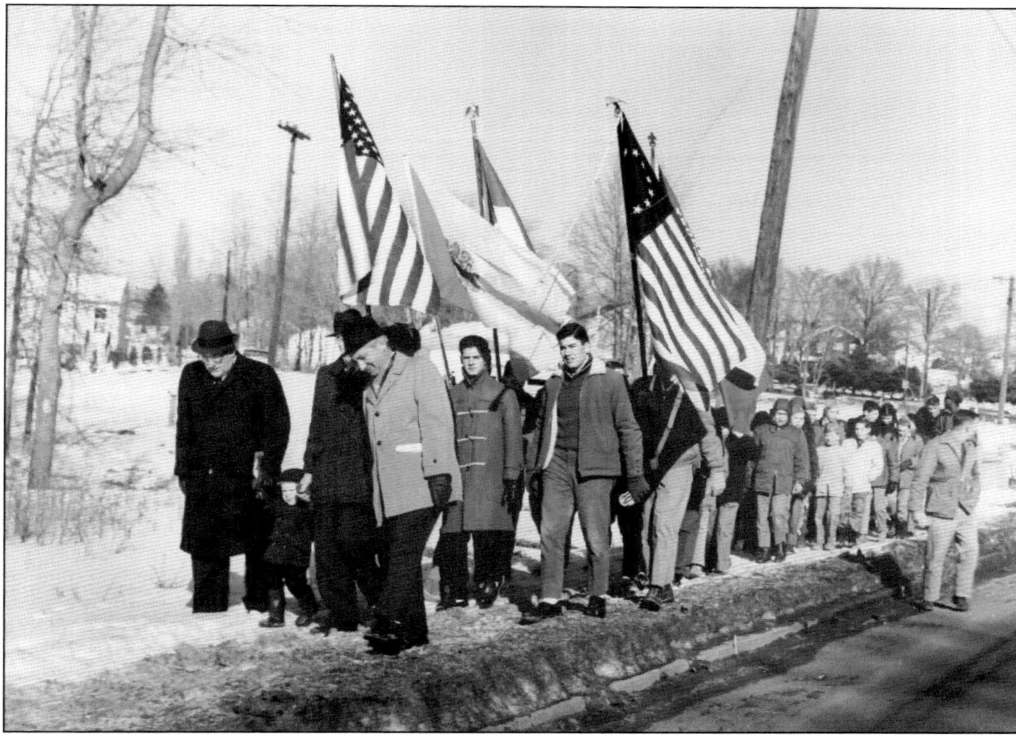

Each year, the township reenacts Col. Edward Hand's Revolutionary War delaying action and march to Trenton. Robert Immordino began the tradition in 1962 with eight marchers from the Junior History Club. This image of the 1963 march shows Mayor Lloyd Carver (first row, left) joined by Robert Immordino (first row, right); Bob DeLorenzo (sixth from left), one of the original marchers from 1962; and descendants of Col. Edward Hand.

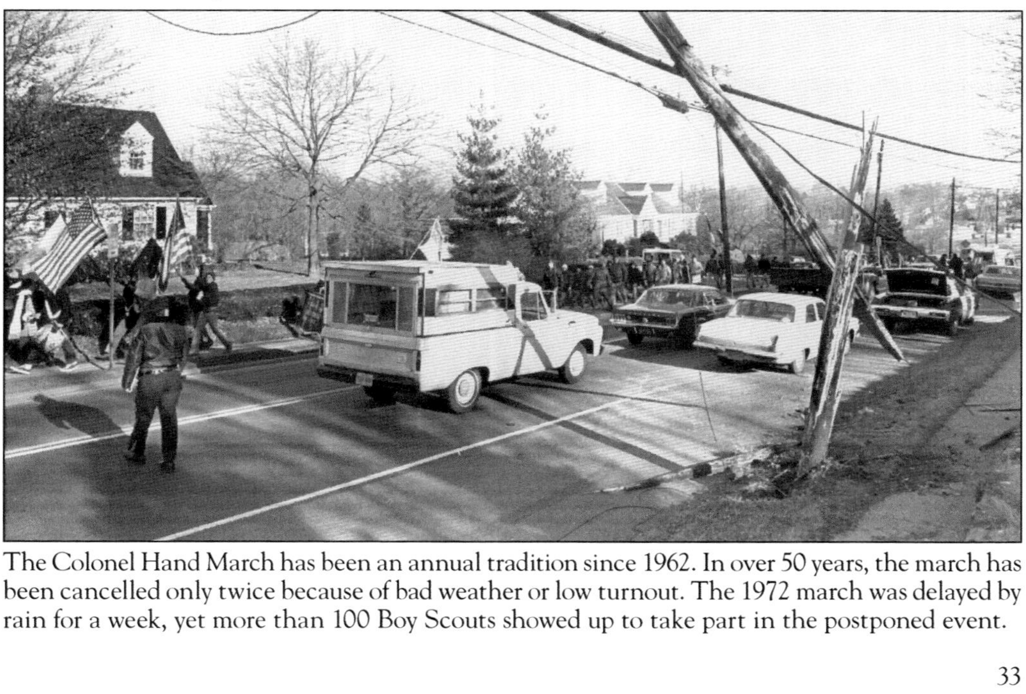

The Colonel Hand March has been an annual tradition since 1962. In over 50 years, the march has been cancelled only twice because of bad weather or low turnout. The 1972 march was delayed by rain for a week, yet more than 100 Boy Scouts showed up to take part in the postponed event.

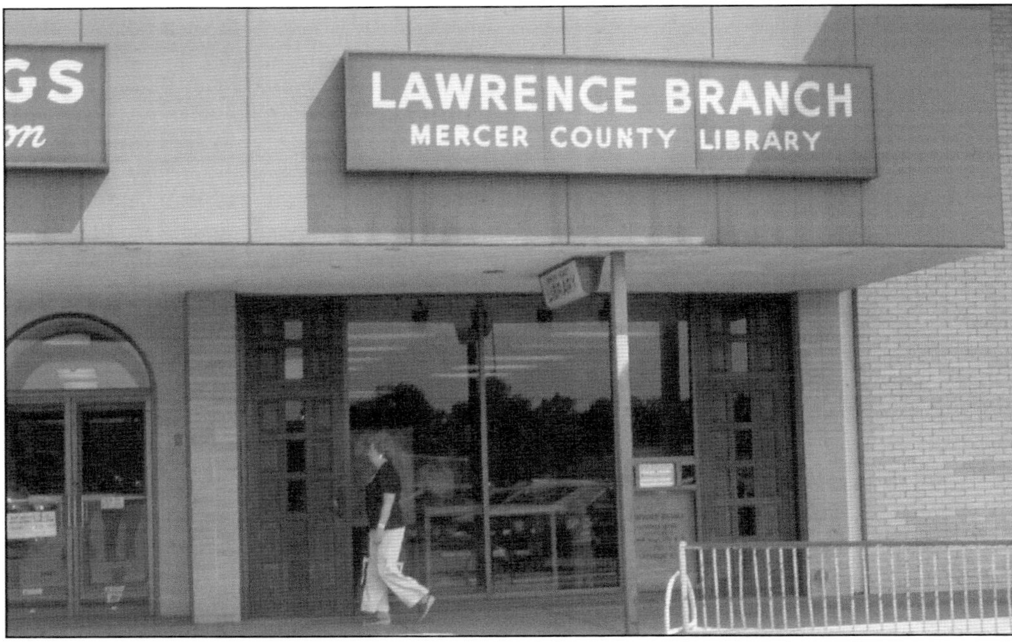

The second location for the Lawrence branch of the Mercer County Library System was in a storefront at Lawrence Shopping Center. The branch, photographed around 1975, was opened in 1969, having moved from its prior location at the rear of the Dunham's Department Store at the shopping center. The original branch, which opened in 1961, was the first public library in the township.

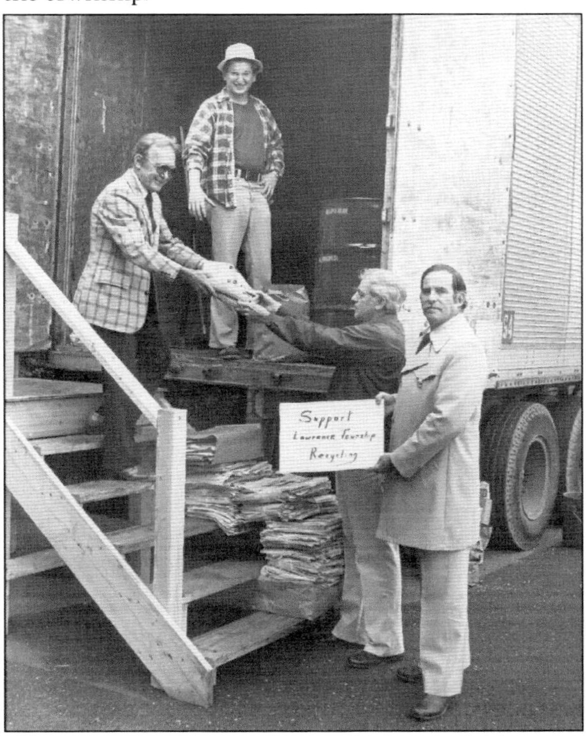

Before there was curbside pickup, Lawrence started a recycling center. A group of citizens formed a Recycling Committee and worked with township government and the owners of Lawrence Shopping Center to create a drop-off area for glass, aluminum and paper. Pictured from left to right are John Wiater (clerk), Edward Curley (committee chairman), Joseph Delle Pazze (mayor), and Norman Bruce (representative of Lawrence Shopping Center). The recycling center opened on June 5, 1982. (Courtesy of the Lawrence Ledger.)

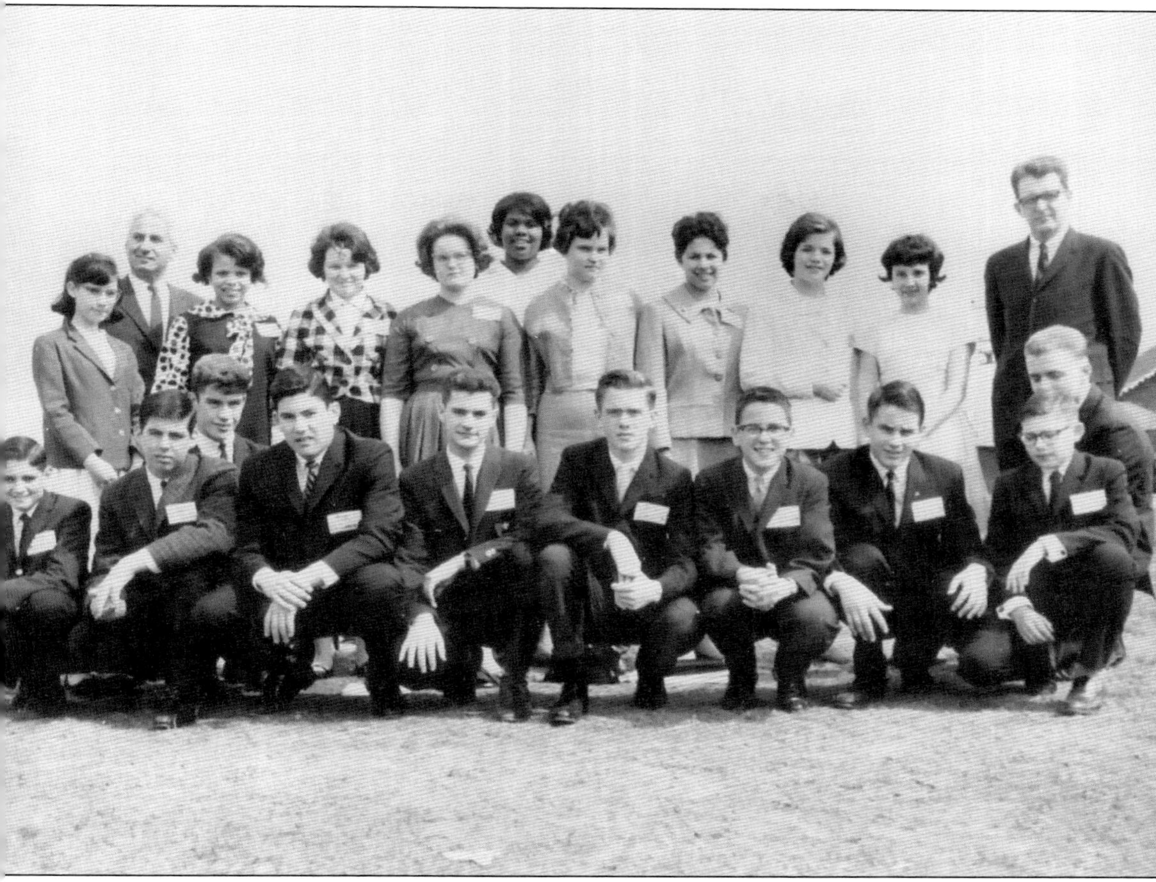

Lawrence sent these delegates to the first Junior Historian Convention in Hightstown on March 30, 1962. The Lawrence Junior Historians was a club for middle and high school students sponsored by the township's Tercentenary Committee and schools during the 1960s. The New Jersey Tercentenary was celebrated in 1964, and many towns created Junior Historian clubs for students to encourage an interest in the state's history and to actively participate in the tercentenary celebrations. The club was affiliated with the Jerseyman program run by the New Jersey State Historical Society. In addition to attending the convention, the Lawrence club took part in several events, including the annual Colonel Hand March and the 150th anniversary program marking the death of Capt. James Lawrence. Aside from helping the Tercentenary Committee plan events, the Junior Historians offered tours of local landmarks and took part in a radio show about New Jersey history.

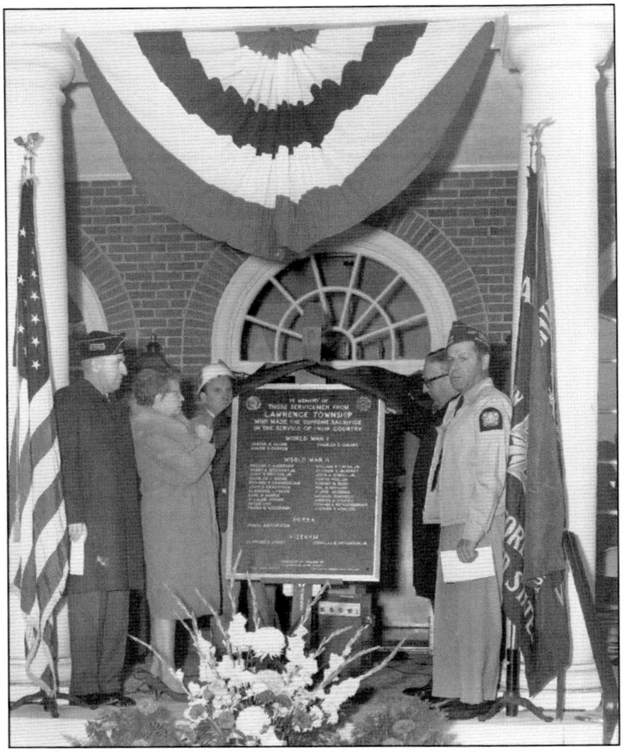

In November 1966, Clifford "Kip" Stout died in combat in the Vietnam War. The following year, his parents suggested the township create a memorial to honor Lawrence residents killed in action while serving in the armed forces. The committee charged with the task of creating a memorial settled on a plaque (seen below), which was placed in the municipal building. The plaque was dedicated in November 1967, following a Veterans' Day parade. Left, Carolyn Stout (left) and George Clifford Stout (right, with glasses), unveil the plaque on the steps of the municipal building. It is now affixed to a wall along the main corridor inside the building.

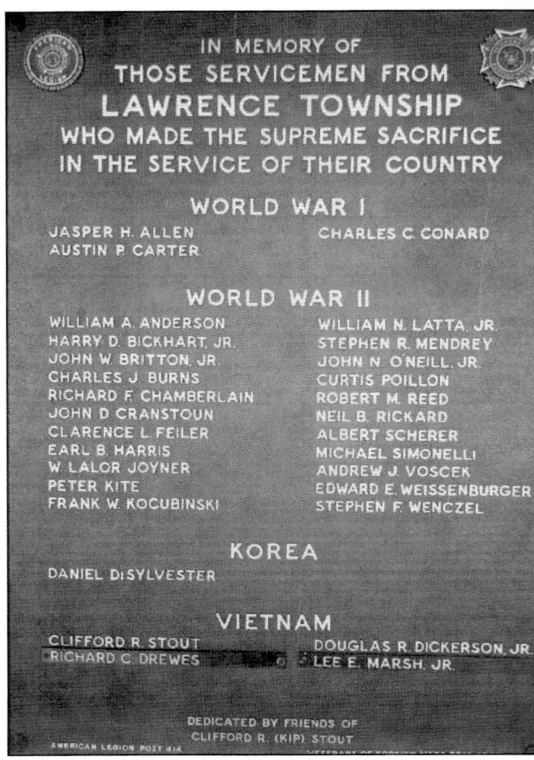

This c. 1920 image shows Leroy "Roy" Applegate in his World War I Army uniform, possibly before a parade. Applegate was one of 99 Lawrence men who fought in the war, three of whom (Austin P. Carter, Charles C. Conrad, and Jasper H. Allen) were killed. Carter Road in north Lawrence is named after Austin P. Carter, the sole Lawrence resident to die in combat. (Courtesy of Kathleen Topley.)

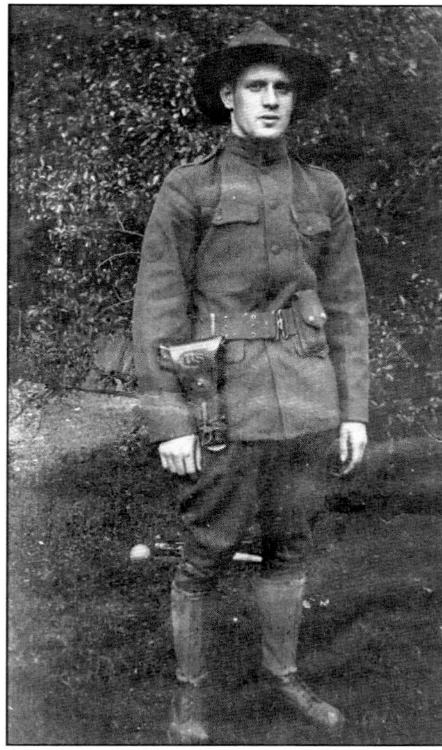

The World War I memorial that now stands in front of the municipal building was once on the grounds of Public School Number 4. When the school was slated for demolition in October 1970, the memorial was moved to its current location. The stone monument was dedicated by the Mercer County Board of Freeholders as a countywide memorial to all of the Mercer residents who lost their lives during World War I.

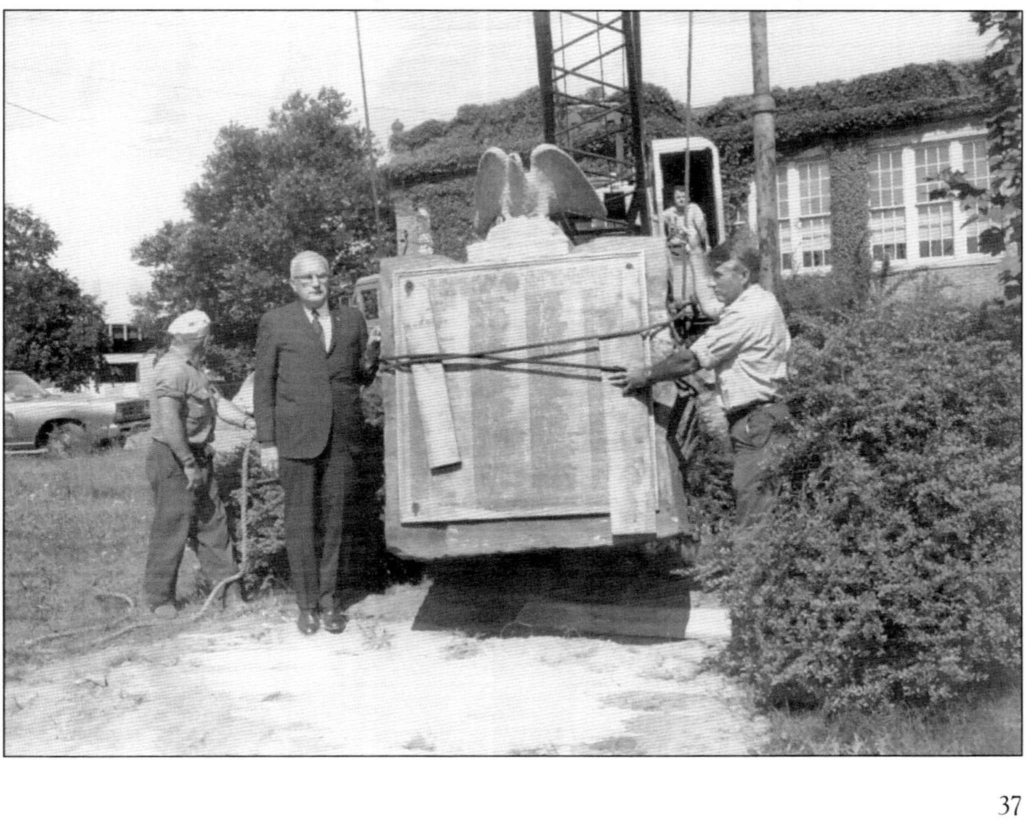

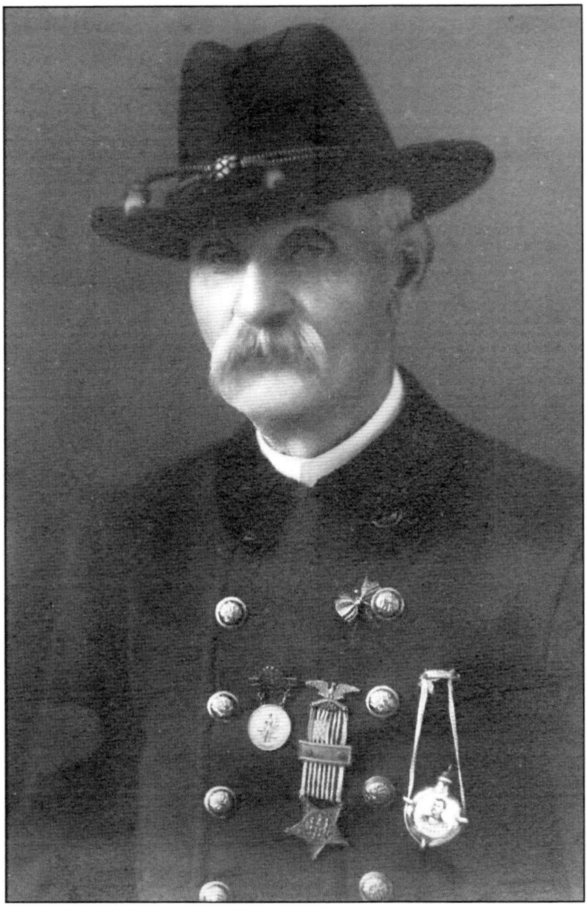

Capt. William H. Bilbee of the New Jersey National Guard had a long military career, serving in the New Jersey 38th Regiment during the Civil War and until his resignation on October 20, 1884. Bilbee was tabbed to command the provisional Company E of the New Jersey regiment during the centennial celebration of the Battle of Yorktown in 1880. Bilbee often visited Lawrence schools on Memorial Day to talk about his experiences in the Civil War.

The Veterans of Foreign Wars (VFW), Post 3022 Ladies Auxiliary, photographed around 1940, met at the VFW Post on Cherry Tree Lane. The Ladies Auxiliary was formed as a support group for the VFW in late 1934, the same year the post had been established by Herbert Mount and 38 other World War I veterans.

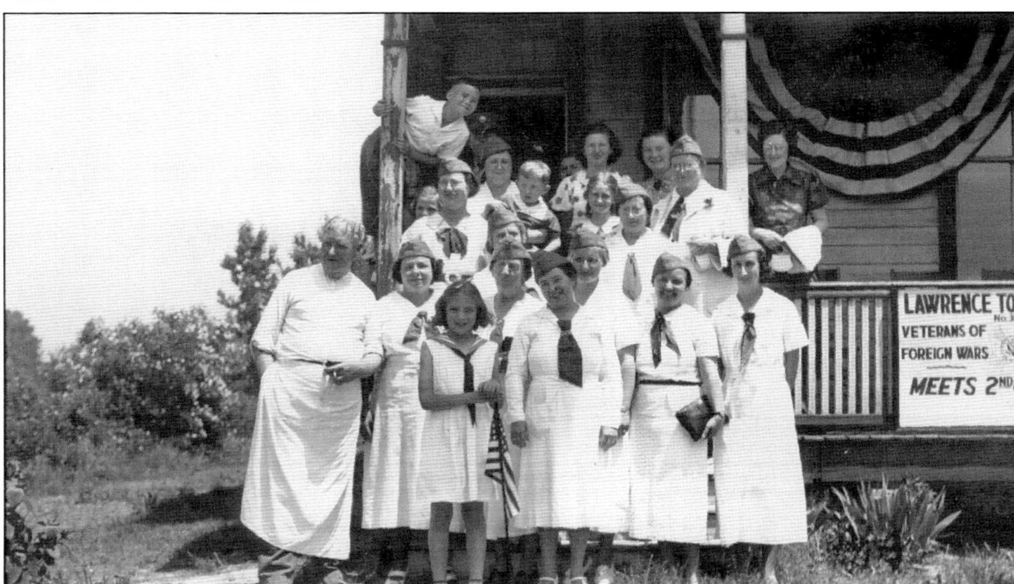

Three

Emergency Services

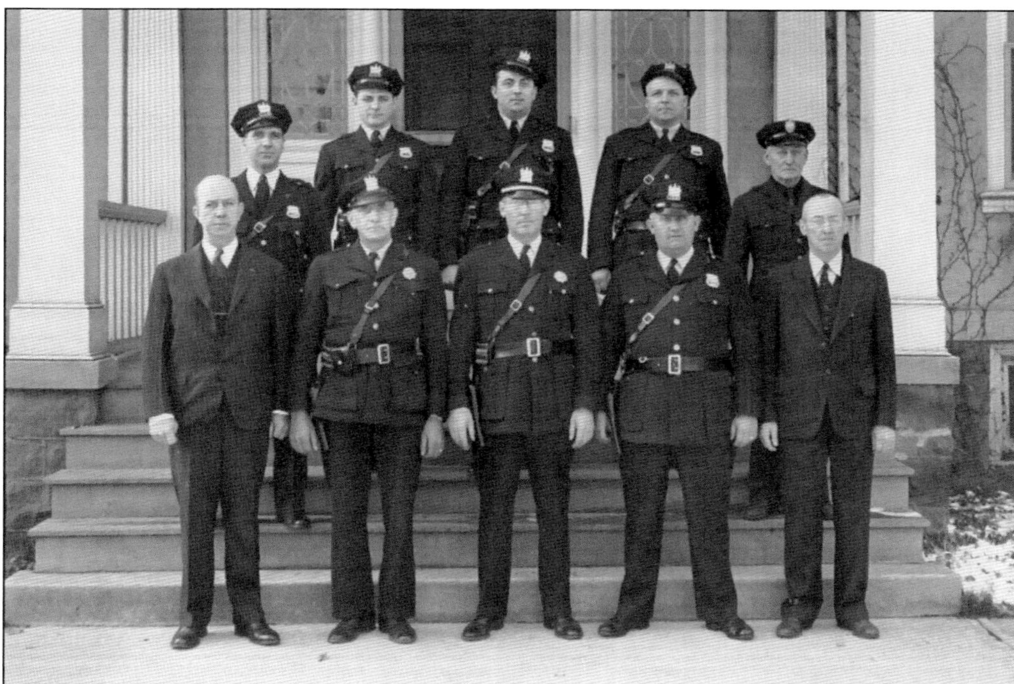

This police department picture, from 1947, was taken in front of the second Town Hall. Pictured from left to right are (first row) Foster Jemison (township committeeman in charge of police), Capt. George Wood, police chief Joseph P. Stonicker, John T. Ball, and Frank Harris (township recorder); (second row) Joseph Olessi, William F. Seabridge, William R. Hullfish, Wesley A. Gronikowski, and John Toft (court clerk and special police officer).

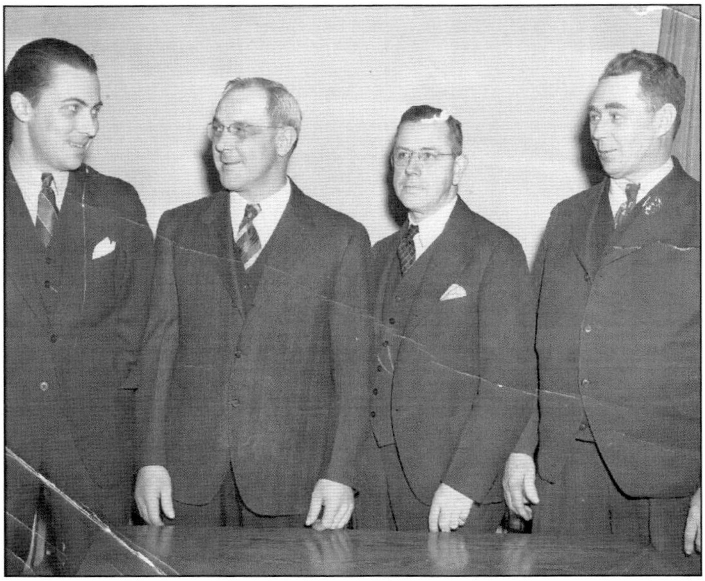

The Lawrenceville Fire Company was founded in 1915. Early members, pictured from left to right, included William R. Hullfish (company president, 1940), Oscar Eggert (chief, 1925–1946), Archibald Garfield Hullfish (president, 1915–1916), and Urias Pierson (first chief, 1915–1921).

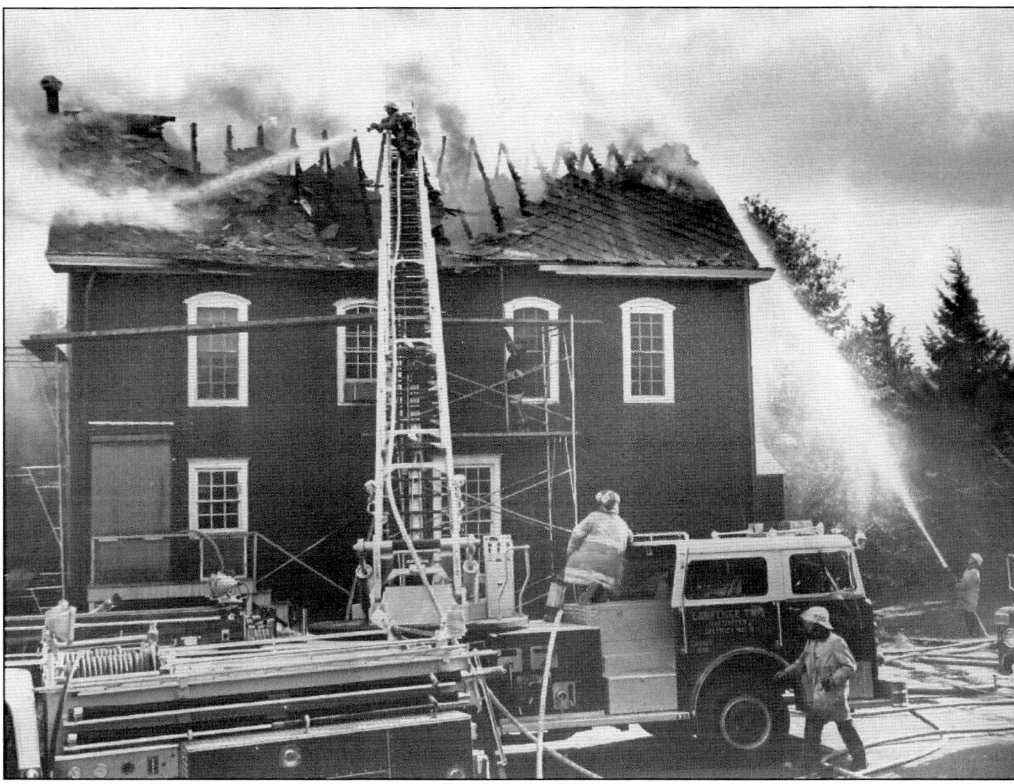

The Auto Engine Shop on The Lawrenceville School campus caught fire on October 14, 1982, when a roofer's solder torch ignited the shingles on the roof during a renovation. The building suffered another fire in 1994. The Lawrenceville Fire Company battled the 1982 blaze with their ladder truck and received assistance from the Slackwood and Lawrence Road Fire Departments. (Courtesy of the Lawrence Ledger.)

Harry Butterfoss, a charter member of Lawrence Road Fire Company, houses the department's new Maxim engine on October 17, 1964. The engine housing was part of a 50th anniversary celebration at the fire station. Butterfoss had served as first assistant chief (1917–1918) as well as chief (1919).

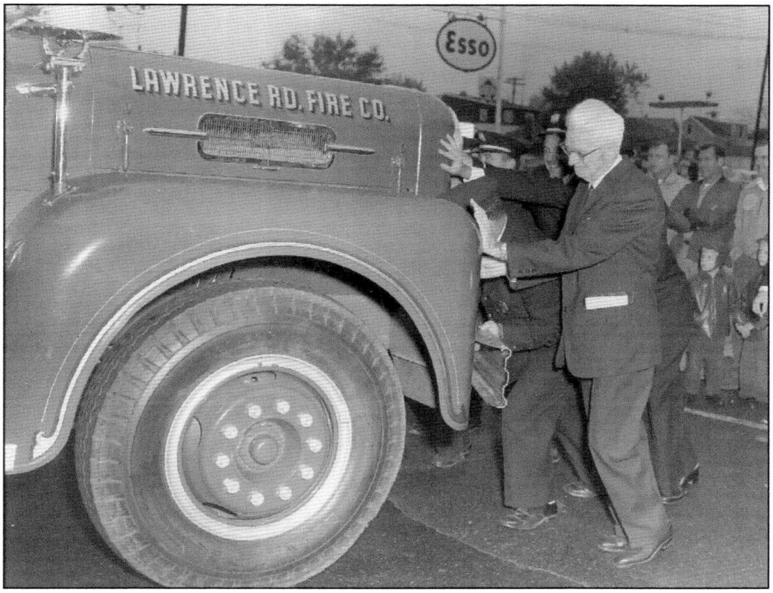

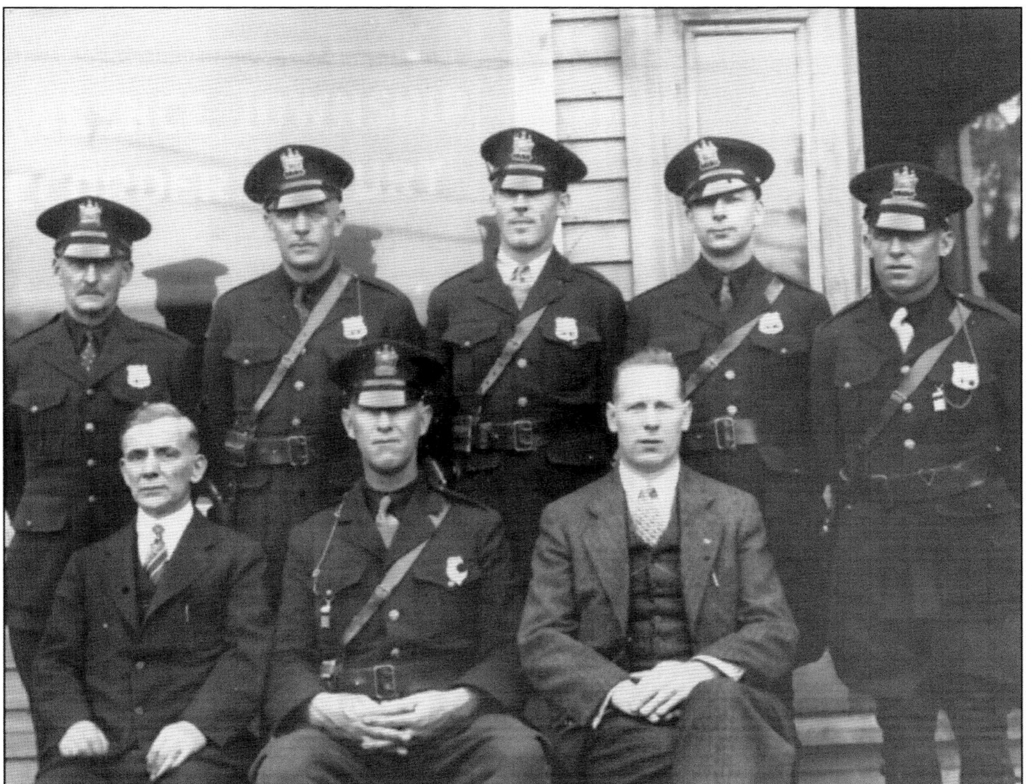

The first police department and recorders court was located in a building at Harney's Corner. Pictured in this 1929 department picture, from left to right, are (first row) Judge Edwin Carpenter, Chief Leland Hopkins, and Police Commissioner George Turner; (second row) John Toft, George Wood, Joseph P. Stonicker, ? Ackroyd, and ? Bond.

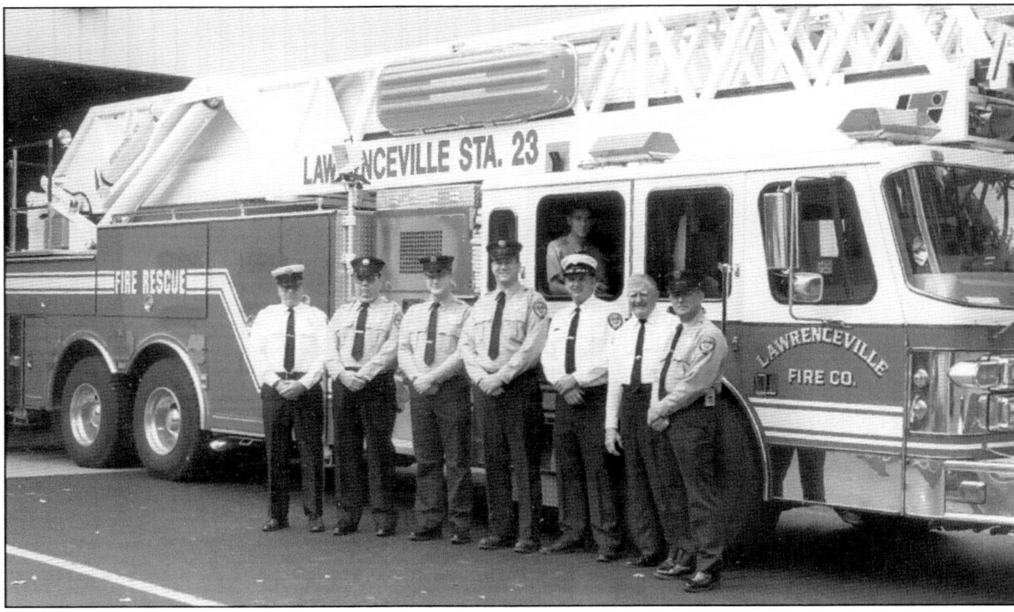

Members of Lawrenceville Fire Company line up with a new rescue truck. Pictured from left to right are 1st Asst. Chief Donald Huber, Tim Dalton, William Gray, Brian Gibbins, Kevin Reading Jr. (seated in truck), Fire Chief Kevin Reading, Franklyn "Bud" Reading, and Fred "Butch" Bentley. The Readings represent three generations of firefighters at the Lawrenceville Company.

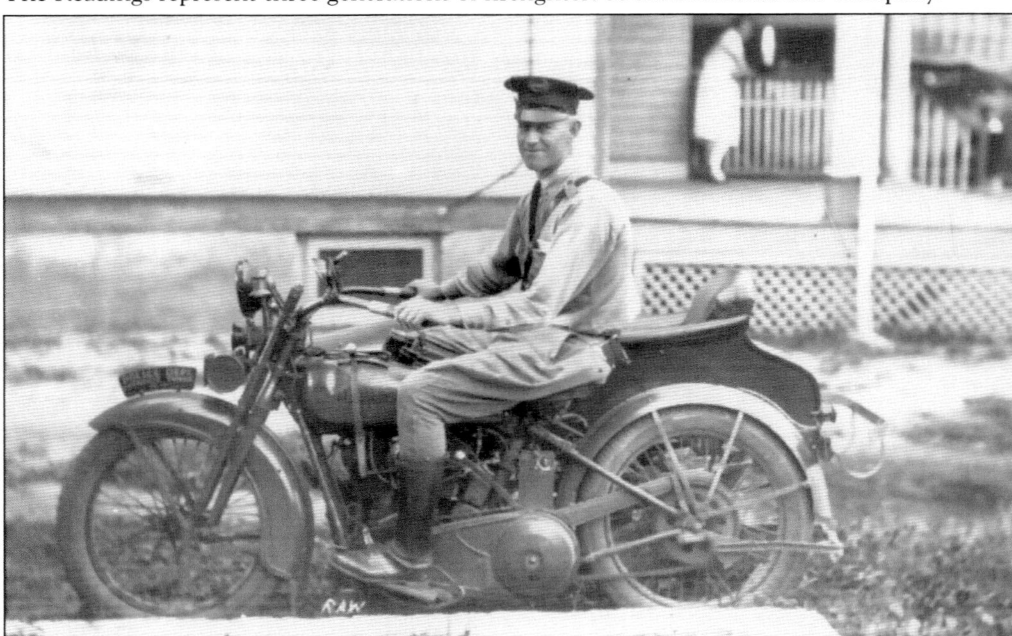

Joseph Leland Hopkins was named Lawrence Township's first police chief on February 24, 1924. He began his duties with the township as a truant officer before becoming a part-time—and later, full-time—policeman. He was chief when he passed away on August 30, 1935. As chief, Hopkins was often seen riding around town on his department-issued motorcycle.

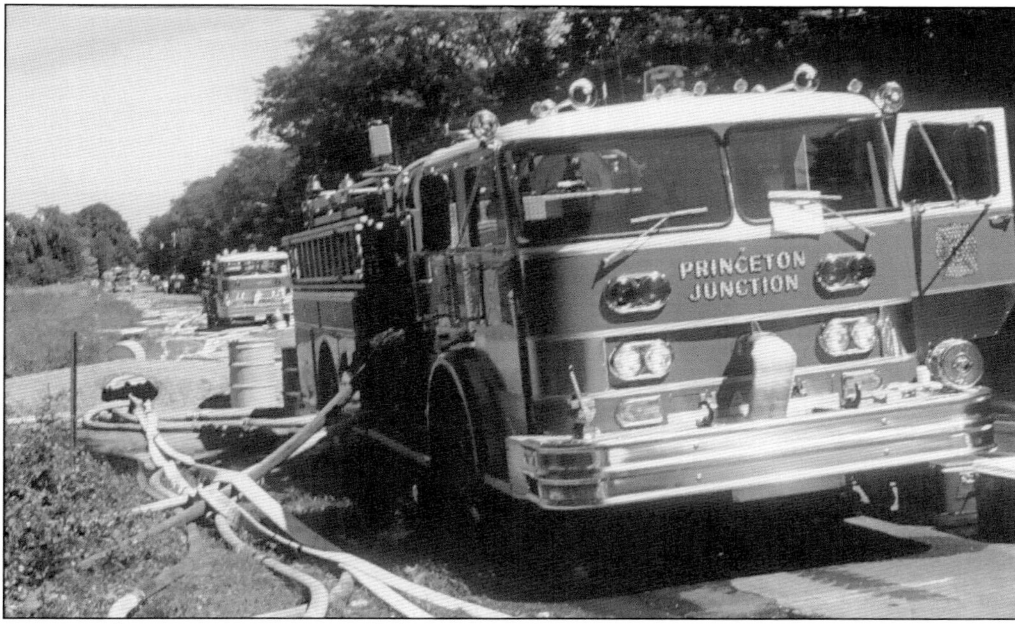

In September 1975, an equipment failure at the filtration plant of the Trenton Water Works cut off water service for a week, affecting 200,000 customers, including many Lawrence residents. In order to get water into the city's system, fire departments from the region set up a line of hoses and engines (above) to pump water from Princeton. The lines ran down the entire length of Princeton Pike in the township and needed to be manned 24 hours a day for the entire week. Below, two Slackwood volunteers take a break from manning a pumper to grab a snack and catch up on the news.

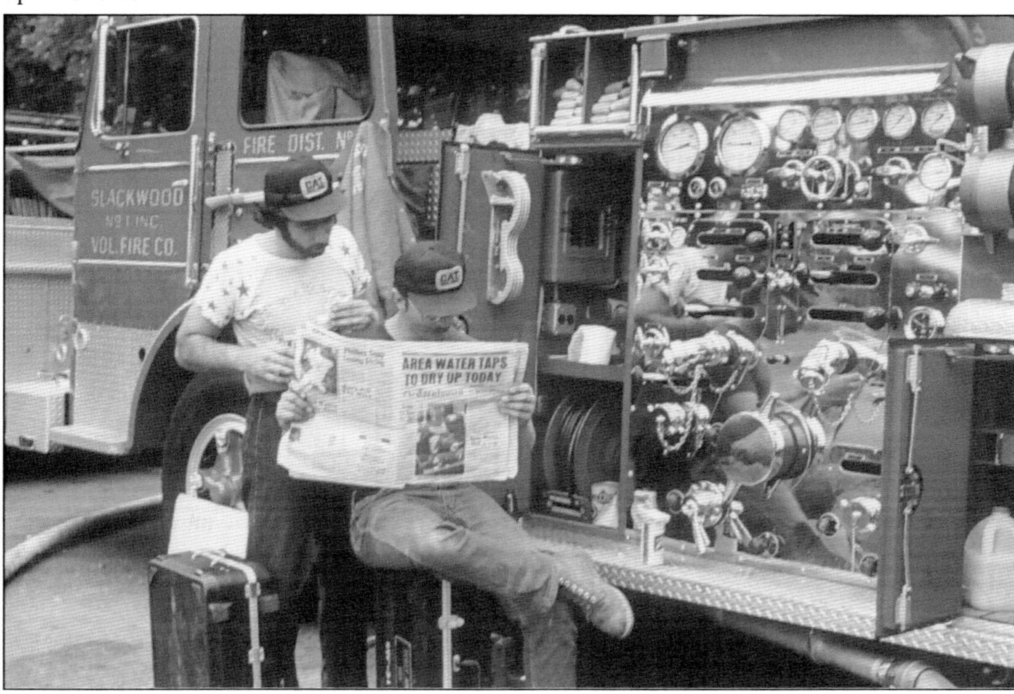

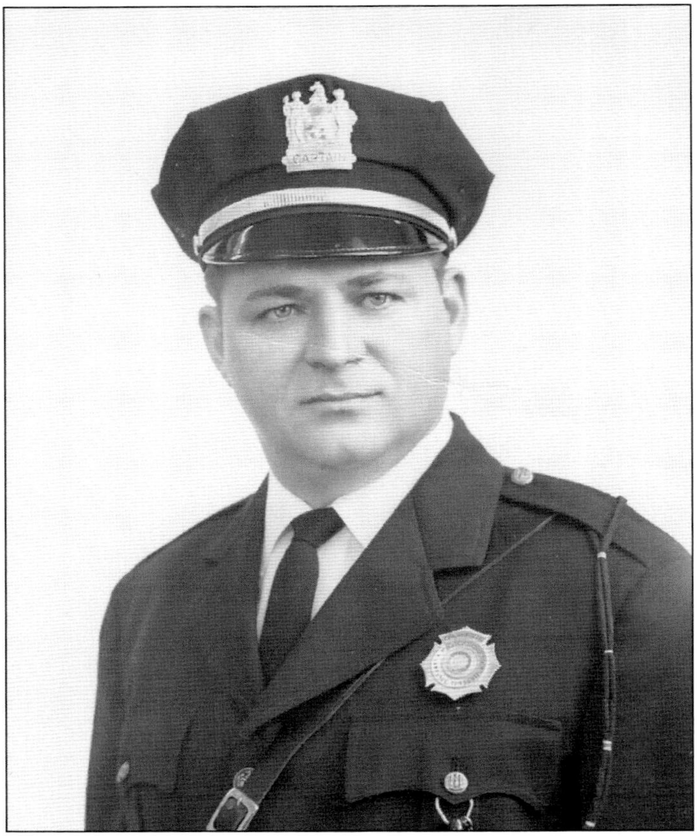

William F. Seabridge is photographed around 1957 as a police captain (left), and showing off a new cruiser as chief of police in 1987 (below). Seabridge served on the police force for 41 years, starting as a patrol officer in 1946 and progressing to captain in 1957. In 1966, he was appointed to the position of chief, becoming the third person to lead the department. As captain and chief, he helped oversee the growth of the department from a force of about 10 officers to one equipped to handle the increased population of the numerous subdivisions built during his term. Prior to his service in the police department, Seabridge was a US Army Air Corps gunner on a B-17 crew stationed in England during World War II.

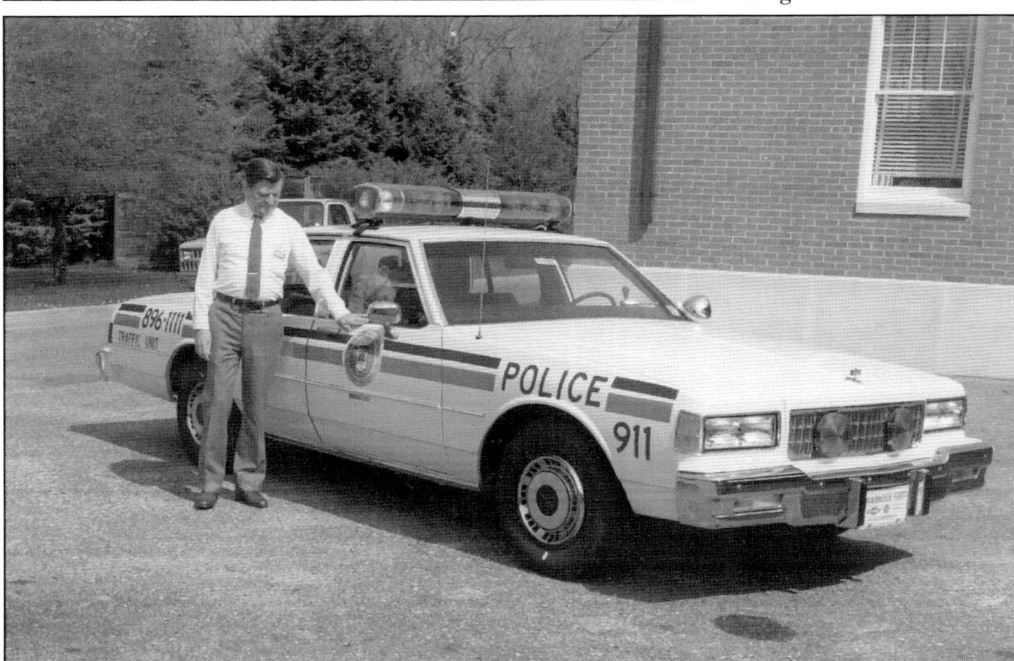

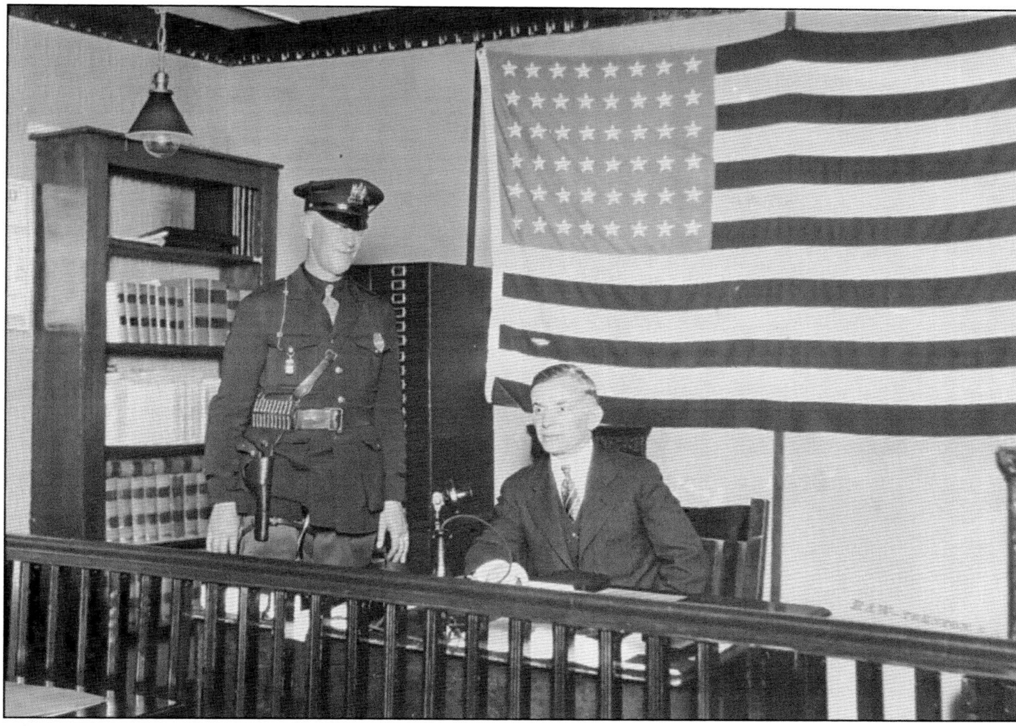

The Recorder's Office at Harney's Corner was located in the rear of Swain's Grocery Store, next to the courtroom. Police chief Joseph Leland Hopkins (left) and Judge Edwin Carpenter (right) are photographed in the office around 1929. The Recorder's Office served as a clerk to the court and the police department, collecting fines and keeping the official records for both departments.

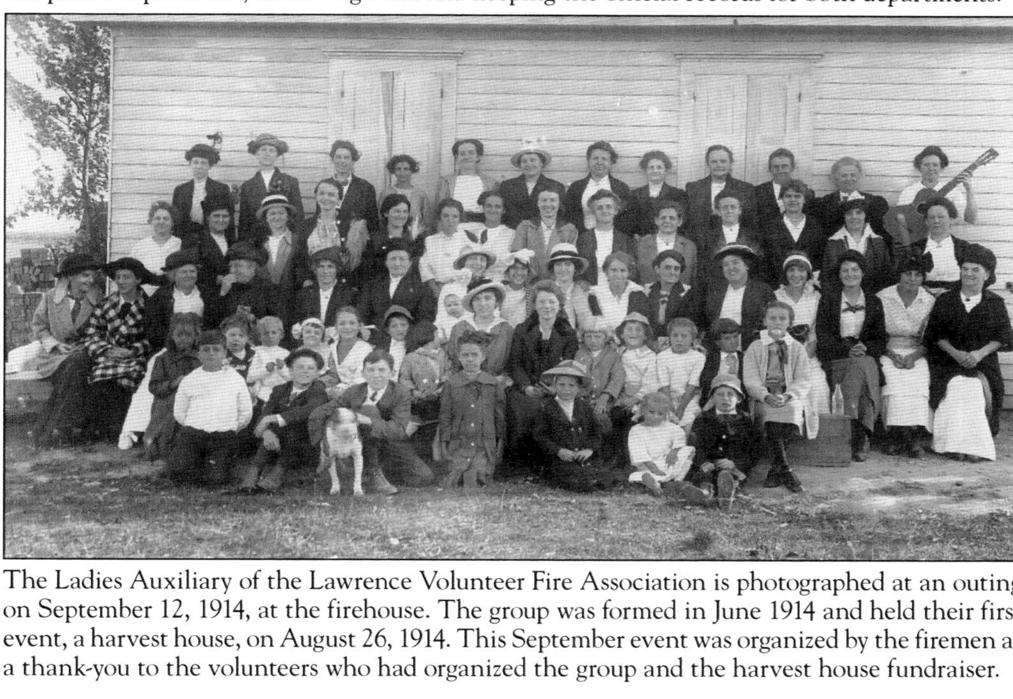

The Ladies Auxiliary of the Lawrence Volunteer Fire Association is photographed at an outing on September 12, 1914, at the firehouse. The group was formed in June 1914 and held their first event, a harvest house, on August 26, 1914. This September event was organized by the firemen as a thank-you to the volunteers who had organized the group and the harvest house fundraiser.

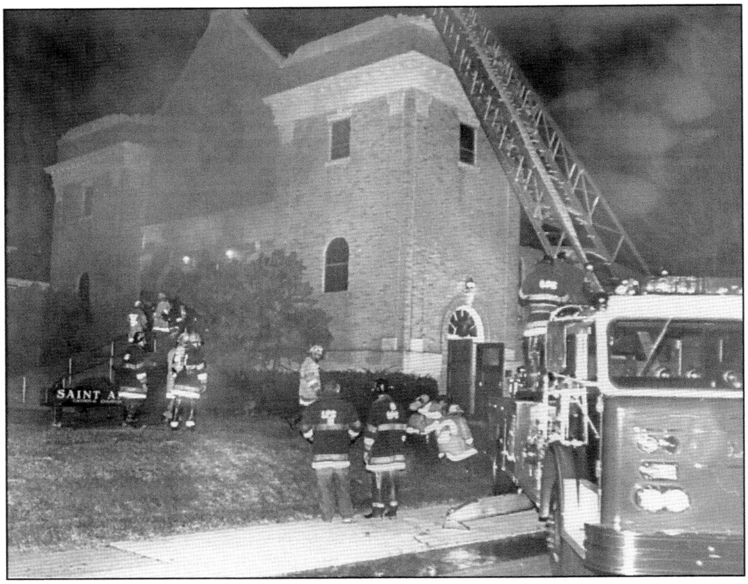

Members of the Lawrenceville Fire Company fight the blaze that destroyed the original St. Ann's Church in the early morning hours of January 2, 1982. The church, built in 1937, was nearly gutted by the fire, which was fought by six area fire companies (including all three Lawrence volunteer departments). (Courtesy of the Lawrence Ledger.)

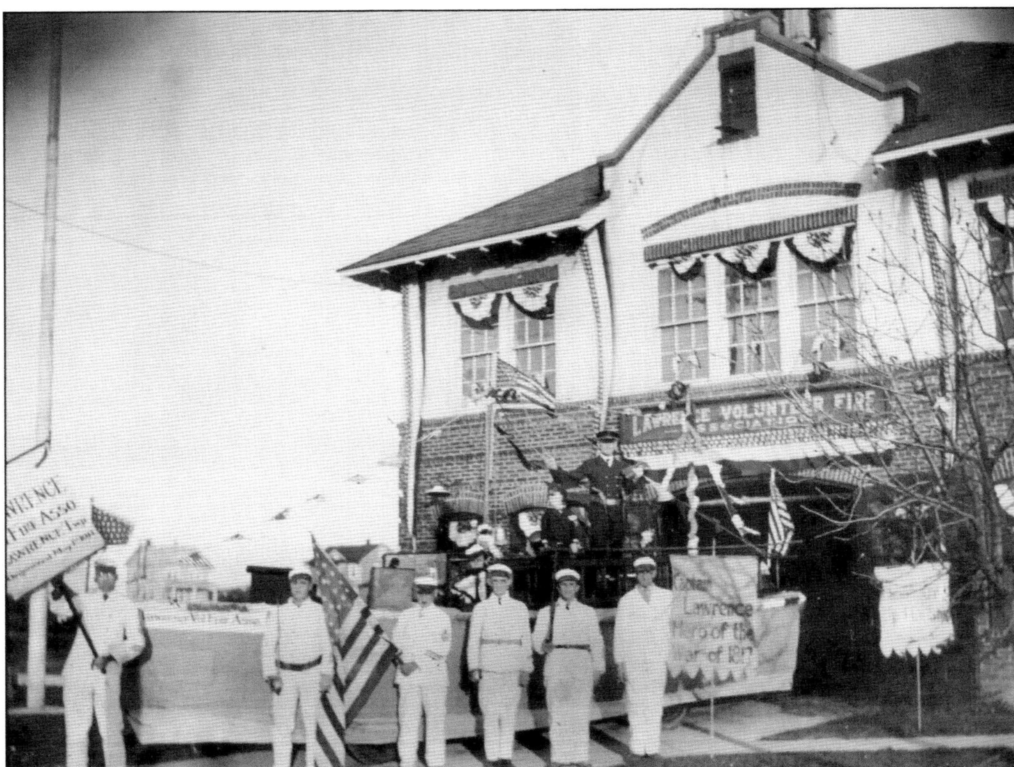

Members of the Lawrence Road Fire Company, then known as Lawrence Volunteer Fire Association, stand with a float depicting Capt. James Lawrence and his ship during the War of 1812. The float was entered in a 1929 Fireman's Parade commemorating the 250th anniversary of the founding of Trenton. From left to right are (first row) Spencer Cornell, Pat Pilla, Joe Pilla, Jim Hindley, Paul Paak, and Robert Ross; (second row, on bridge) George Ziegler, and Tony Pilla.

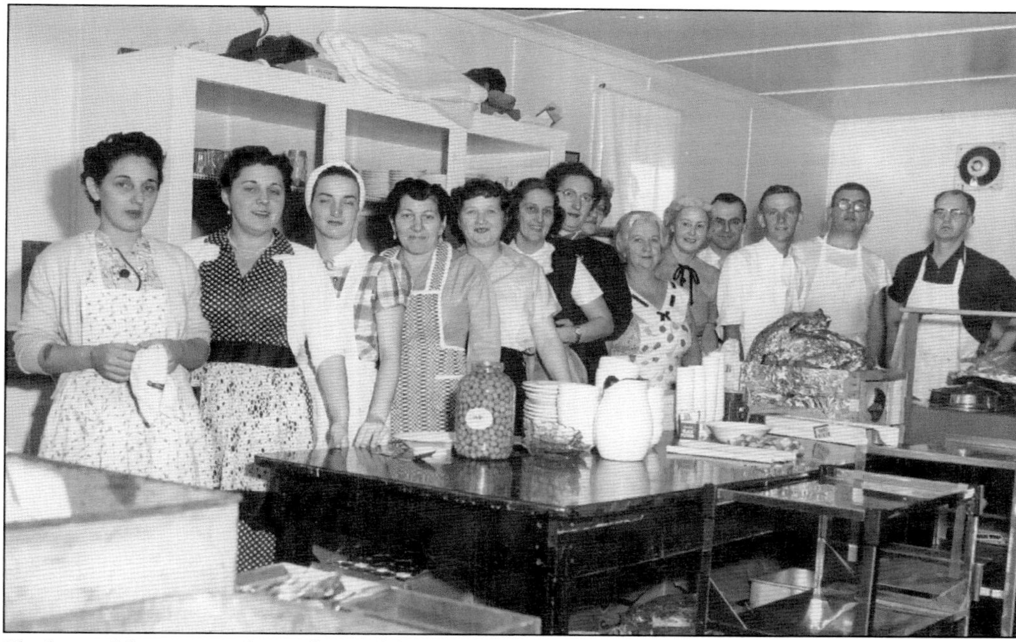

Slackwood firemen and members of the Ladies Auxiliary prepare for a fundraising turkey dinner in the firehouse, around 1950. Pictured from left to right are Winona Nash, Lamina Hollandonner, Virginia Ratcliffe, Dorothea Mohr, Mary Turner, Peg Dyer, Vivian Weigel, Ida Mason, Lillian Smith, Dot Goodwin, Howard Feiler, Harry Ratcliffe, Charles Turner, and Fred Weigel.

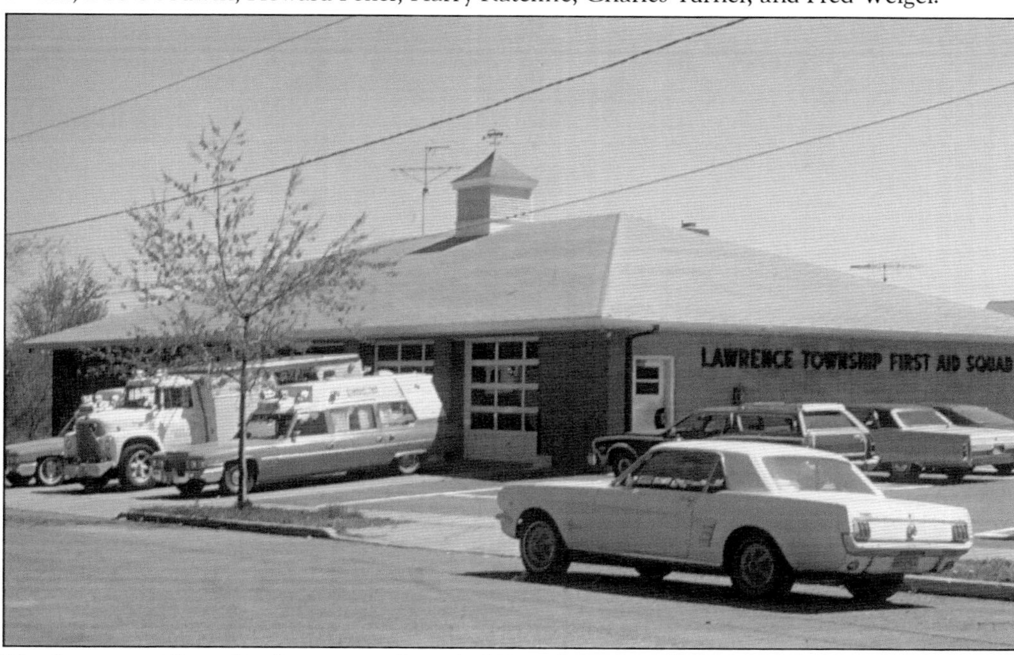

The Lawrence Township Emergency First Aid Squad was founded in 1946 to provide ambulance service to township residents. The squad was formed with the help of the Lions Club and was ready for service in October 1947. By the 1960s, the squad had their own building on Wilson Avenue (later renamed Pilla Avenue) and housed multiple ambulances.

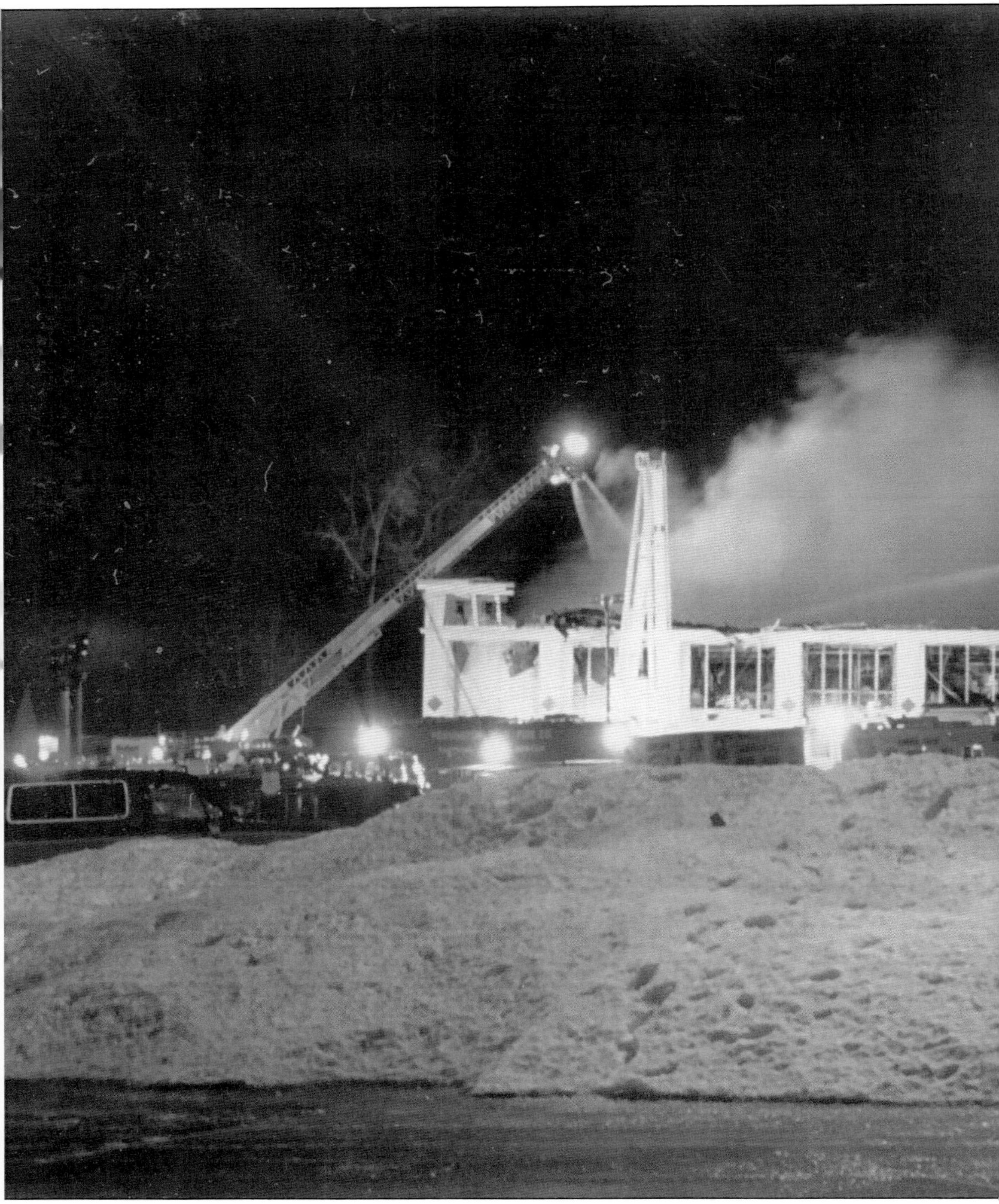

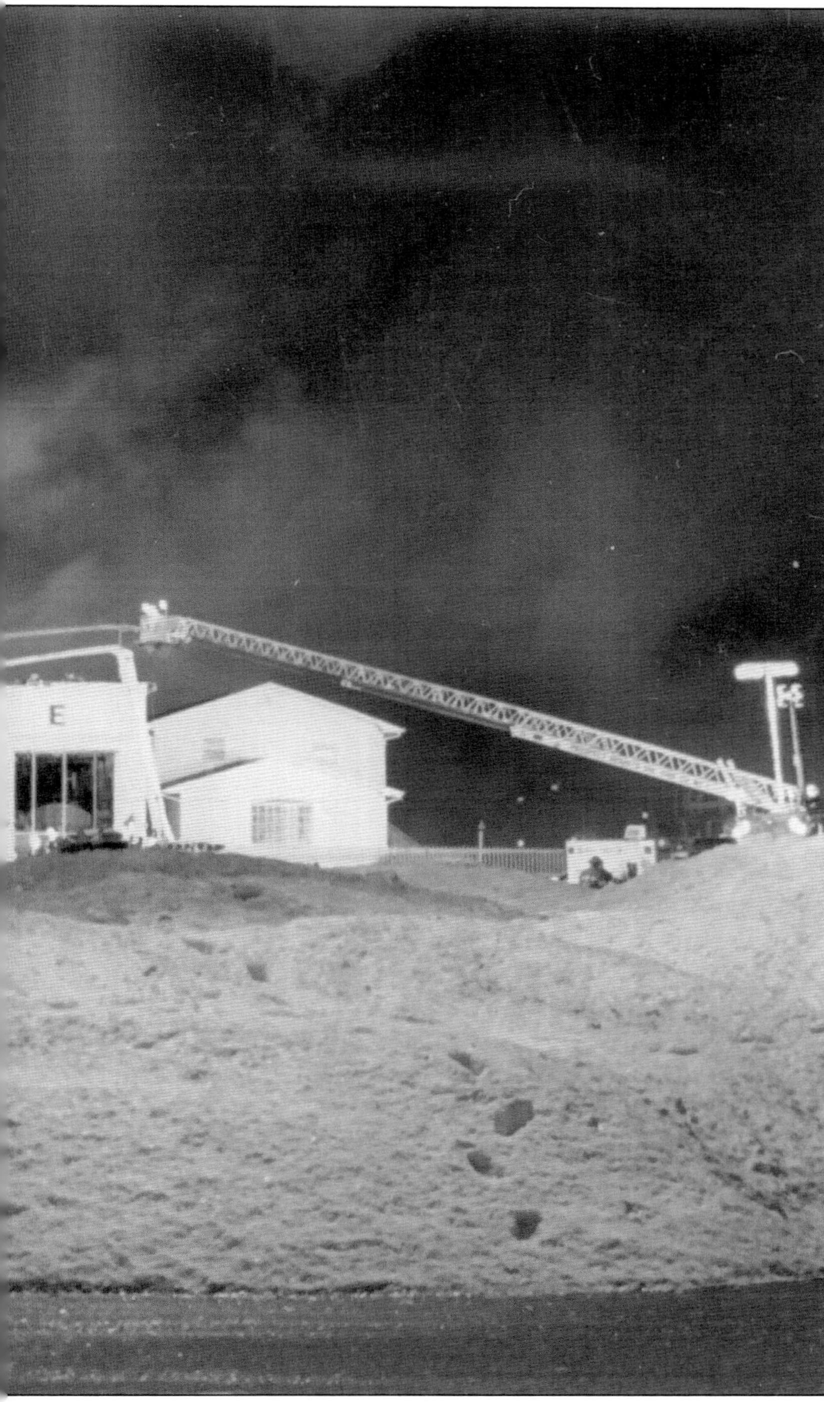

A fire broke out in the Huffman-Koos furniture store at Lawrence Shopping Center on the evening of January 19, 1996. The fire started in the store's sign on a windy night and became a fast-spreading blaze that took over 11 hours to extinguish. Hot spots flared up over the weekend, requiring a few return visits from the fire department. Here, aerial trucks from Lawrence and Ewing are seen fighting the fire, which destroyed the building. Huffman-Koos was the original occupant of the space when the shopping center opened in the 1960s, but had closed in the early 1970s. Park Lane Furniture occupied the location until the late 1990s, when Huffman-Koos returned to the center.

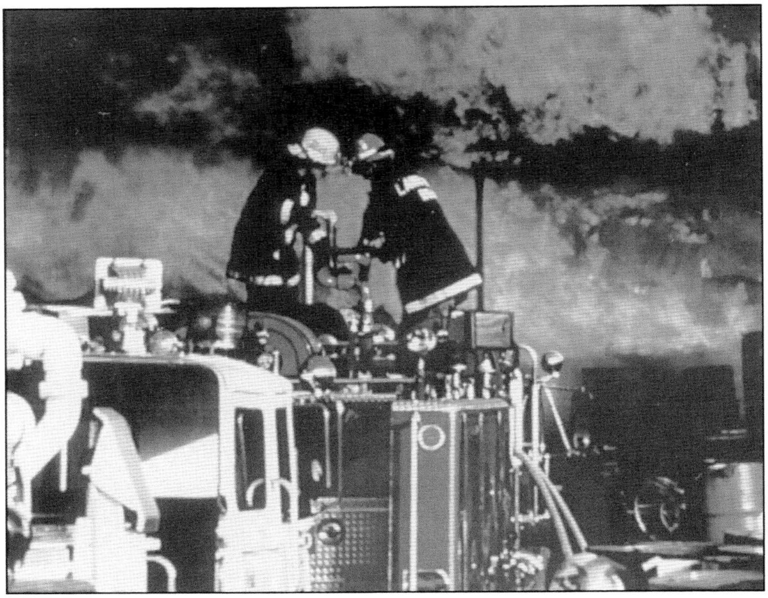

Firefighters Jim Yates (left) and Lt. Wayne Hannon (right), from Lawrence Road Fire Company, fight a blaze at Trenton Fiber Drum Company on September 22, 1984. Trenton Fiber Drum cleaned and recycled barrel drums at their property on New York Avenue. The fire produced thick, dark smoke, which could be seen from as far away as New Brunswick.

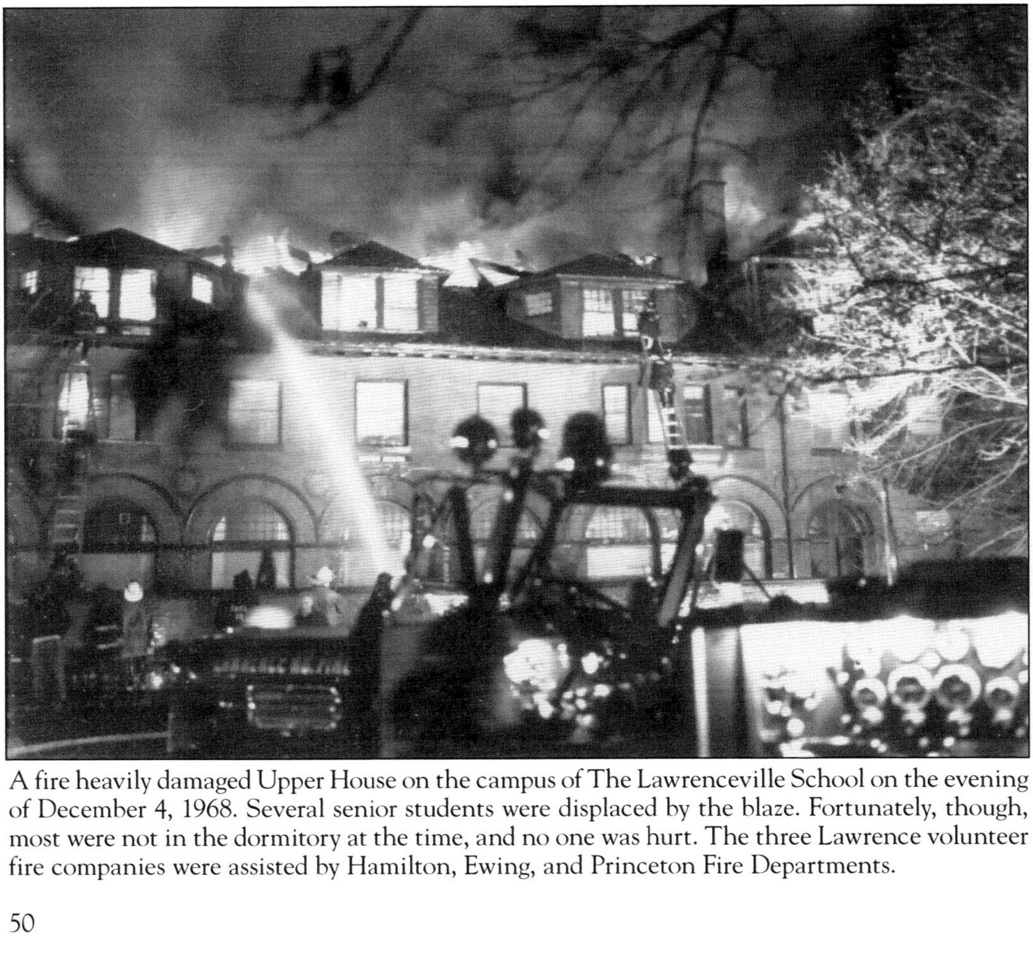

A fire heavily damaged Upper House on the campus of The Lawrenceville School on the evening of December 4, 1968. Several senior students were displaced by the blaze. Fortunately, though, most were not in the dormitory at the time, and no one was hurt. The three Lawrence volunteer fire companies were assisted by Hamilton, Ewing, and Princeton Fire Departments.

Smoke billows from the windows of the Nash home on Brunswick Avenue as numerous spectators watch firemen work to put out the fire. The spectacular blaze engulfed the home around 1958. The Nash family had lived in the house for several decades, having been one of the first families to settle in the Slackwood neighborhood.

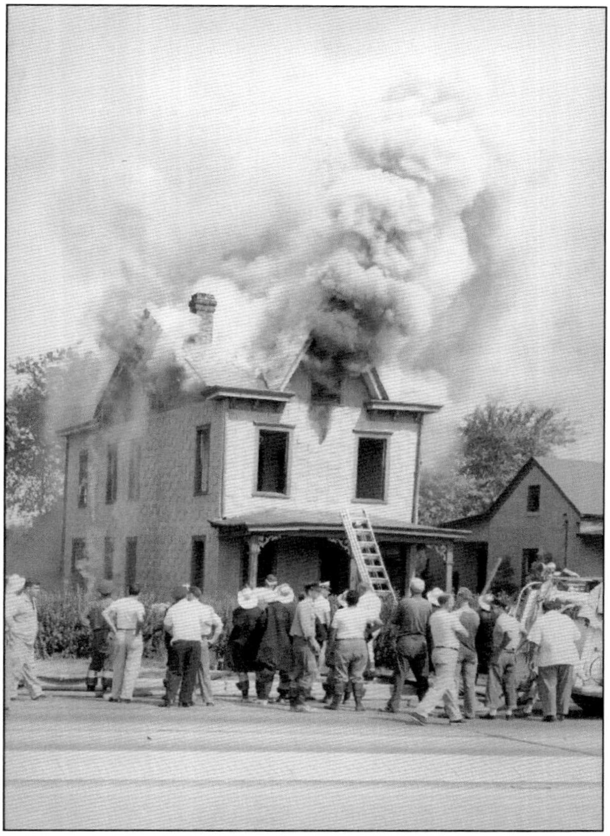

Slackwood Fire House on Slack Avenue (photographed in November 1939) was built in 1921, replacing the original building, which had become too small to fit new fire engines. A sign in front of the firehouse warns drivers to slow down because of unreliable traffic lights. The sign may have been put up following a tragic accident that occurred on January 20, 1934, killing seven firefighters at a nearby intersection.

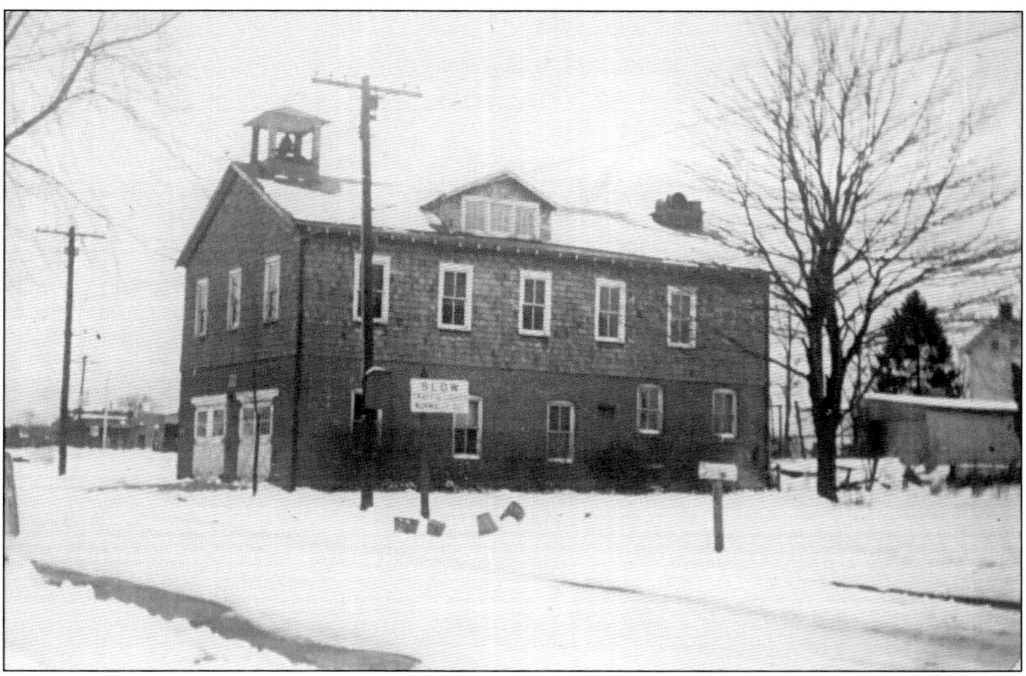

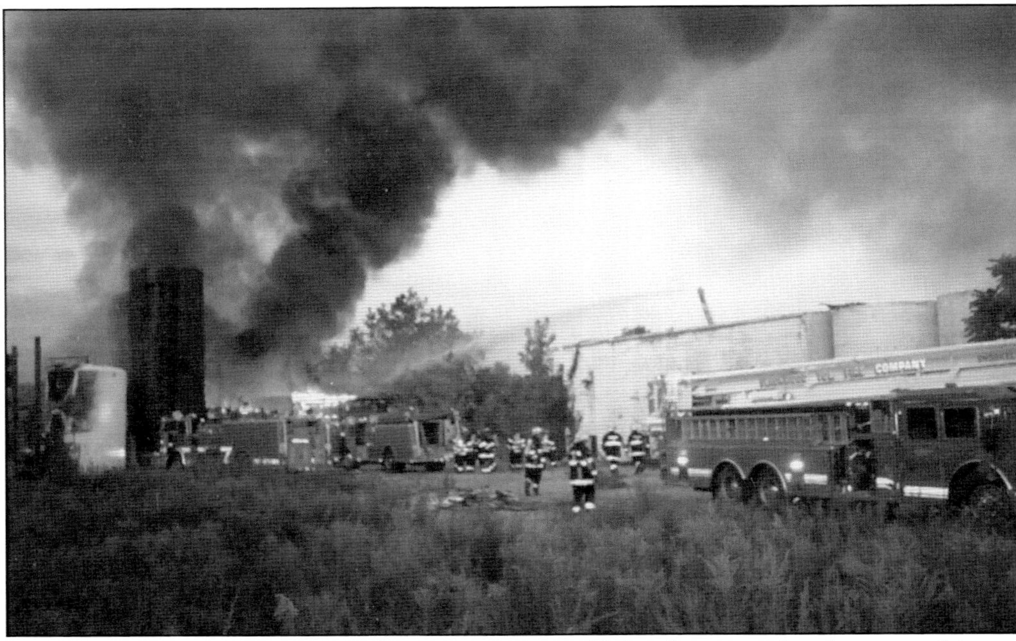

Saturn Chemical, Inc., on New York Avenue, was engulfed in flames on the afternoon of August 21, 1981. The fire was remarkable for a series of explosions that occurred, as well as for the dark cloud of smoke that covered the area. Fears of either a major explosion or possible toxic fumes led fire officials to order a partial evacuation of the surrounding neighborhood. Residents near the plant had long expressed concerns about the safety of chemicals used by Saturn to produce ink and paint. Just over a year earlier, the plant had suffered a lightning strike to an above-ground tank, and the resulting gas leak had forced the closure of a portion of Route 1 while firefighters worked to contain it.

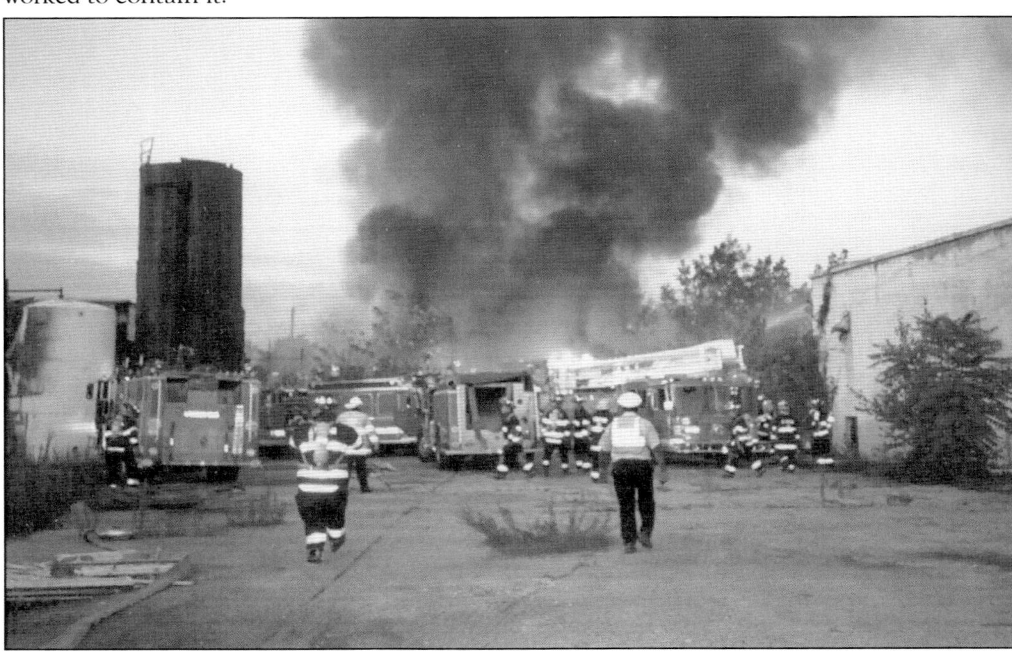

Four

Houses and Neighborhoods

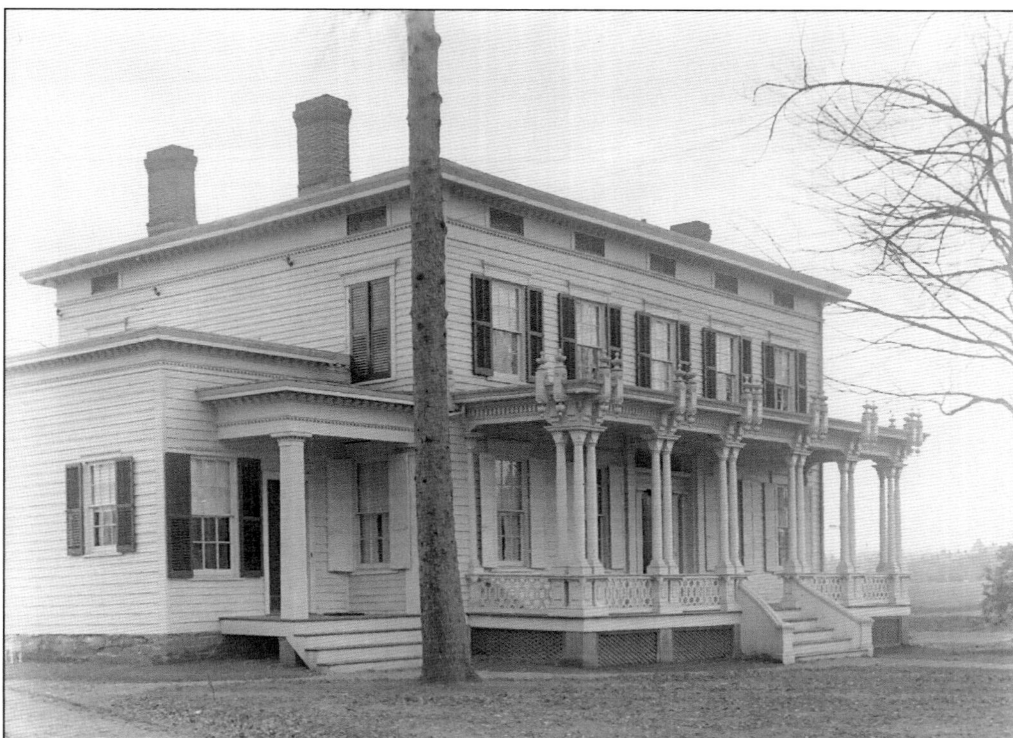

The William Grover House was located on Lewisville Road on Lawrenceville School property, near the Biles/Monroe House. The house burned down in the 1960s after years of disrepair. The land was once owned by General Joseph Brearley and later by the federal government, which used the farm as a work-skills training facility for soldiers returning from World War I with disabilities.

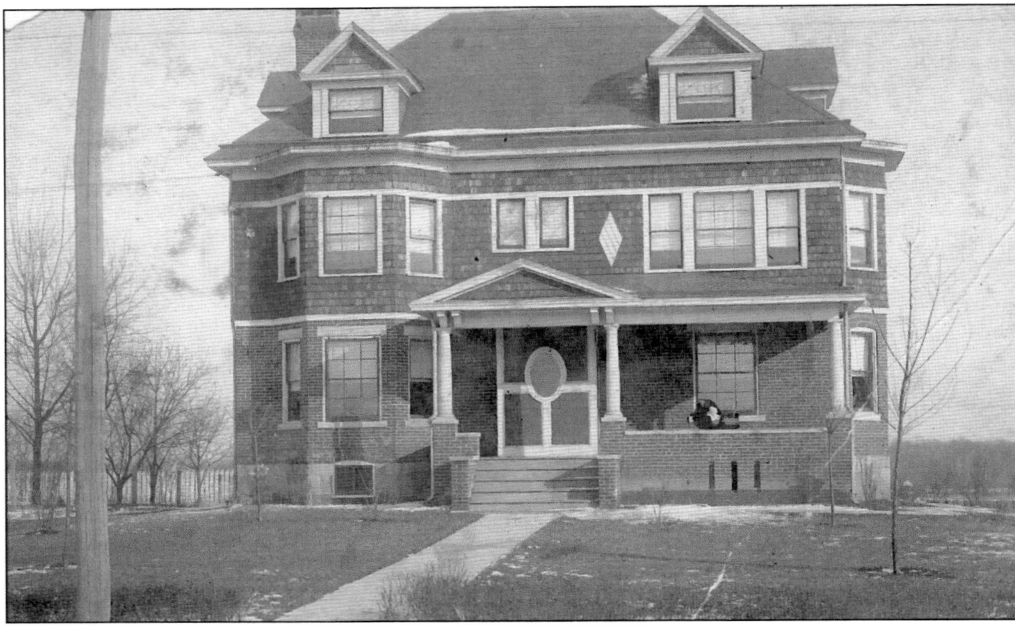

The Goulding House was featured on a c. 1910 postcard. The house, located on Lawrence Road, is an example of Victorian architecture in Lawrence Township. It is in an area that developed along with the trolley lines that ran from Trenton to Princeton. Residents could live in Lawrence and commute to work in either town via trolley.

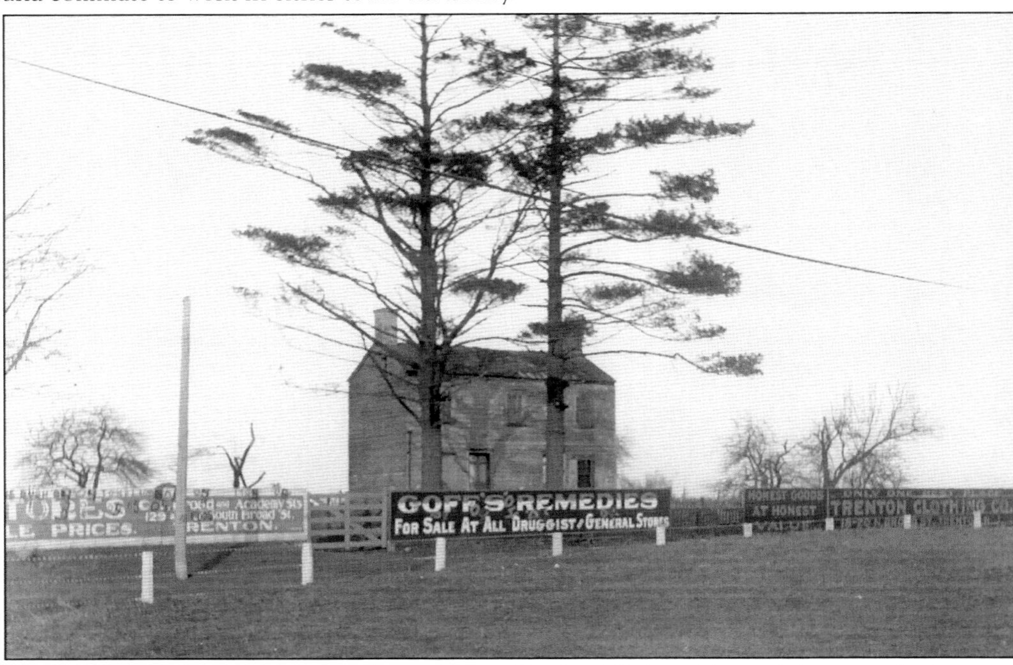

The advertising on the fence in front of the Elizabeth Labaw House (photographed around 1902) on Fackler Road targeted passengers on the trolley, which ran in front of the property. The house later served as the McCrae family home and was razed in March 1994 to make way for construction of a new home.

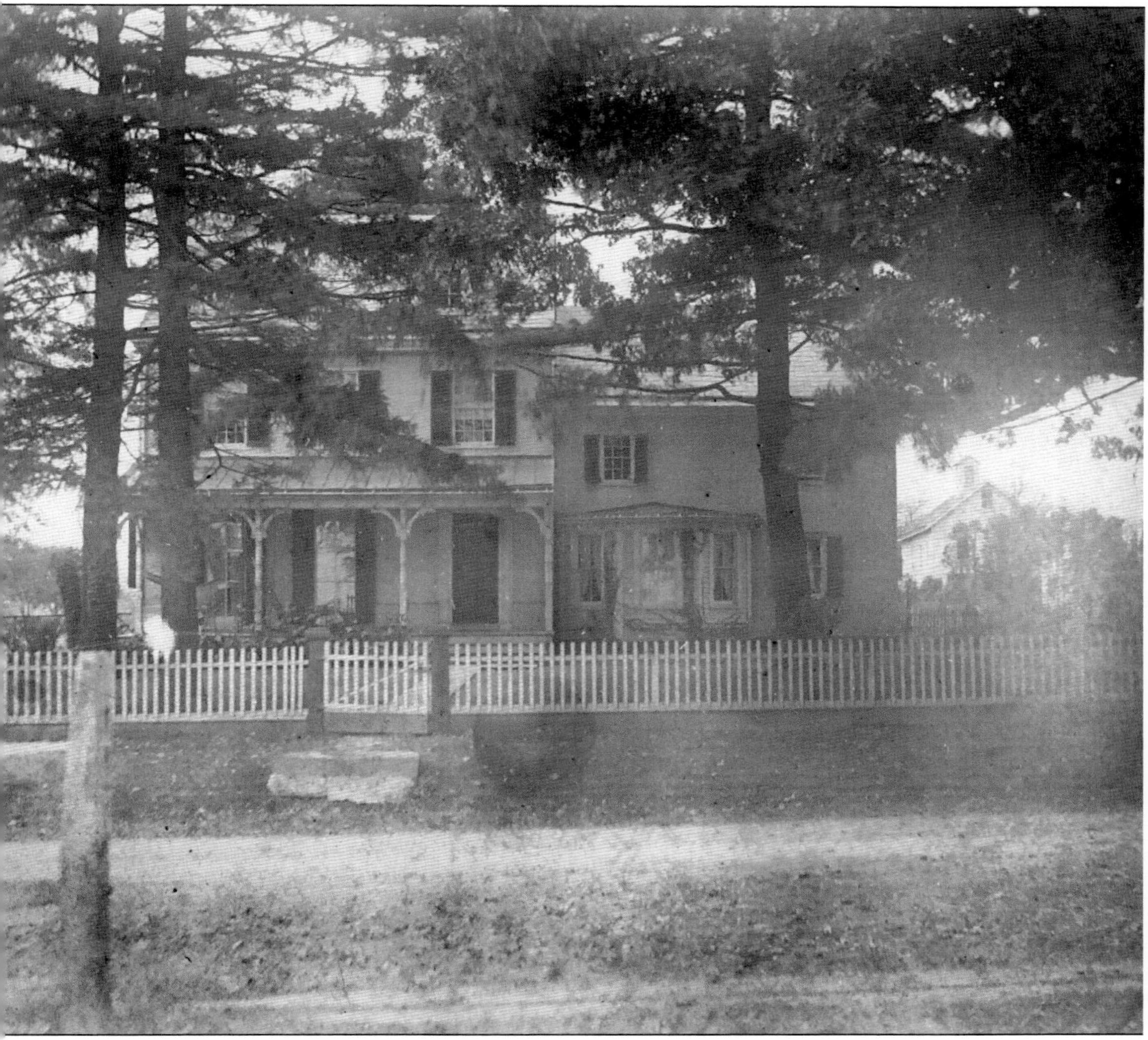

The Jasper Smith III house, located on a large plot of land on Lawrence Road, was destroyed by fire in 1904. Smith was a prominent lawyer and died without direct heirs, so he willed the farm and house to the Lawrenceville Presbyterian Church. The house was briefly occupied by the church's minister, and the property was subsequently dubbed the Parsonage Farm. Despite stipulations in Smith's will that made it difficult to sell off parts of the land without first contacting the Smith family, the church was eventually able to divest itself of the real estate. The large parcel was broken up through sales to Rider College, developers, and individuals. Today, Rider University, the Long Acres subdivision, and the township municipal complex are all located on land that was once the Parsonage Farm.

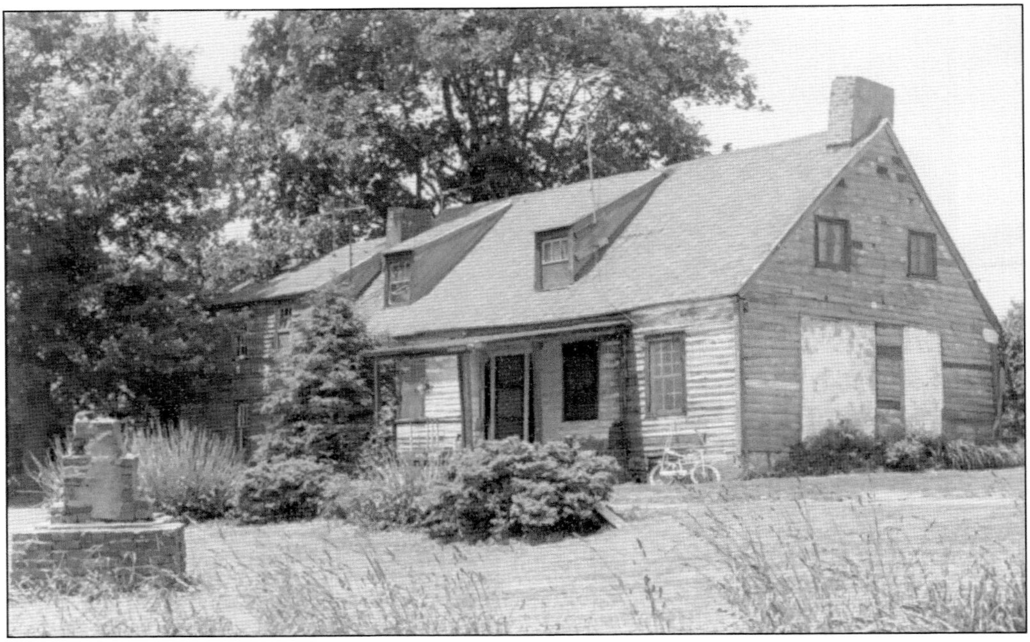

The Joseph/Azariah Reed House, pictured around 1976, was located on Federal City Road, just south of Interstate 295. The wood and stone house was built around 1776. It was preserved during the construction of the interstate, but by 1989 had sat unoccupied and neglected for several years. It was eventually demolished.

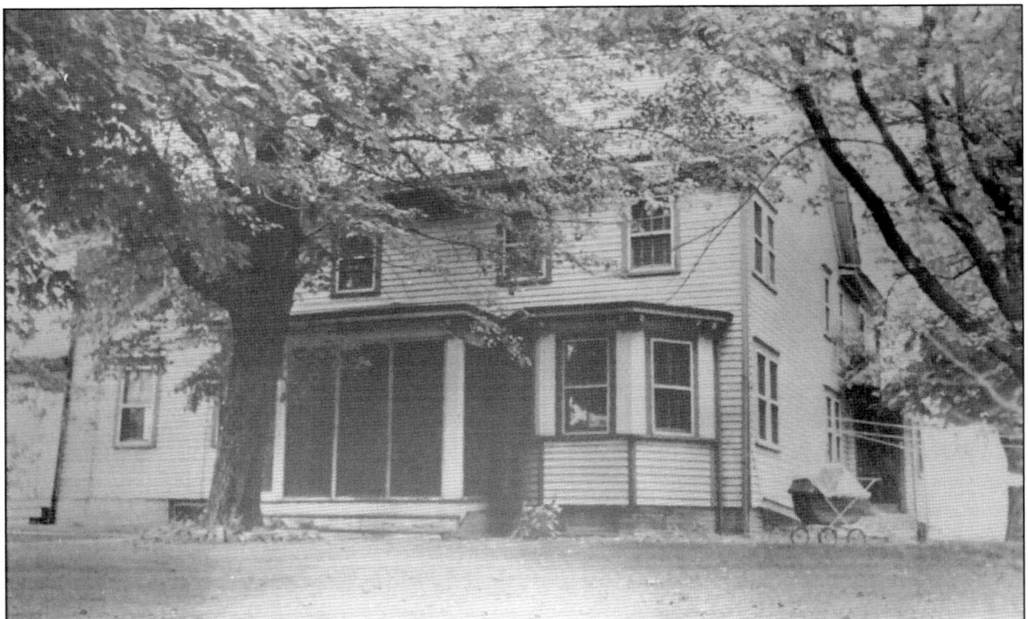

Pictured around 1910, the Joshua Smith/Peter Mershon farmstead on Gedney Road was, at one time, a 106-acre farm. Both the Mershon and Smith families were early settlers of Maidenhead, with the Mershons owning many lots in the northern part of town and the Smiths owning a great deal of land in the southern part.

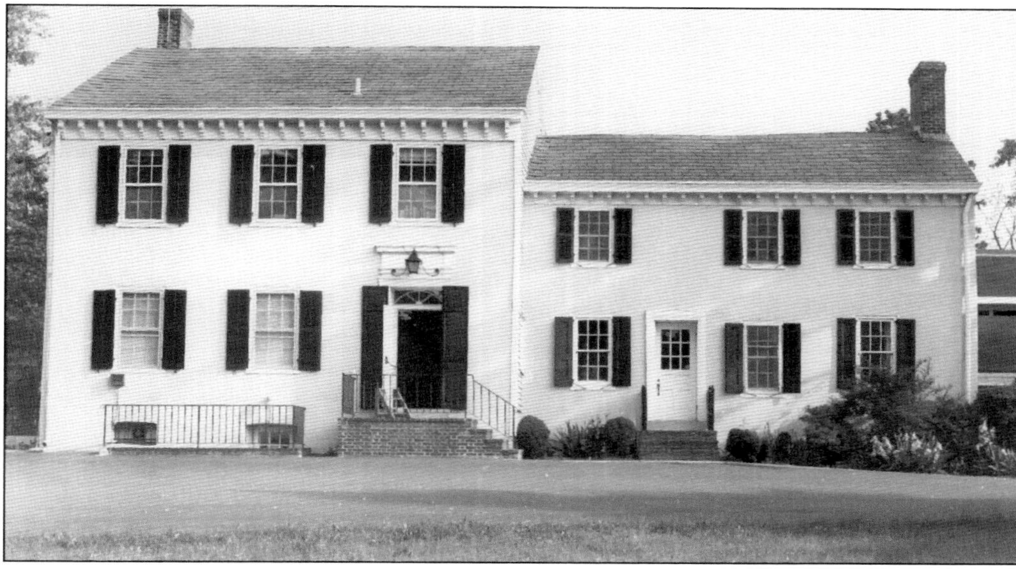

The Edgar Smith estate, pictured around 1970, is also known as the Phillips-Schenck House. It is located just north of Province Line Road on Princeton Pike. The property was purchased by Chapin School in June 1958, and the house was converted to office space. Although the exterior was sided to match the rest of the school, parts of the interior retain their original materials and furnishings.

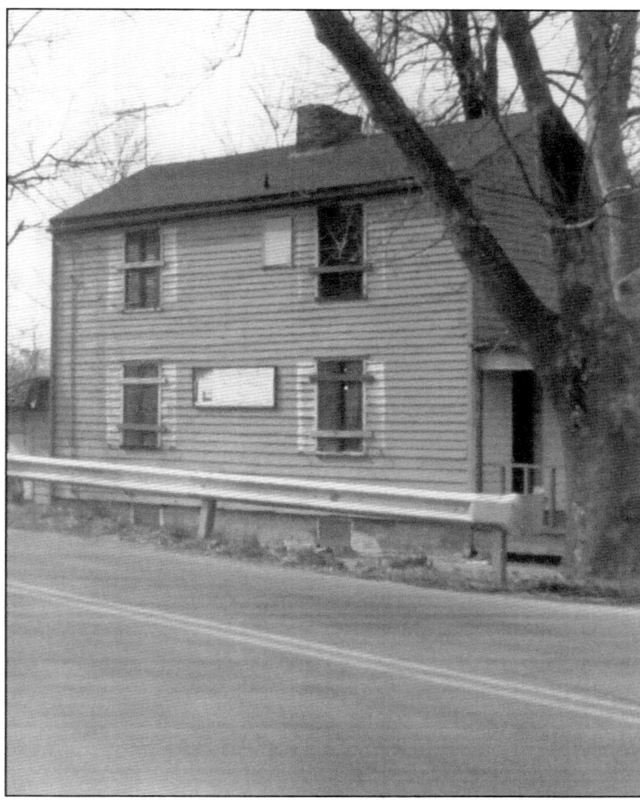

Port Mercer Canal House is pictured here in April 1979, before being restored by the Lawrence Historical Society. The bridge tender's house remained occupied when the canal closed to traffic in 1933, but was vacant by the mid-1970s. It was built around 1833 or 1834, with a rear addition added in the early 1900s. At one time, Port Mercer was a vibrant part of town, with an inn, a general store, warehouses, and a post office serving canal traffic.

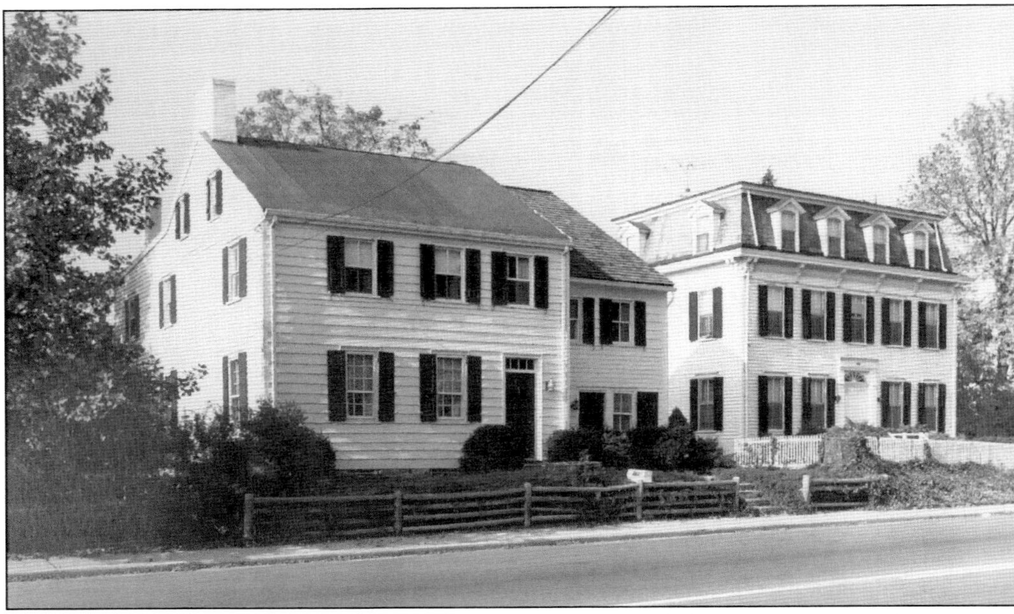

Benjamin Smith owned a large parcel of land on Princeton Pike that is now at the corner of Darrah Lane. The house on the left is the Rising Sun Tavern, which the Smith family ran until the late 1800s. Drovers would stay at the tavern overnight, and their animals would pasture in the fields behind the building. The Johnston house (right) was once part of a larger family home and was moved to the roadside in the early 1900s. (Courtesy of Laurin McCracken.)

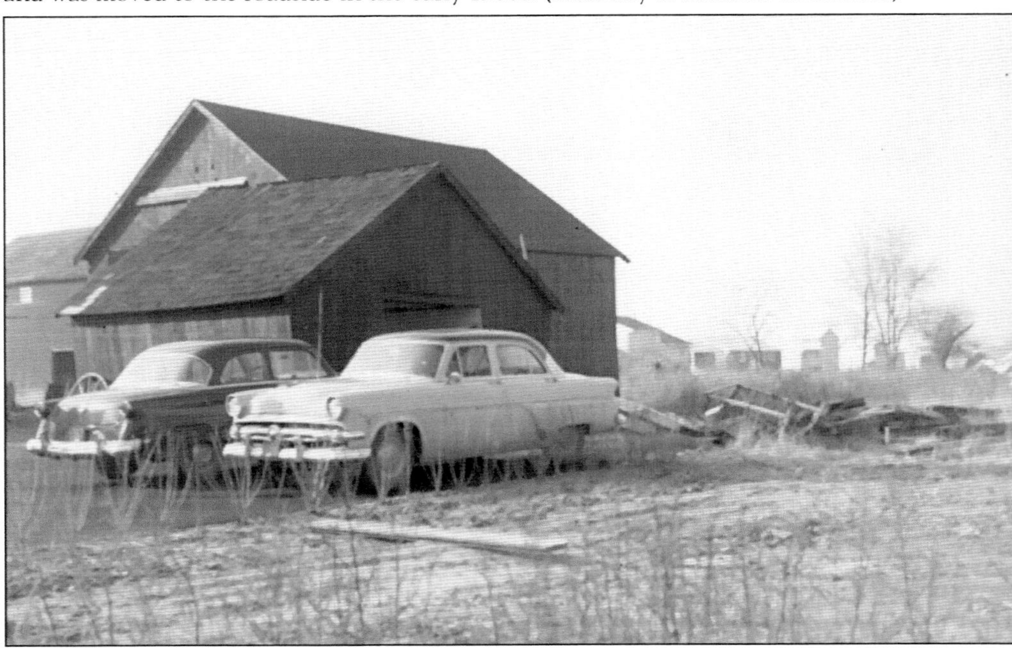

After the Smith family closed the Rising Sun Tavern, they converted the land into a farm. Barns were built between the tavern and the Johnston house, where they remained until burning down in the 1970s. In 1957, the barns functioned as storage and as a garage. To the right (in the distance) are new houses on Darrah Lane that were built as part of the Nassau I development.

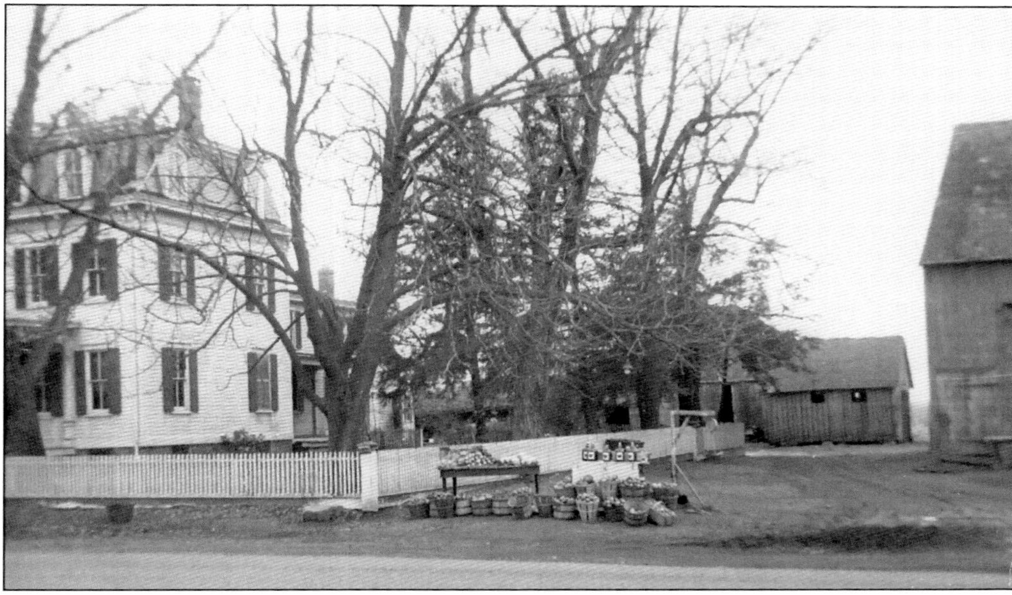

Another view of the Johnston house on Princeton Pike shows even more barns to the right of the Smith property in October 1955. When it was a working farm, the family often set up a roadside stand, where they sold fruit, vegetables, and farm-made products like cider and jam. The farm was replaced by housing in the early 1960s.

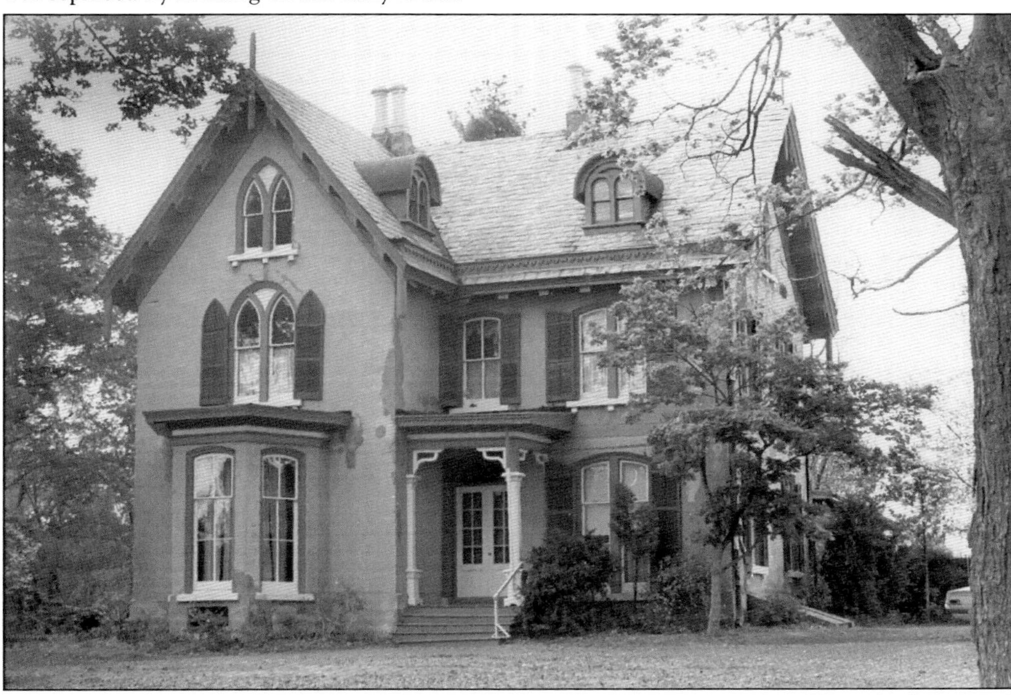

This c. 1965 photograph shows the J. Brewer House, also known as Sunny Gables, which was built in the 1870s by the Bruere (Brewer) family. The house is an example of Gothic Revival Victorian, which was a style typical of the Rosedale section of town. The house, located on Rosedale Road, was restored by a private owner in 1993.

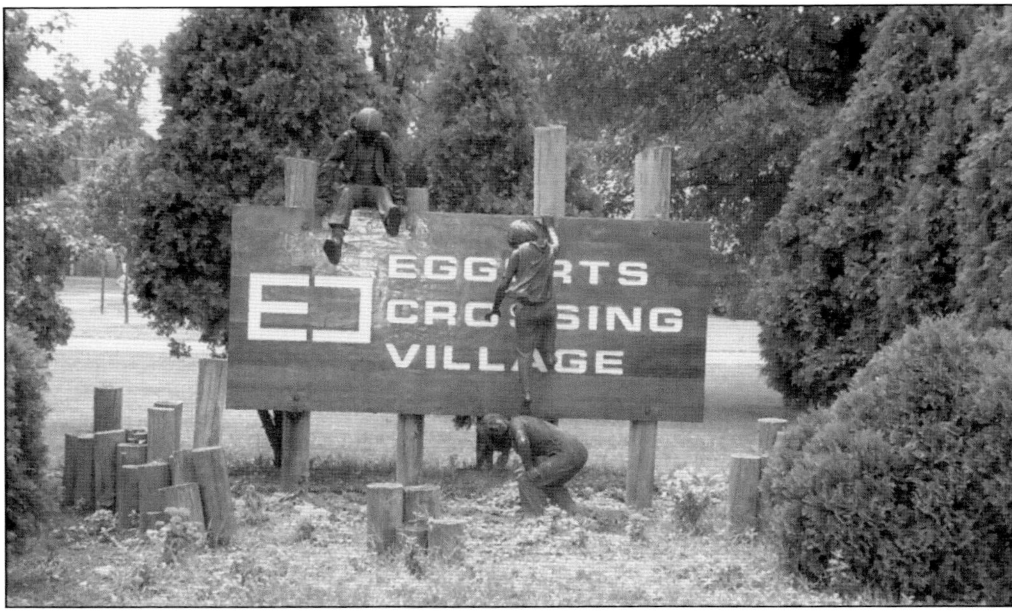

A sign, pictured above, welcomes visitors to Eggerts Crossing Village; below is an example of the housing units in the complex, which opened in May 1974. In 1965, the Lawrence Community Action Council (CAC) was formed to address the issue of poverty in the township. By 1969, a housing committee within the CAC was considering ways to rehabilitate substandard housing and decided to pursue new building instead. The Lawrence Non-Profit Housing Corporation was created, and planning for the village began in fall 1970. Funded by state loans and federal grants, the village included 100 units for low- and moderate-income families. The sculpture around the sign is titled "Adventure." (Courtesy of Fred Vereen.)

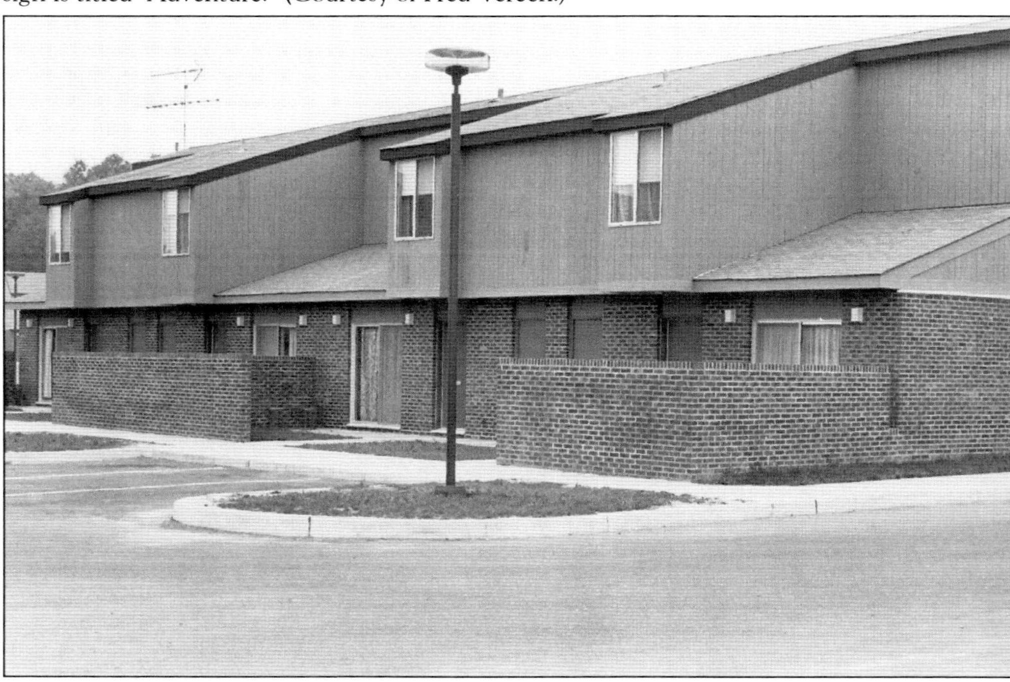

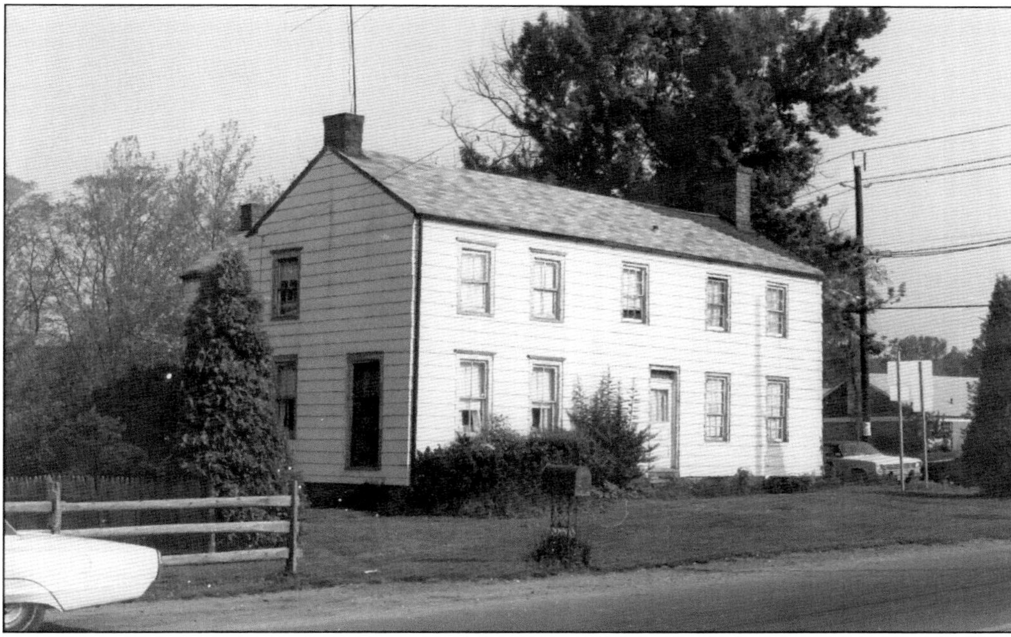

The Baker House, photographed in 1962, was the home of Benjamin Baker and was located at the corner of Franklin Corner Road and Princeton Pike. Baker built a hotel in 1806 on the northbound side of Brunswick Pike and later built a basin near the hotel after the Delaware and Raritan Canal was constructed. The wharf, hotel and house are long-gone, but the name Bakers Basin is still used to refer to the area.

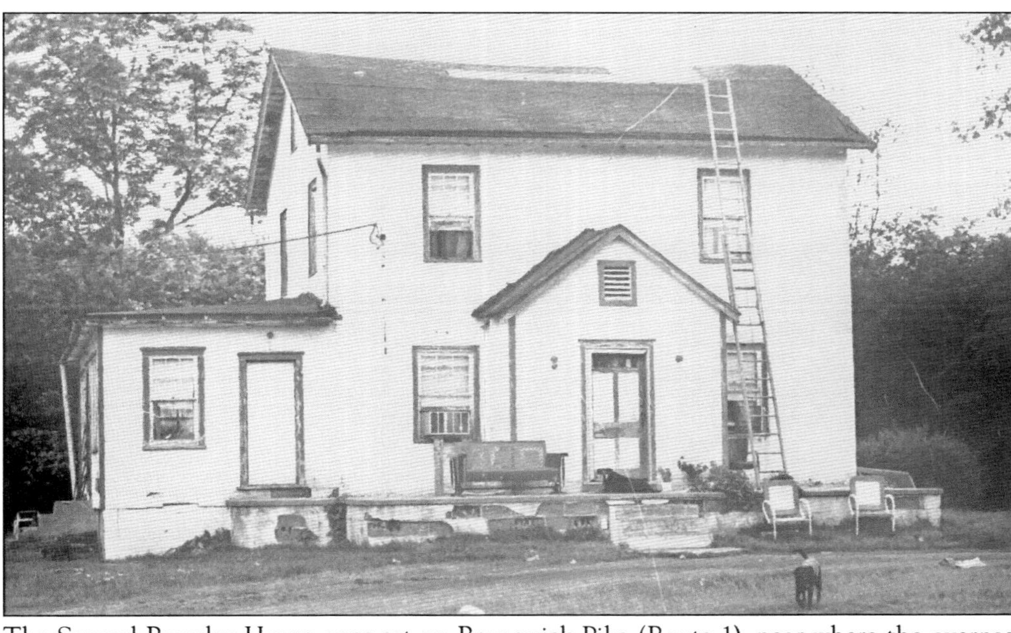

The Samuel Brearley House once sat on Brunswick Pike (Route 1), near where the overpass for Interstate 295 is located today. Samuel was the grandson of John Brearley (who built the Brearley house at the end of Meadow Road) and a distant relative of David Brearley (a signer of the US Constitution).

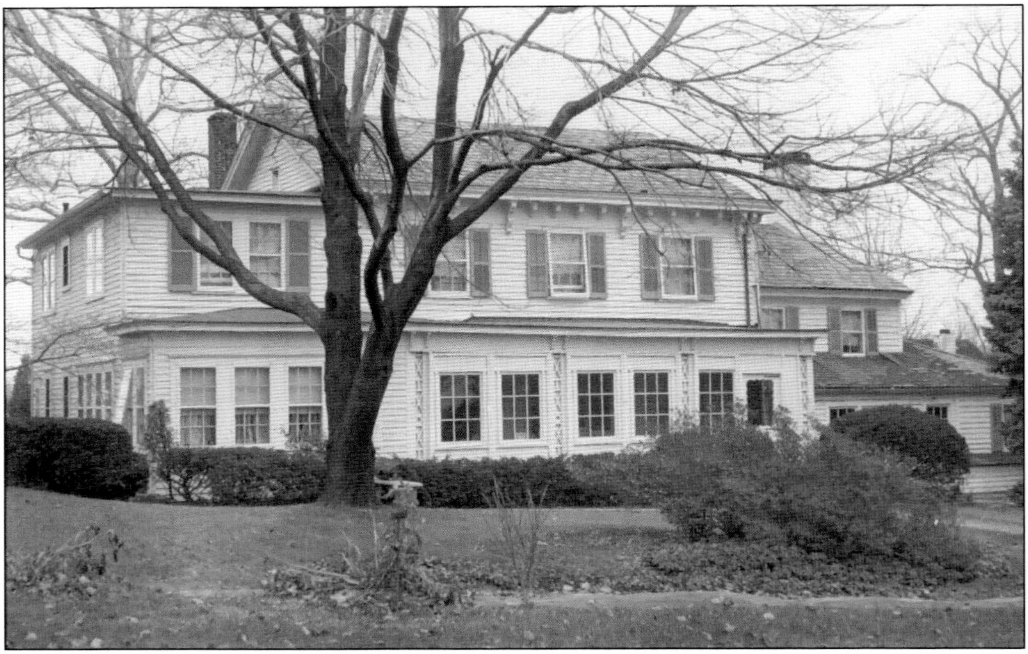

The Jasper Smith II house on Pine Knoll Drive, pictured in November 1964, is one of the oldest in the township. Built in the mid-1700s, the farmhouse served as the home of the earliest generations of Smiths. By the 20th century, the property was owned by the Ribsam family, and the house became known as the Smith/Ribsam house. The farmland had become the Pine Knoll Tree Farm.

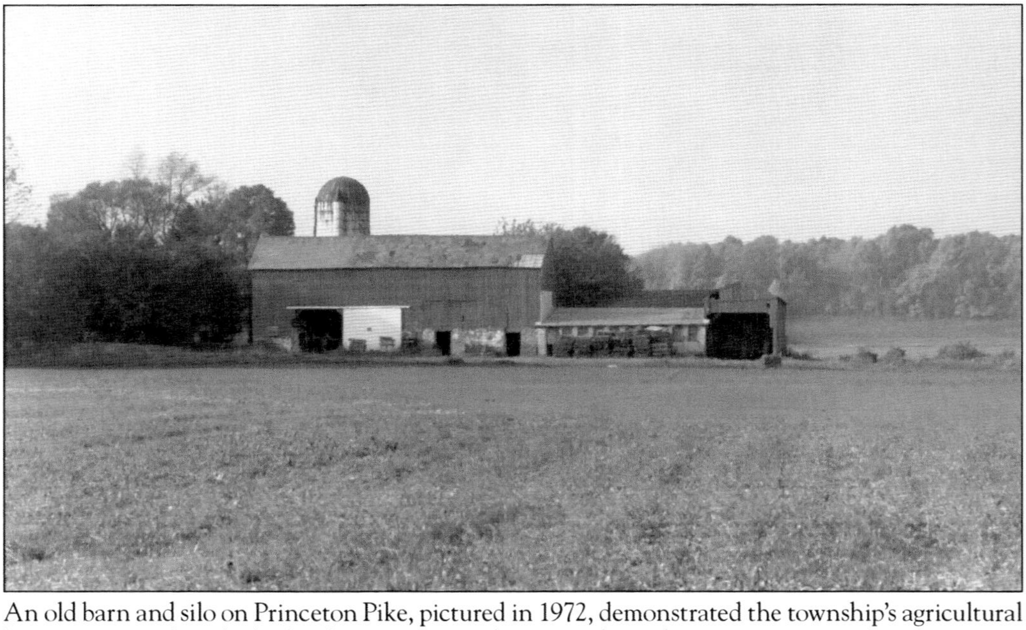

An old barn and silo on Princeton Pike, pictured in 1972, demonstrated the township's agricultural heritage, even though the land was no longer being used as a farm. It was not uncommon to see abandoned farm structures in the 1970s, as the township transformed from a farming community to a suburban center. (Courtesy of Laurin McCracken.)

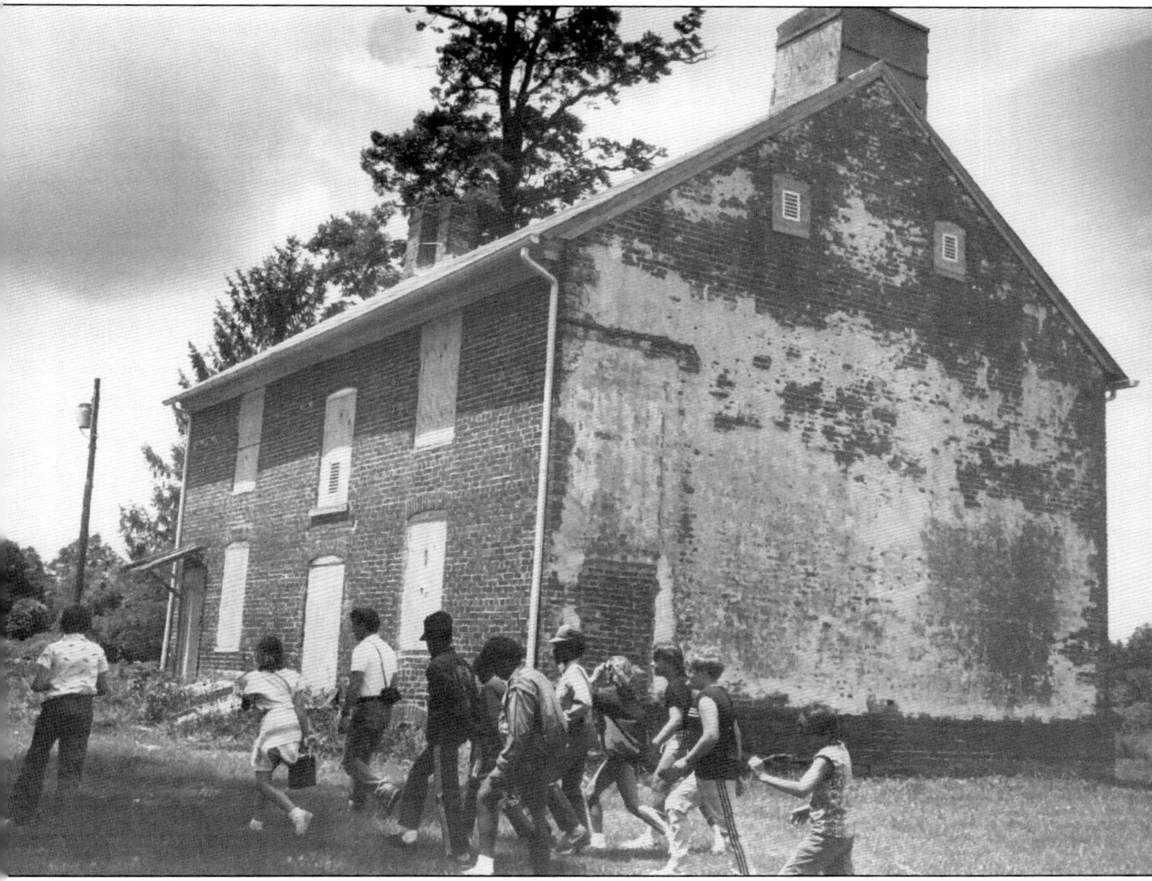

In this c. 1990 photograph, Dick Beach leads a group of students past the boarded-up Brearley House on an outdoor education field trip. The house was built by John Brearley and owned by the Brearley family until the early 1900s. The Fawcett family was the last to live in the house, and it was left vacant by subsequent owners. In 1977, the township purchased a large parcel of land that included the house, with the intention of making the area a park with athletic fields and picnic areas. The park was never built, and a pig farmer began using the house in the 1980s. The township and the historical society came together in the 1990s to raise funds and obtain grants to restore the house. The project was successful, and the restoration was completed by May 2000. The area around the house has been made into a park for passive recreation and includes a bike and walking trail. (Courtesy of the Lawrence Ledger.)

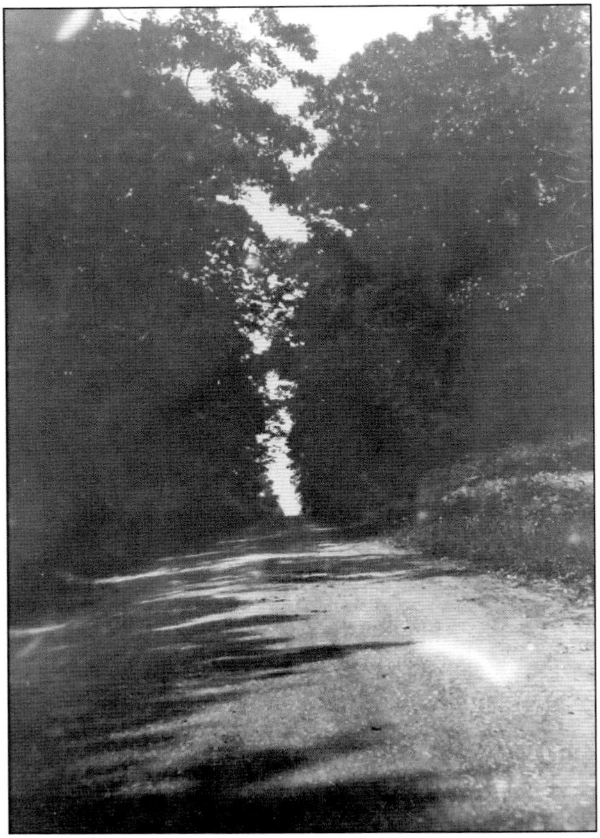

Sattherwait's Woods (pictured left, around 1900), on the east side of Brunswick Pike, had a dirt lane opposite Texas Avenue that lead to the farm of Henry Mershon III. Benjamin Sattherwait, having already purchased four lots of adjacent land, bought the Mershon property after the death of Henry's widow, Sarah (around 1874). The Mershon farmhouse was destroyed by fire around 1912. Below, a 1974 view of the same area shows the Colonial Lakelands development and businesses along Brunswick Pike. The body of water is Colonial Lake, a man-made retention basin for the Shabakunk Creek, which ran through the woods. The creek was a flood concern when the subdivision was built in the late 1920s, so the lake was created to catch excess rainwater.

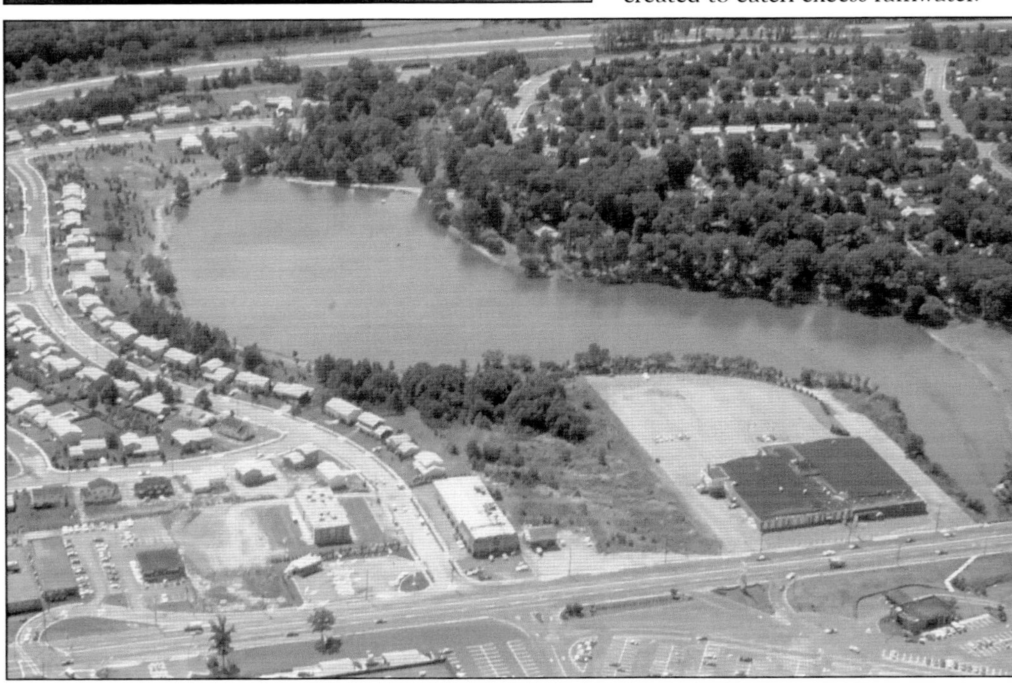

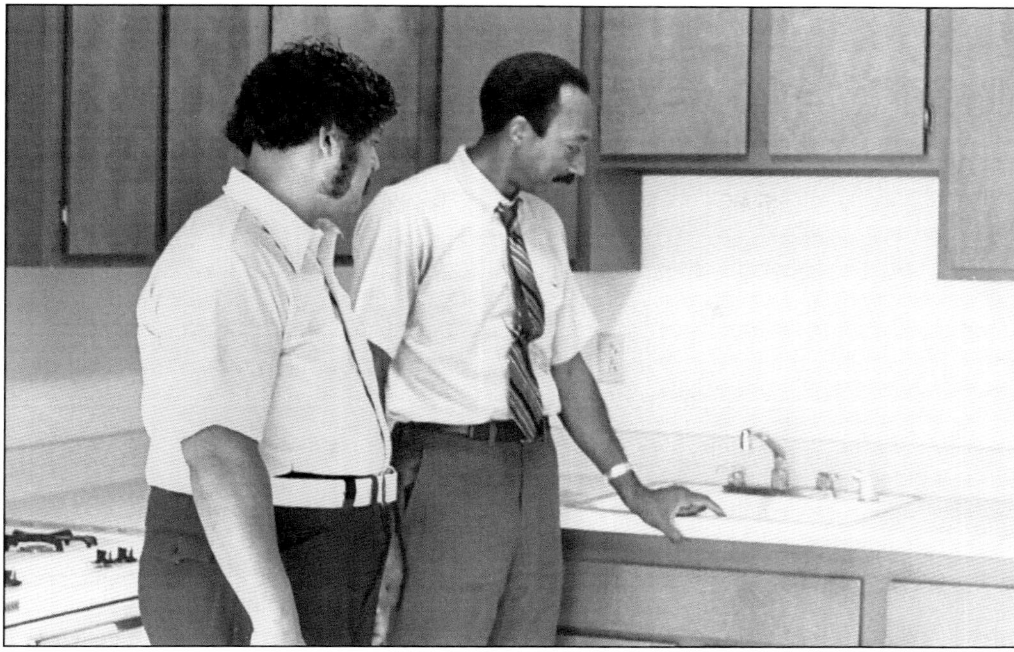

Eggerts Crossing Village opened in May 1974. In this image, Fred Vereen (right) gives a tour of a kitchen to Harold Brown in one of the units during a press preview of the housing development. The village was sponsored by Lawrence Non-Profit Housing, Inc. and built by Eggerts Development Corporation. Both groups were formed under a 1967 New Jersey law aimed at providing housing opportunities for families with a moderate income.

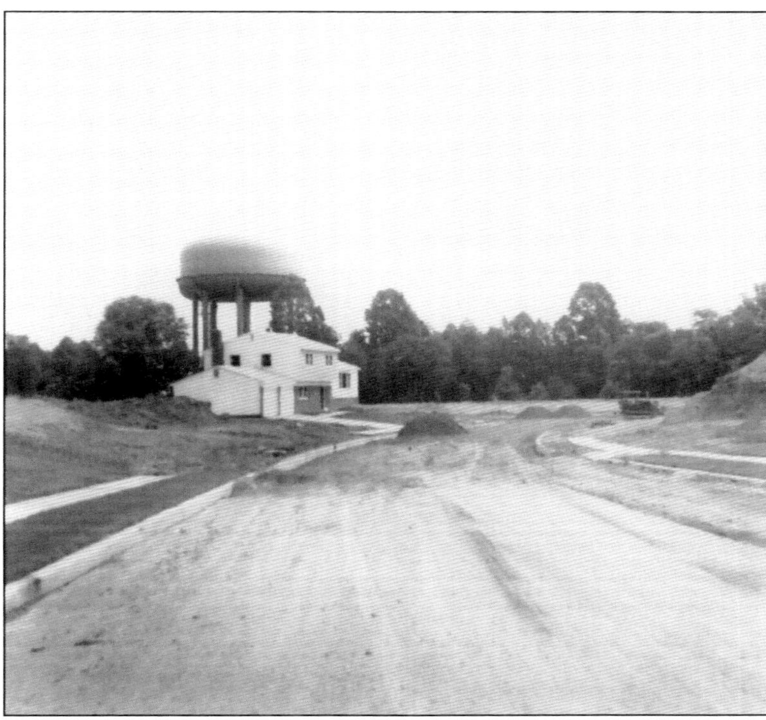

A lone completed house sits on Lawnside Drive in the Norgate II Estates in 1961. Hampton Estates, Inc. built the Norgate, Nassau, and Pine Knoll subdivisions during the 1950s and 1960s. Some of the land was once the Pine Knoll Tree Farm, and a wide variety of trees that survived the building can be found in the neighborhood today.

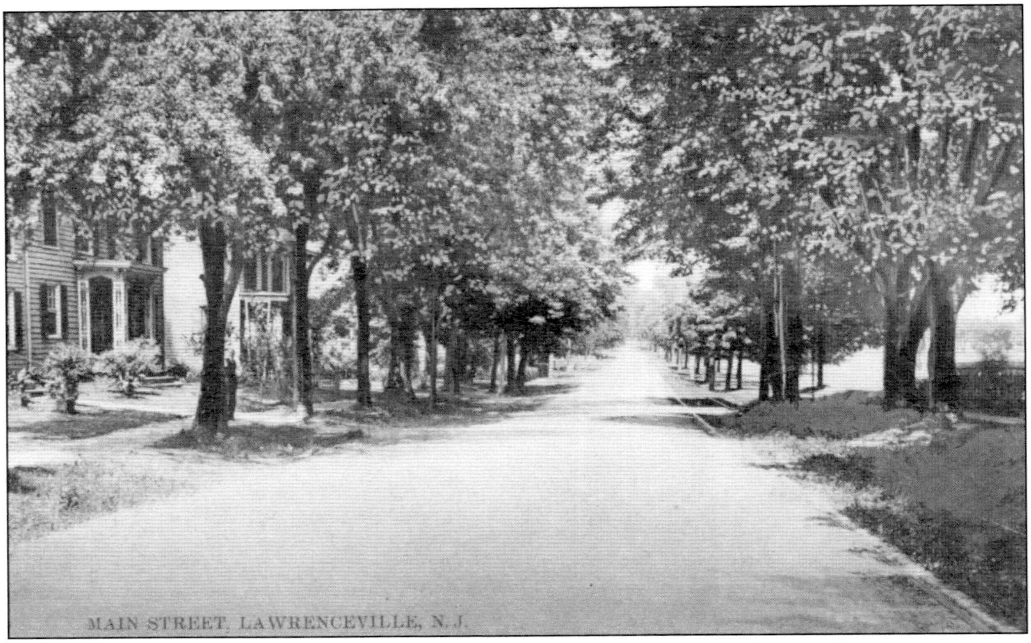

A postcard of Main Street in the village of Lawrenceville, from around 1900, shows a quiet tree-lined street with houses just to the side of the road. The Lodge and Store of The Lawrenceville School (below, around 1910) are two such houses sitting next to each other on the school's property. The Lodge was used as a residence hall by the school. Tracks for the trolley can be seen under the grove of trees on the right. Main Street is now part of Route 206, and the houses now sit further back from the busy highway.

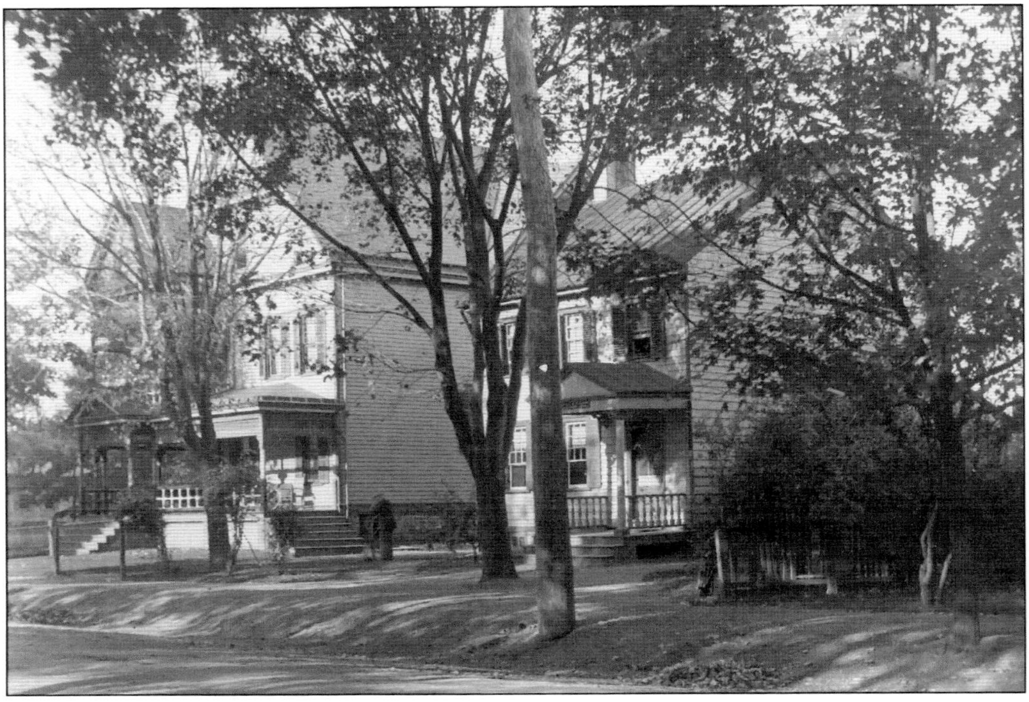

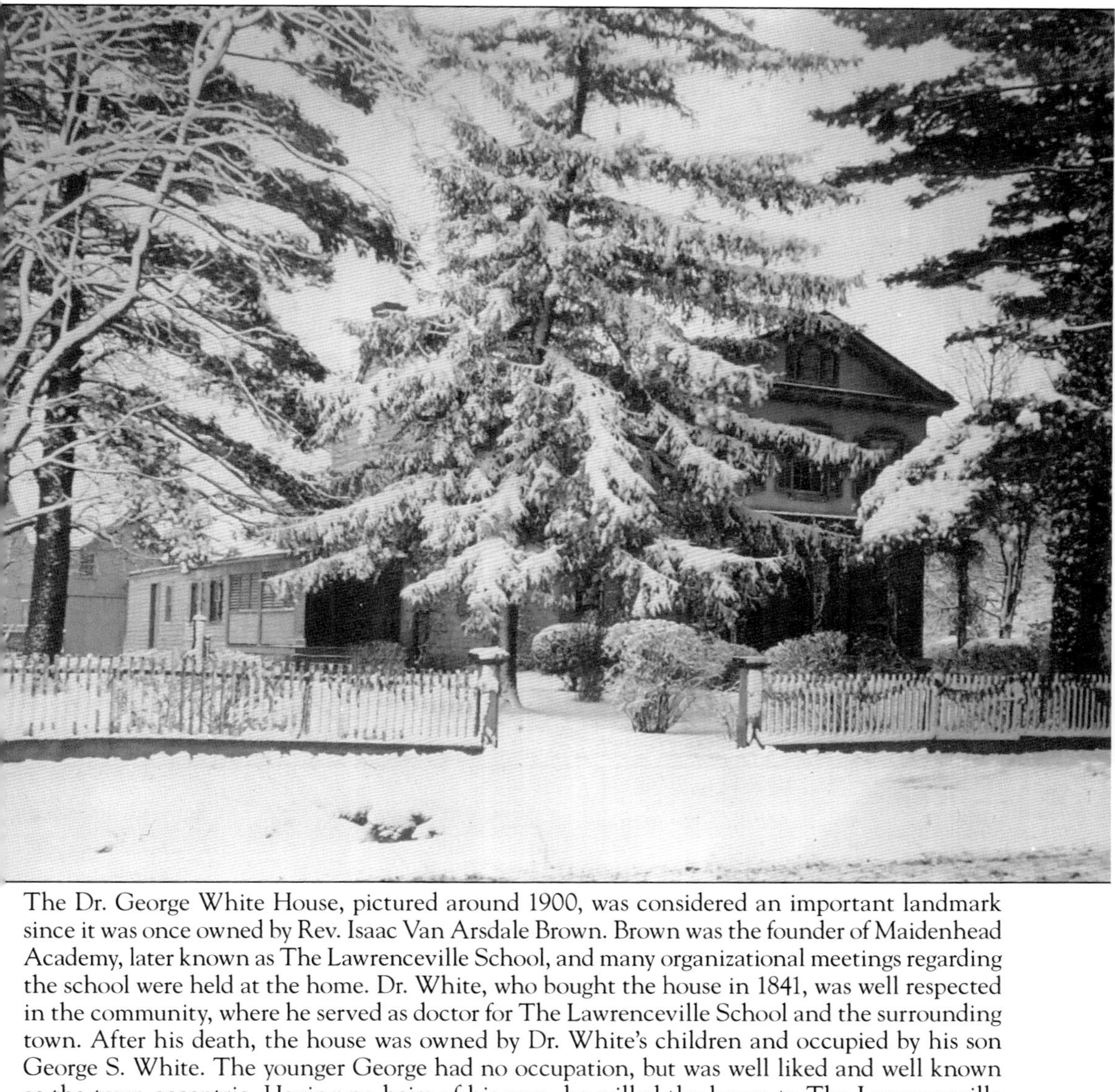

The Dr. George White House, pictured around 1900, was considered an important landmark since it was once owned by Rev. Isaac Van Arsdale Brown. Brown was the founder of Maidenhead Academy, later known as The Lawrenceville School, and many organizational meetings regarding the school were held at the home. Dr. White, who bought the house in 1841, was well respected in the community, where he served as doctor for The Lawrenceville School and the surrounding town. After his death, the house was owned by Dr. White's children and occupied by his son George S. White. The younger George had no occupation, but was well liked and well known as the town eccentric. Having no heirs of his own, he willed the house to The Lawrenceville School. Years of neglect made it too costly to repair, however, and it was torn down. The village post office was built in its place.

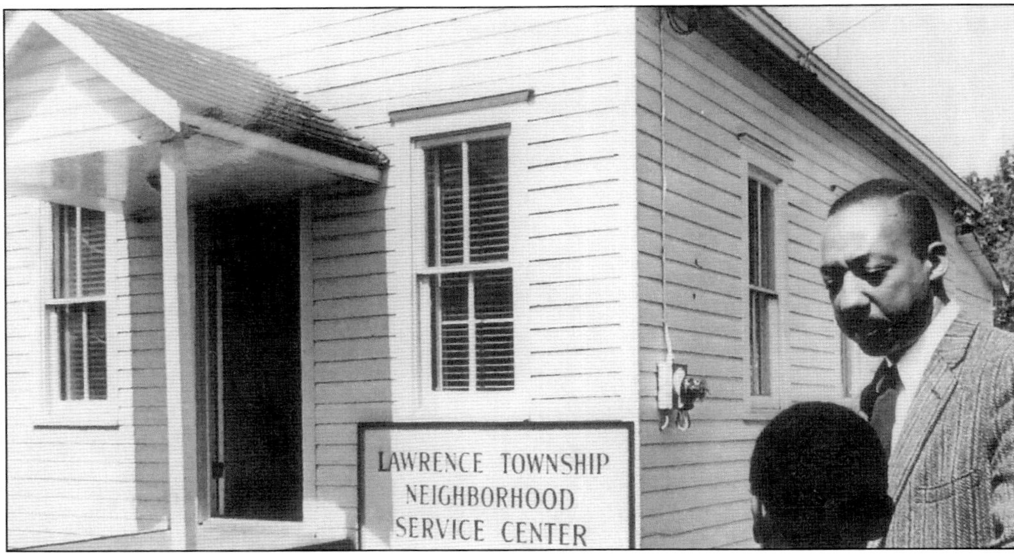

Above, Fred Vereen Jr., speaks to a child in front of the first Neighborhood Service Center on Landover Road in Eggerts Crossing in 1969. The center was initially housed in an abandoned church, but had moved to a new building on Eggerts Crossing Road (below) by 1976. Vereen was the main force behind the creation of the center, which offers educational, recreational, and social opportunities to Lawrence residents, particularly those with lower incomes. The center was started with the support of the Lawrence Community Action Council, which was able to secure federal funds for the project. Vereen was the longtime director of the center. In addition to his work there, Vereen also played a key role in the building of affordable housing in the Eggerts Crossing neighborhood and in addressing civil rights issues in Lawrence. (Top, Courtesy of Fred Vereen.)

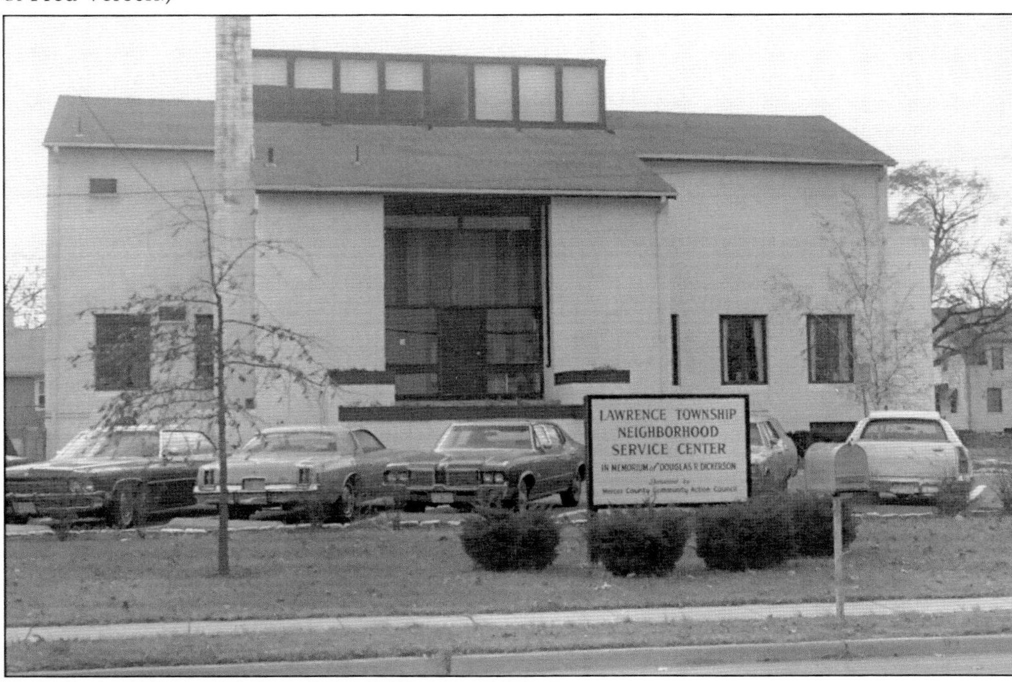

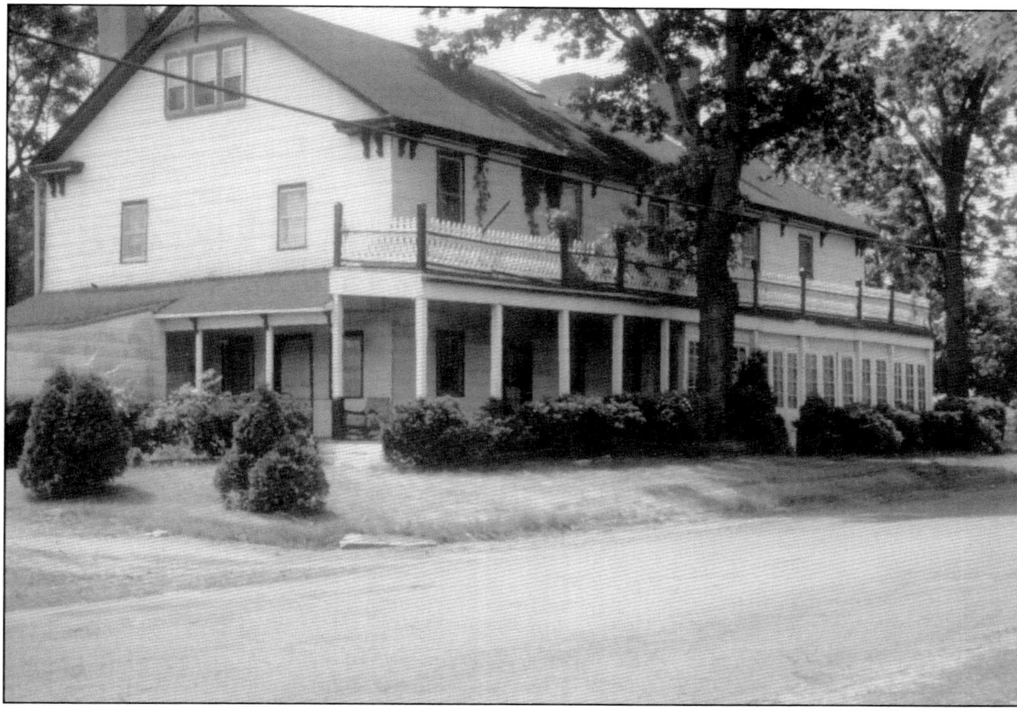

The Princessville Inn on Princeton Pike had a storied history as one of the premier inns in Hunterdon (and later, Mercer) County. Built in 1808, the inn served as both a stopping point for travelers along the Princeton Turnpike as well as a meeting place and reception hall for large local events. During its peak (1837–1918), it was run by William Webster Mershon and, following his death, by his daughter Susan Pierson. During that time, the inn was picked to be the host of several conventions, including the county Republican convention from 1850 until 1890. It is rumored that Abraham Lincoln may have been a speaker or guest at one of these conventions. The inn was destroyed by fire in January 1982. (Top, Courtesy of the Mershon Family Association; Bottom Courtesy of the Lawrence Ledger.)

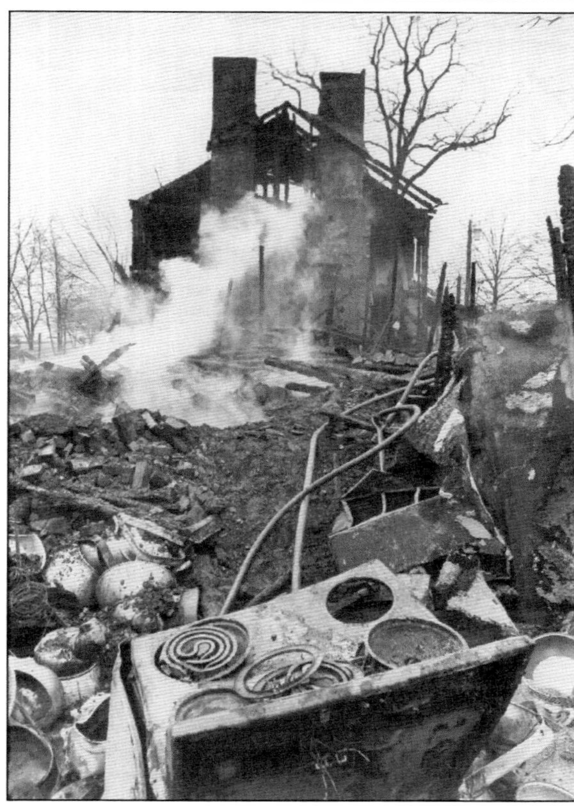

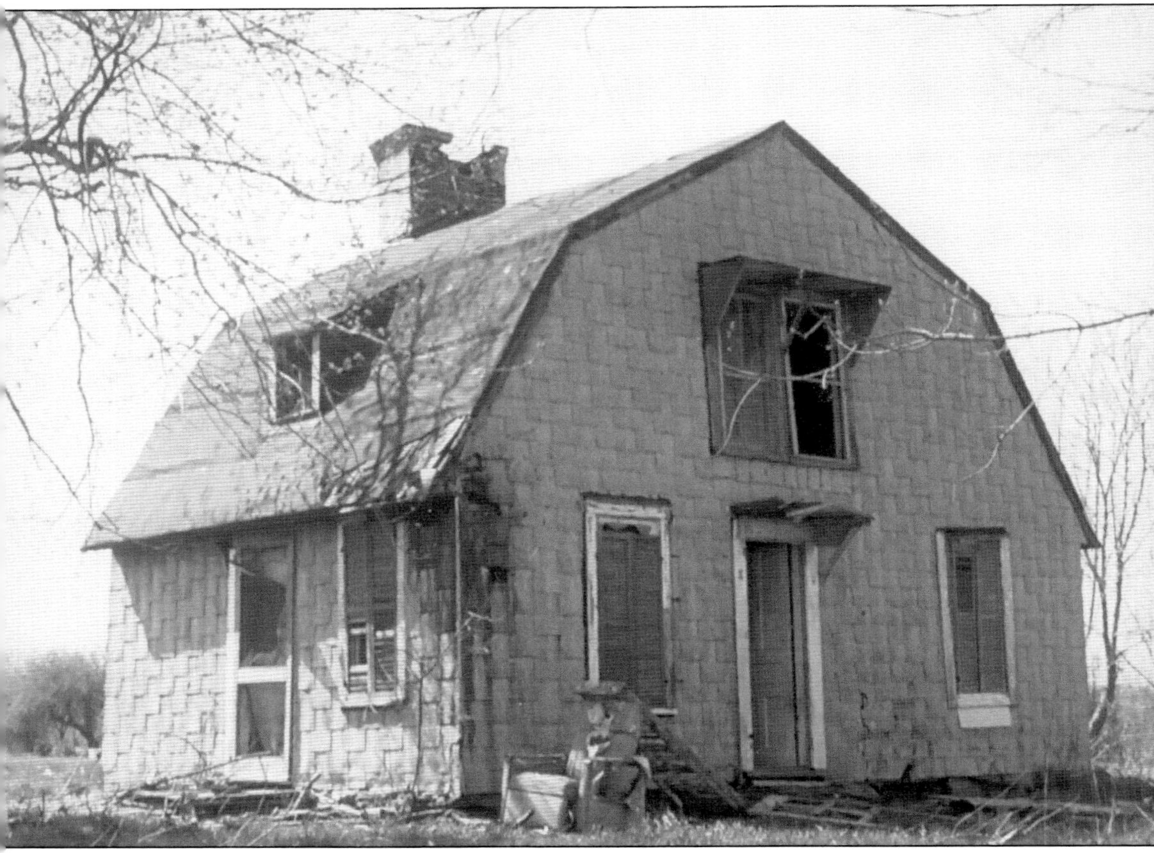

The Anne Knight farmhouse was built around 1725 on either Lewisville or Meadow Road (the historical record is not clear). Rachel Collins owned a farm on Meadow Road near the Princessville Inn, and Anne Knight resided with the Collins family in the late 1800s. John Knight, Anne's husband, was a runaway slave who was brought to the farm via the Underground Railroad. When Rachel Collins passed away, the ownership of the land transferred to Anne Knight's son, John Wood. Wood sold the farm and house to his mother, who was still living there while working as a cook at the Princessville Inn. Anne farmed the land with the help of her cousins, the Bosley family, who moved from Philadelphia specifically to work on the farm. Eventually, Anne decided to sell the land to the Piersons, owners of the Princessville Inn. A later owner burned the house down in the 1970s.

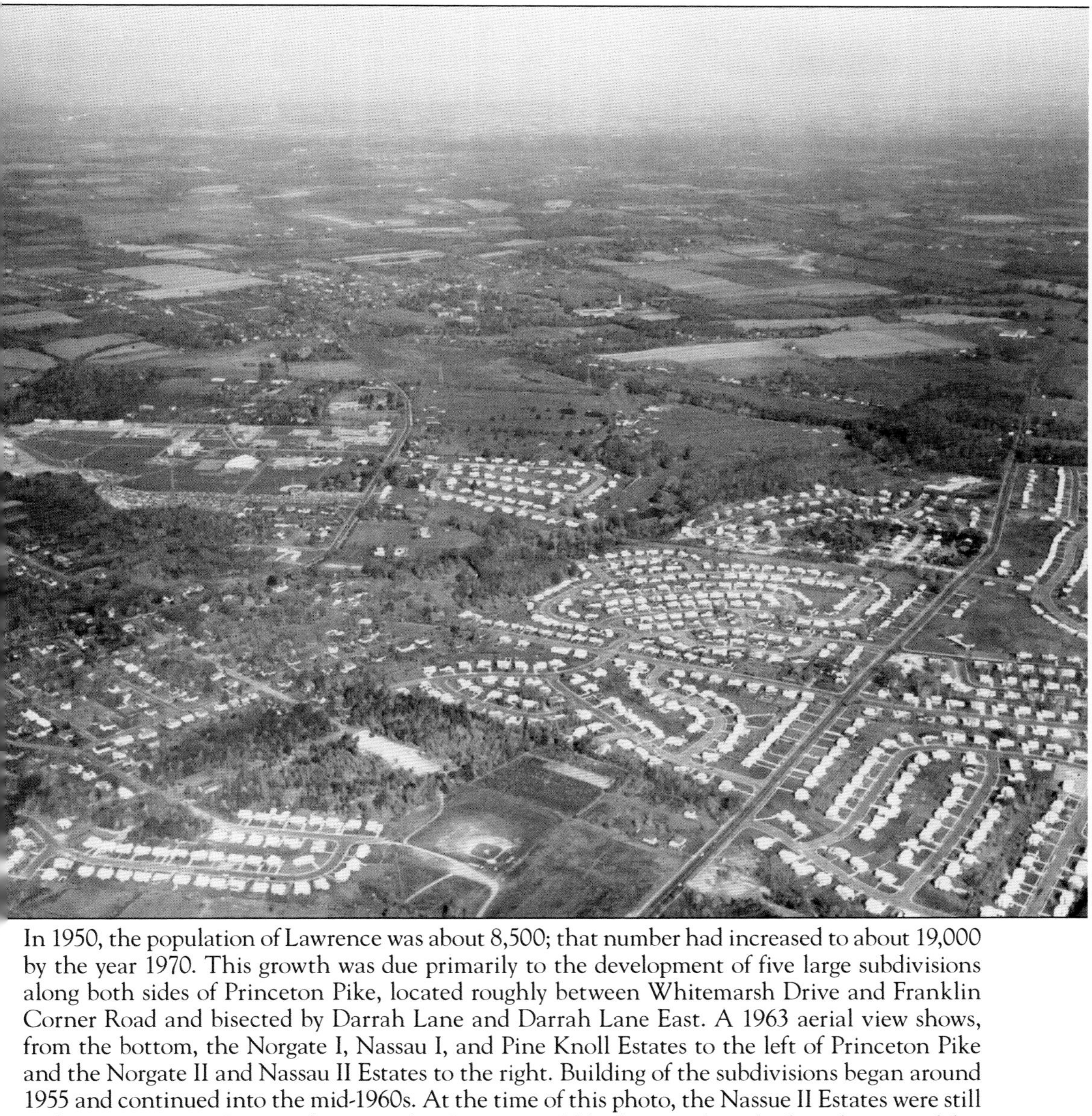

In 1950, the population of Lawrence was about 8,500; that number had increased to about 19,000 by the year 1970. This growth was due primarily to the development of five large subdivisions along both sides of Princeton Pike, located roughly between Whitemarsh Drive and Franklin Corner Road and bisected by Darrah Lane and Darrah Lane East. A 1963 aerial view shows, from the bottom, the Norgate I, Nassau I, and Pine Knoll Estates to the left of Princeton Pike and the Norgate II and Nassau II Estates to the right. Building of the subdivisions began around 1955 and continued into the mid-1960s. At the time of this photo, the Nassue II Estates were still under construction. It is worth noting that Interstate 195 had not yet been built at the time of this picture, and most of the area north of Franklin Corner Road remained farmland. Development paused briefly in the 1970s, but picked up again in the later part of the 20th century, bringing the population to just under 34,000 by the 2010 census.

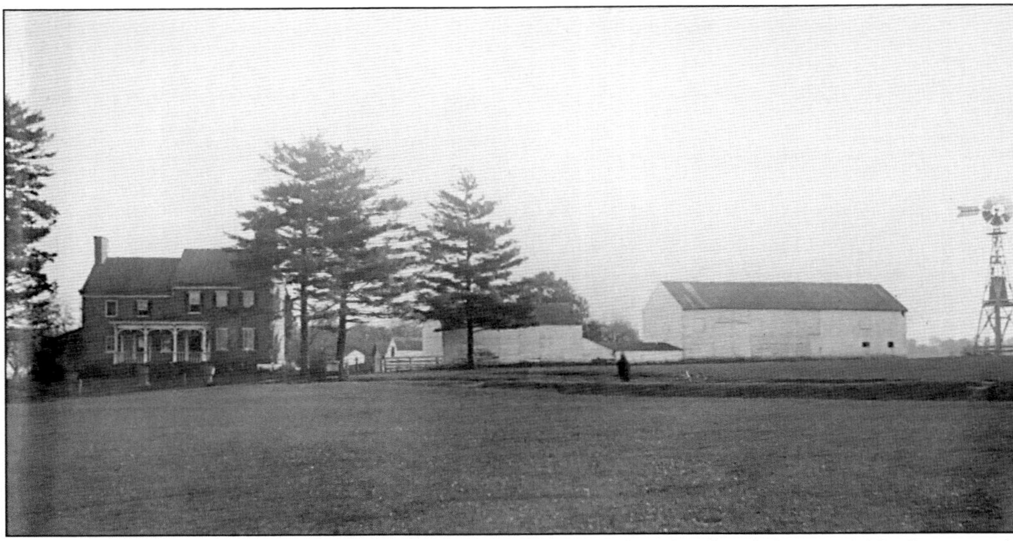

The Mershon farmhouse, "Old Brick," is seen on the left-hand side of this c. 1900 photograph. The house stood on what is now the golf course at The Lawrenceville School. The land remained a farm after the school purchased it from the family, possibly to provide food for students. The windmill and barns to the right of the house no longer exist, but Old Brick remains, situated next to the third tee on the golf course. (Courtesy of the Mershon Family Association.)

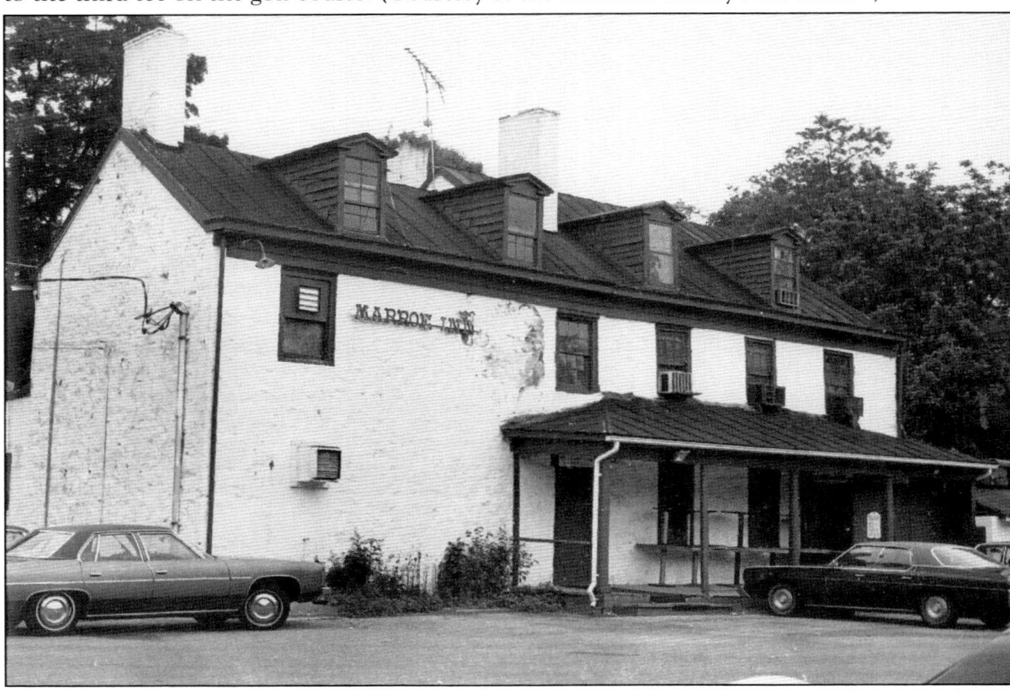

This c. 1970 image shows the Henry Mershon IV House, later known as the Welling Farmhouse, located on what later became the Heinemann Electric Company property on Brunswick Pike. The company did not want to demolish the house when it purchased the land, so it was leased and converted into a restaurant. The Marroe Inn was a popular dinner spot for many decades until it was demolished in 1999 to make way for a car dealership.

Five

Houses of Worship

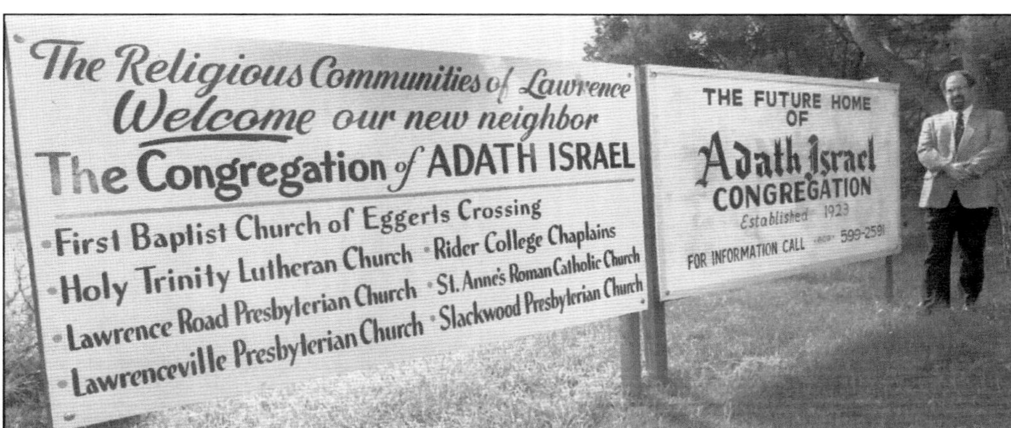

Adath Israel Congregation was established in Trenton in 1923 and built a synagogue on Bellevue Avenue in 1926. Faced with a declining membership in the city, the congregation elected to move to Lawrence in 1987. Rabbi Daniel Grossman stands next to a welcome sign at the construction site of the new synagogue in August 1988. The current building was dedicated in spring 1991. (Courtesy of the Lawrence Ledger.)

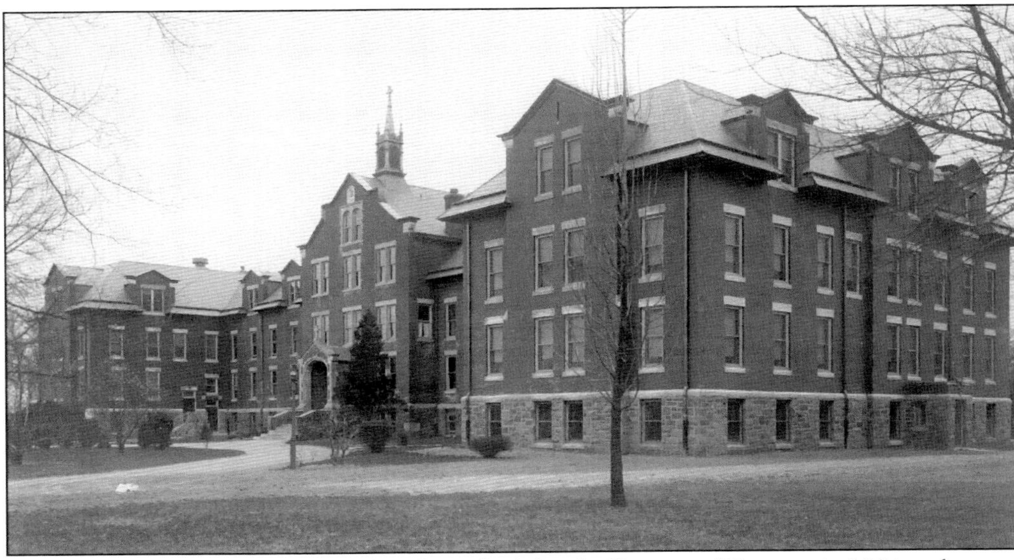

Morris Hall Home for the Aged (above) was built by the Diocese of Trenton in 1904 and named in honor of Col. Daniel Morris. The Morris Hall Health and Rehabilitation Center, a 24-hour care facility, was built on the campus in 1971 and renamed the St. Lawrence Rehabilitation Center in 1980. The original building was demolished in 1994 and replaced by St. Mary's Assisted Living and St. Joseph's Skilled Nursing Center. Until St. Ann's opened in 1937, the Holy Rosary Chapel served as the church for Lawrence Township's Catholic population. Below, from left to right, are Richard J. Coffee, Robert Cleary, Charles E. Connell Jr., and Nicholas Loveless. The four served as altar boys at the chapel in 1936 and remained lifelong friends.

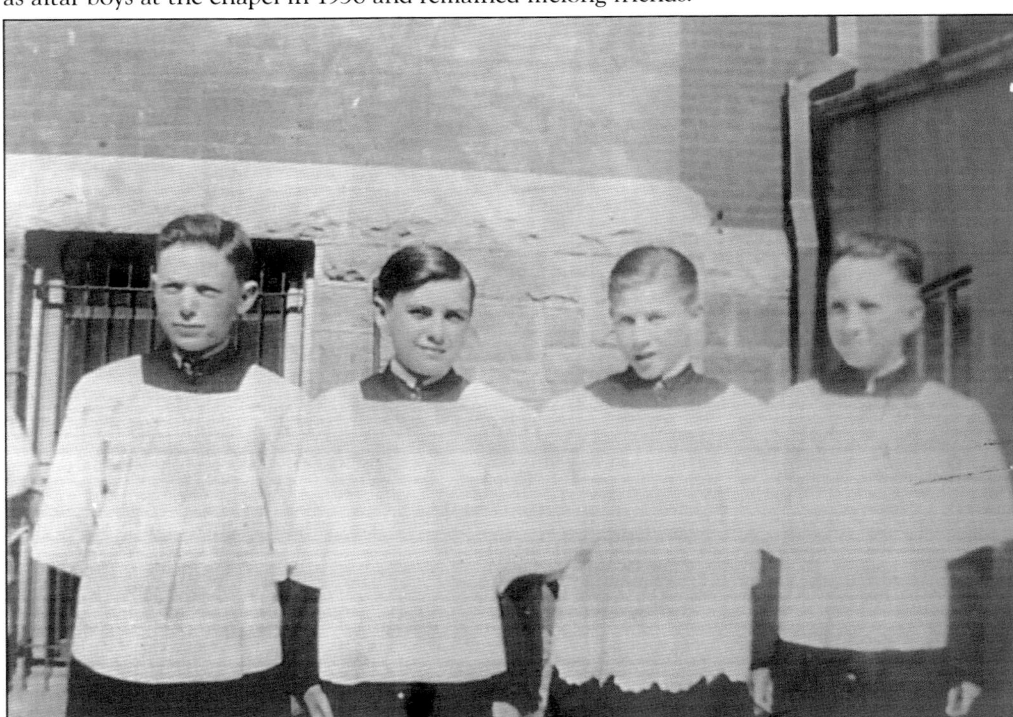

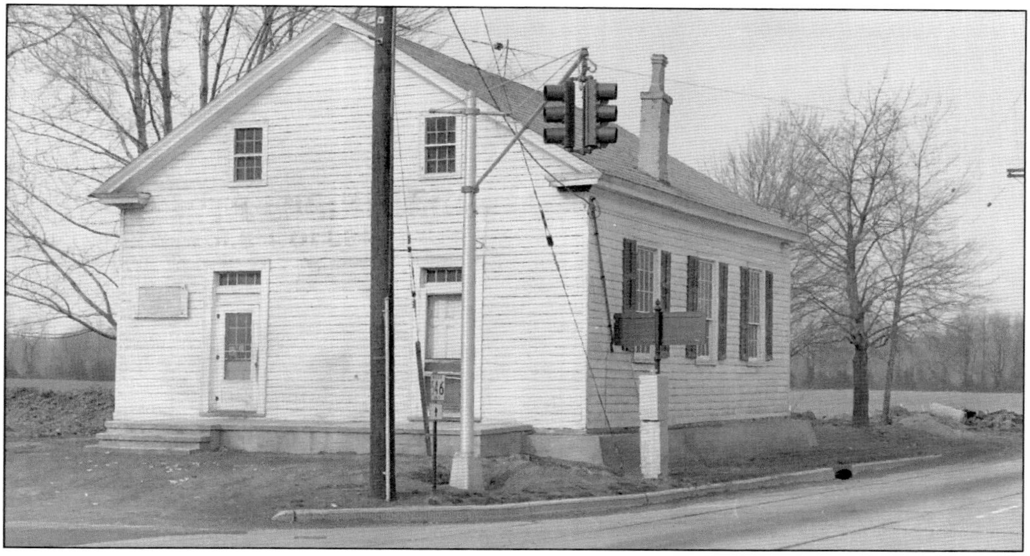

Methodist Episcopal Church, pictured around 1958 at the corner of Route 1 and Franklin Corner Road, was established near the Princessville Cemetery on Princeton Pike, across from Lewisville Road in the early 1800s. The building was moved during the 1870s and was later converted to an antiques store before being demolished and replaced by a Howard Johnson Motel and Restaurant. (Courtesy of James V. Sciocco.)

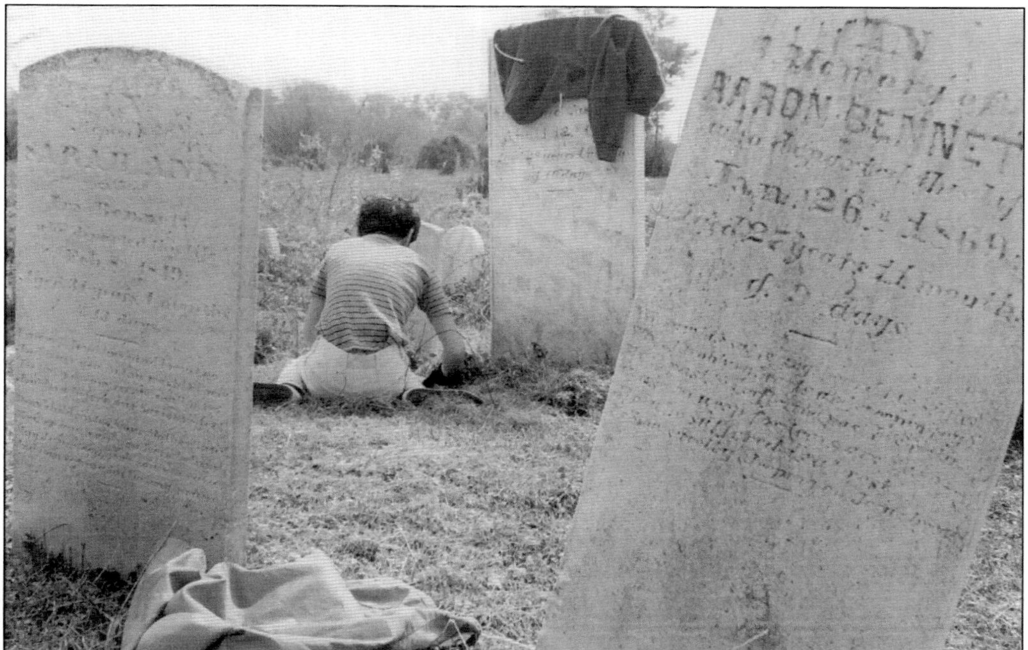

When the Methodist Episcopal church dissolved, the Princessville Cemetery fell into disrepair. Ed Moore initiated a community project to restore the cemetery in 1975. The Methodist Episcopal Church transferred the land to the township, and it became part of the Port Mercer-Princessville-Brearley Park. Volunteers, including local Boy Scout and Girl Scout troops, helped clean and straighten stones as a Bicentennial project in 1976.

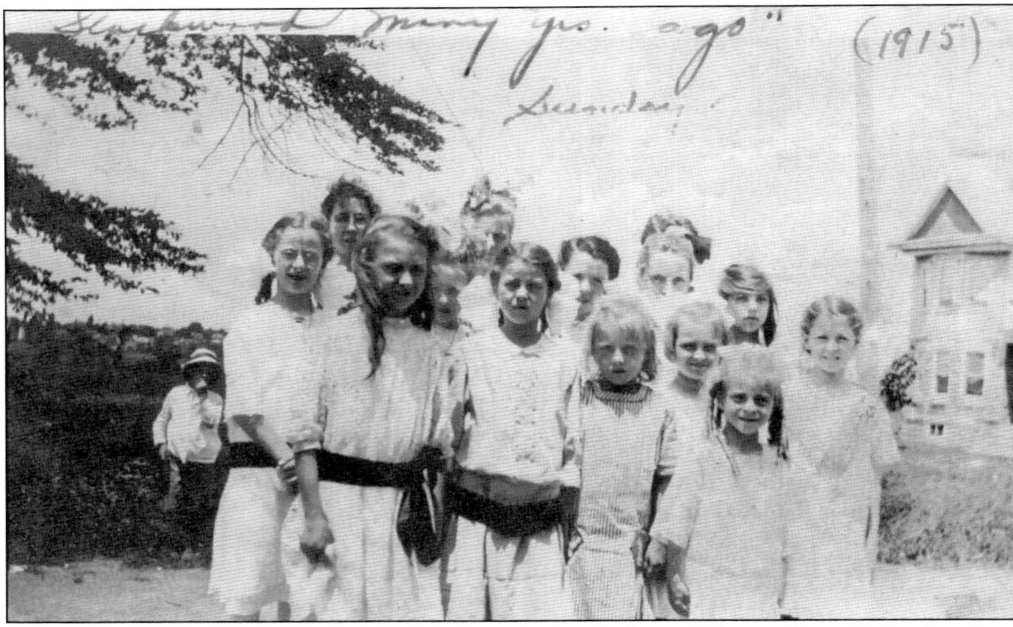

In 1915, this Sunday School group posed in front of the Slackwood Union Chapel. The chapel was built by the Slackwood Union Chapel Association in 1894, with the help of volunteer labor, on land donated by James R. Stevens. The chapel held Sunday school and prayer meetings. In 1914, the chapel became the Slackwood Union Church. In 1935, it became the Slackwood Presbyterian Church, affiliated with the United Presbyterian Church.

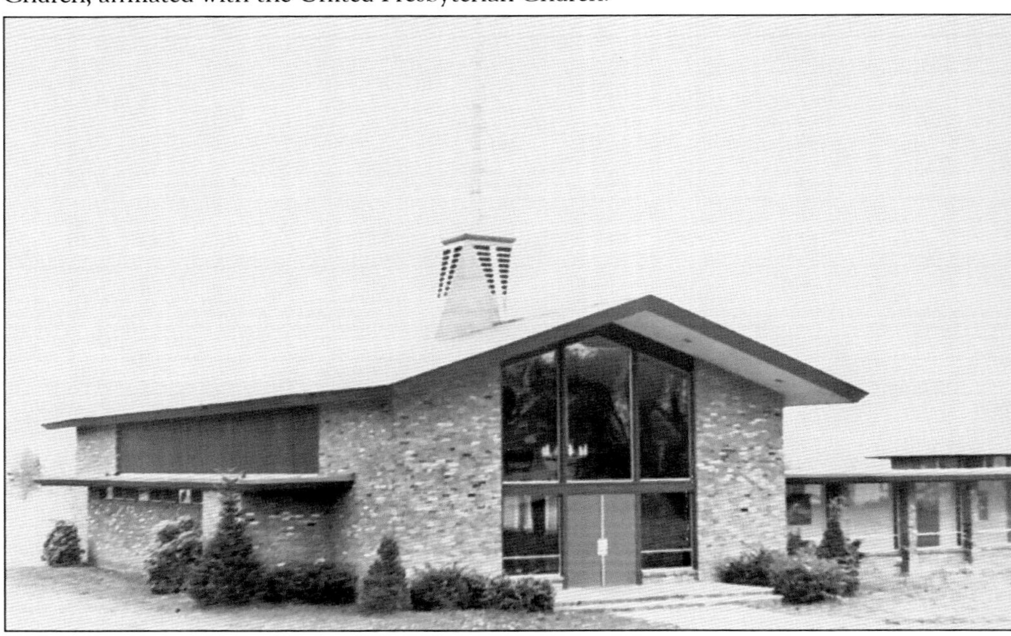

Holy Trinity Lutheran Church, located at the corner of Allen Lane and Princeton Pike, observed its 60th anniversary in 1971. The metal steeple was removed as part of renovations done to the church around 1990. Holy Trinity was originally located in Trenton, but moved to Lawrence Township in 1961.

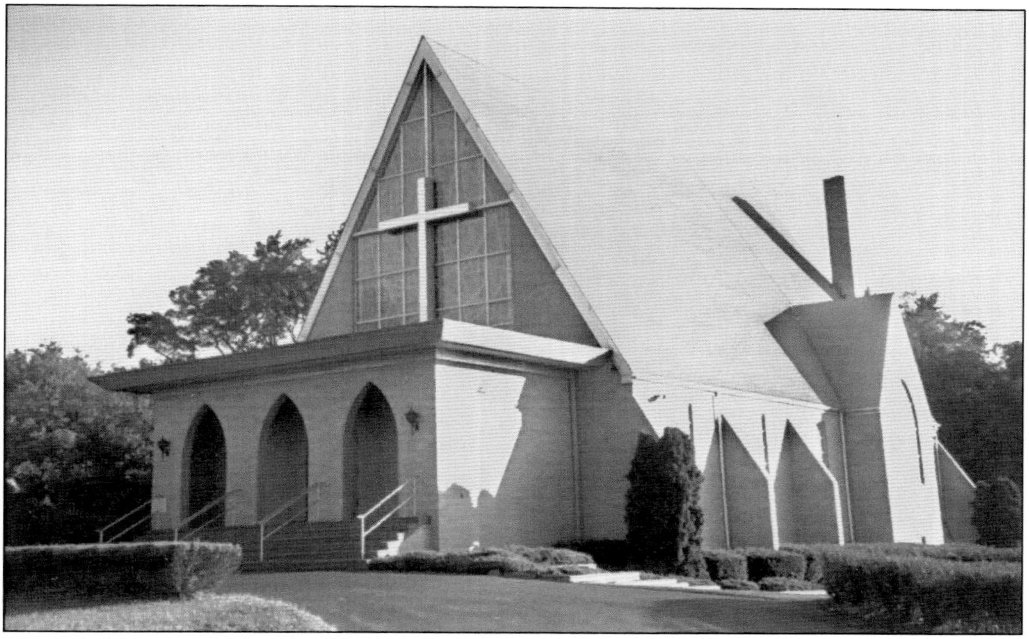

The Polish National Church of Our Savior was originally established in Trenton in 1917. In 1952, the parishioners decided to start a fund to build a new church. The new building, on Princeton Pike near the Lawrence Shopping Center, was completed in April 1968. Parishioners took part in the construction, including the building of the main altar and pews.

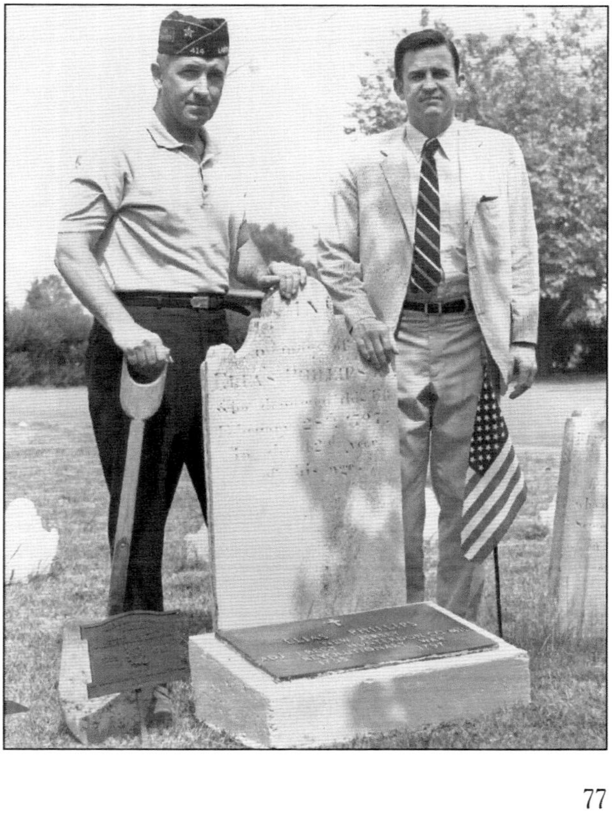

Nicholas Loveless (left) and Rev. Dana Fearon (right) stand at the grave of Elias Phillips in the Lawrenceville Presbyterian Church Cemetery, shortly after the placement of a new marker denoting Phillips's military service. Phillips was one of the guides used by George Washington to lead the American army down back roads toward Princeton after the Second Battle of Trenton on January 2, 1777.

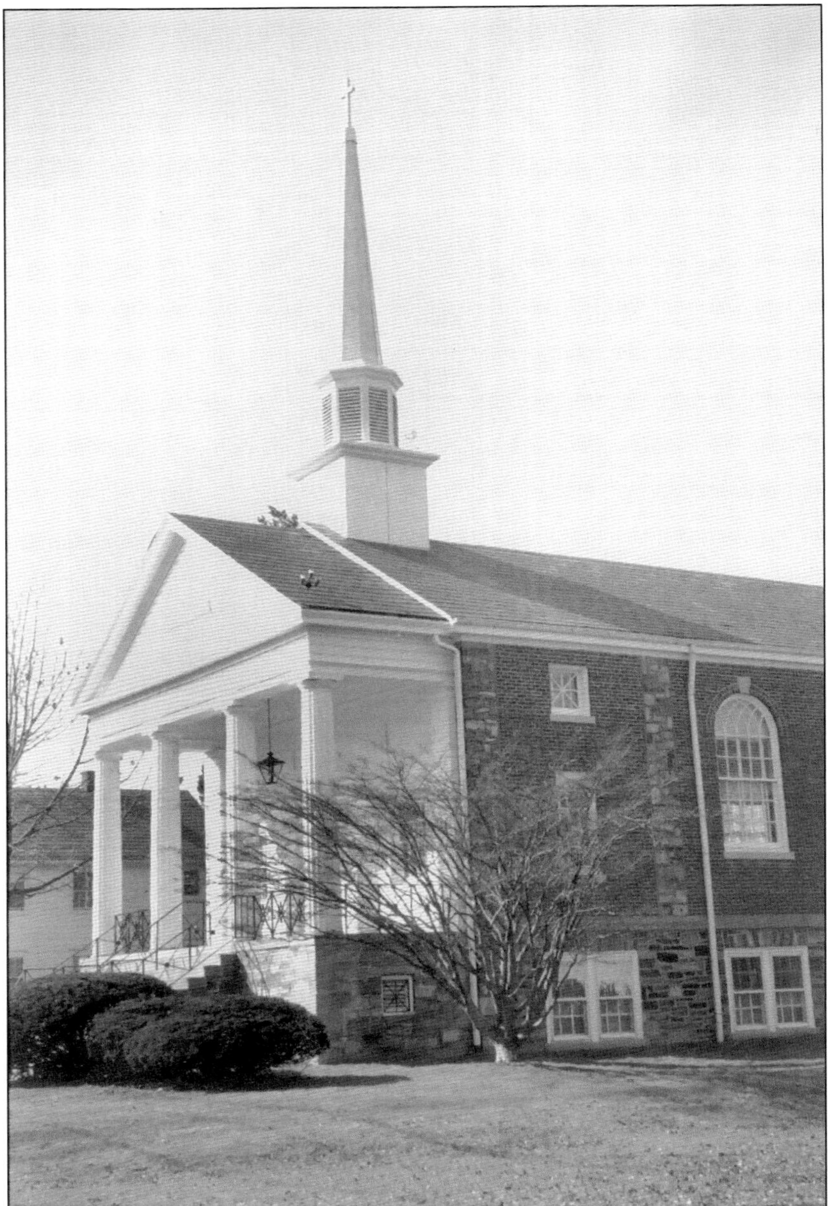

This photograph from around 1996 shows Lawrence Road Presbyterian Church, which was then a few years shy of its 60th anniversary. The church began as the Lawrence Road Sunday School in 1914, when neighborhood residents began meeting to discuss Scripture under a tree near the eventual church location. Rev. Samuel Polk ran the school under the guidance of theology student Merril Winn and the Lawrenceville Presbyterian Church. In 1915, the group changed its name to the Lawrence Road Chapel Association, and members began fundraising to construct the church. The first phase of the building, the construction of a Sunday school room and chapel, was completed in 1922. The foundation for the church was also laid, and the building was completed in time to hold its first service on Christmas Day 1938. Between 1915 and 1938, Sunday school was held at Eldridge Park School.

The Presbyterian Church of Lawrenceville (seen in 1904) was officially established in 1698. In 1710 Ralph Hunt and Benjamin Hardin deeded parts of their land to be used for the building of the church. The original church was replaced in 1764 by what is now the front section of the building. Elias Phillips, who helped George Washington during the Second Battle of Trenton, is buried in the cemetery.

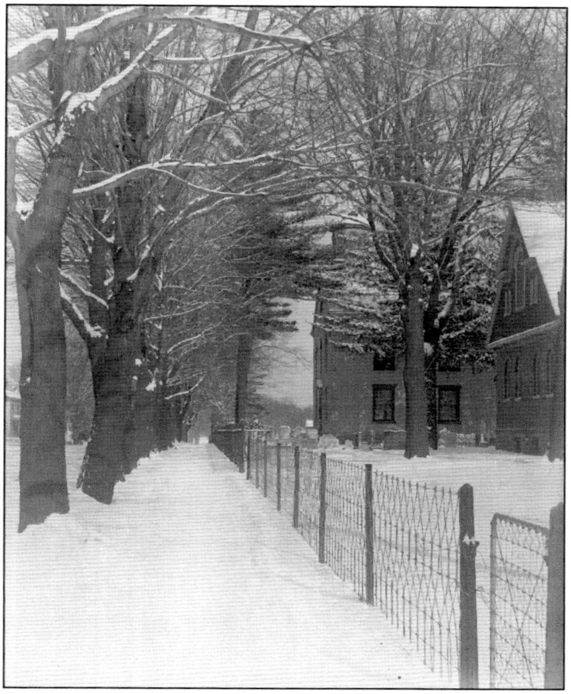

The original Slackwood Presbyterian Church on Brunswick Avenue, photographed around 1939, was destroyed by a fire on April 29, 1951. It has since been rebuilt and remains active today in the same location, just south of Whitehead Road on the northbound side of Brunswick Avenue.

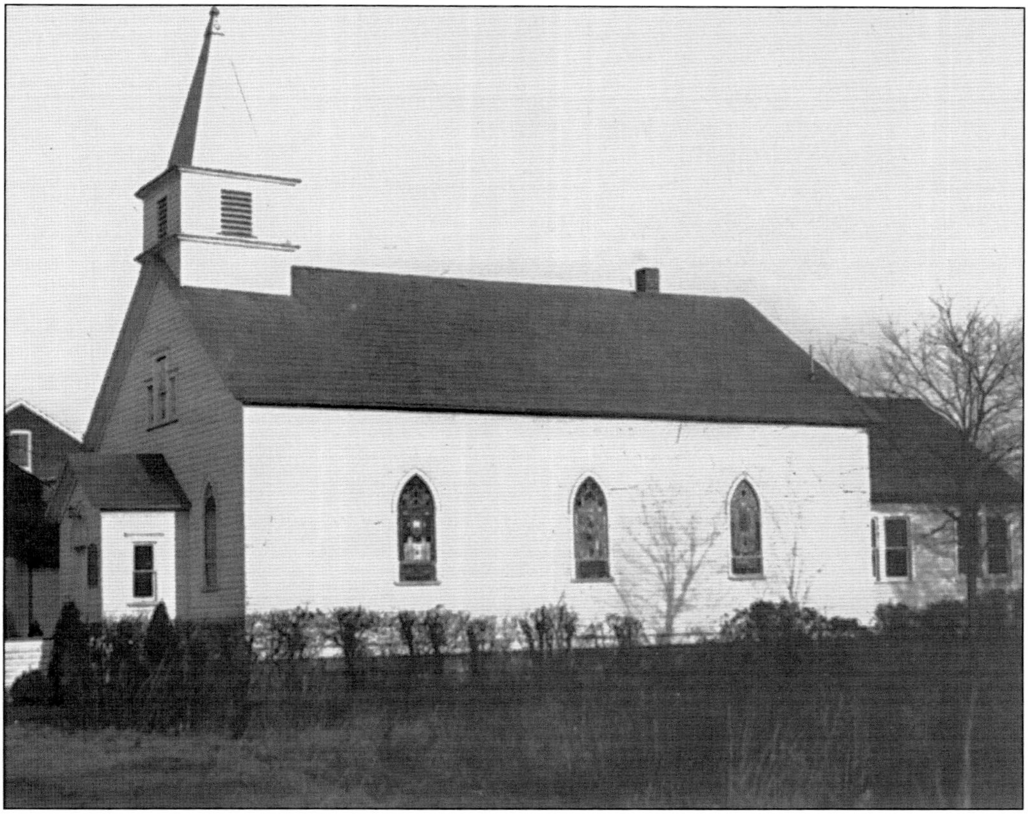

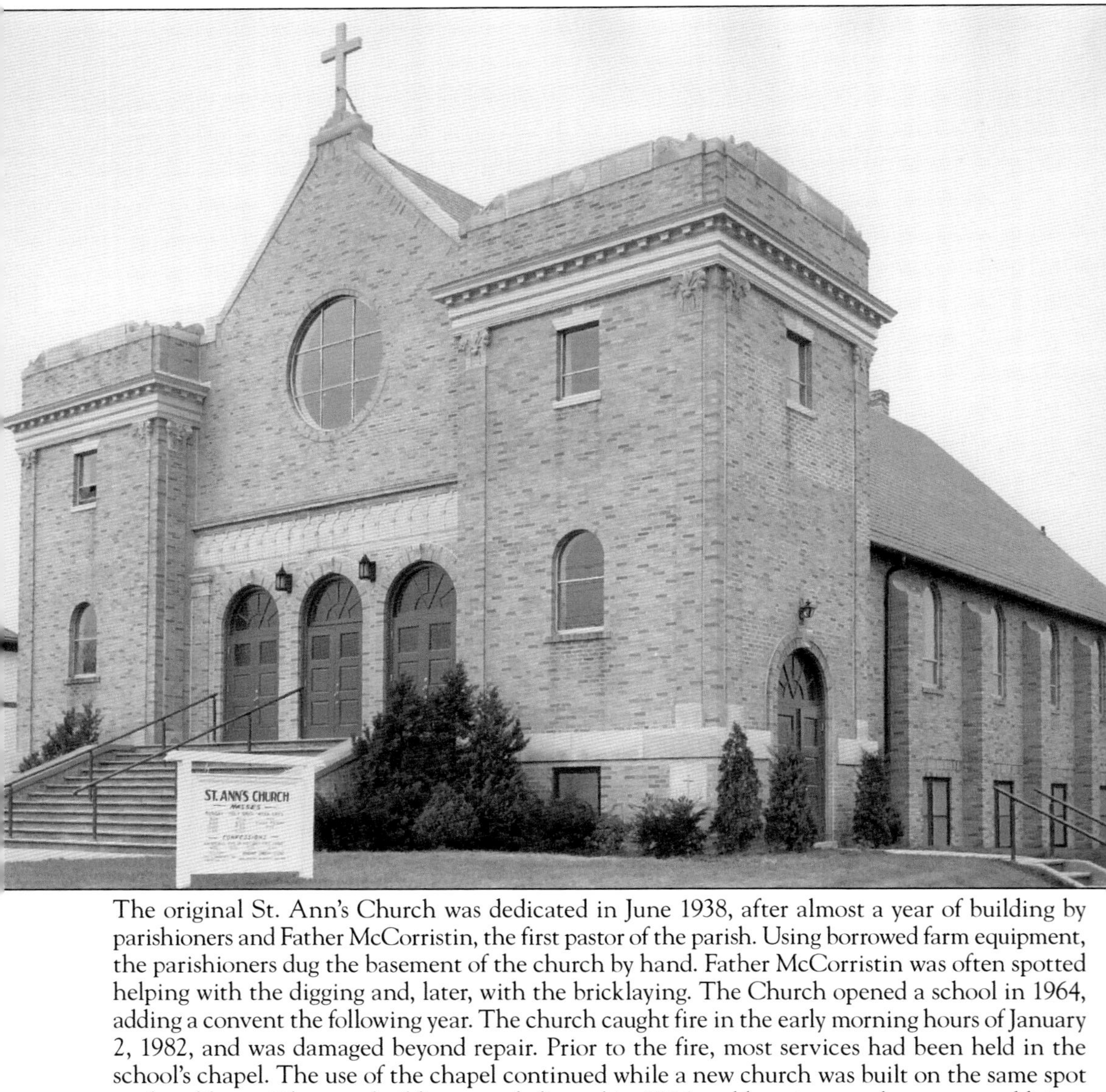

The original St. Ann's Church was dedicated in June 1938, after almost a year of building by parishioners and Father McCorristin, the first pastor of the parish. Using borrowed farm equipment, the parishioners dug the basement of the church by hand. Father McCorristin was often spotted helping with the digging and, later, with the bricklaying. The Church opened a school in 1964, adding a convent the following year. The church caught fire in the early morning hours of January 2, 1982, and was damaged beyond repair. Prior to the fire, most services had been held in the school's chapel. The use of the chapel continued while a new church was built on the same spot as the old one. The new building was dedicated in 1986 and has since undergone an addition. The Faith Development Center was completed in 2006, adding parish offices, meeting rooms, a reflection garden, and a library.

Six

Parks and Recreation

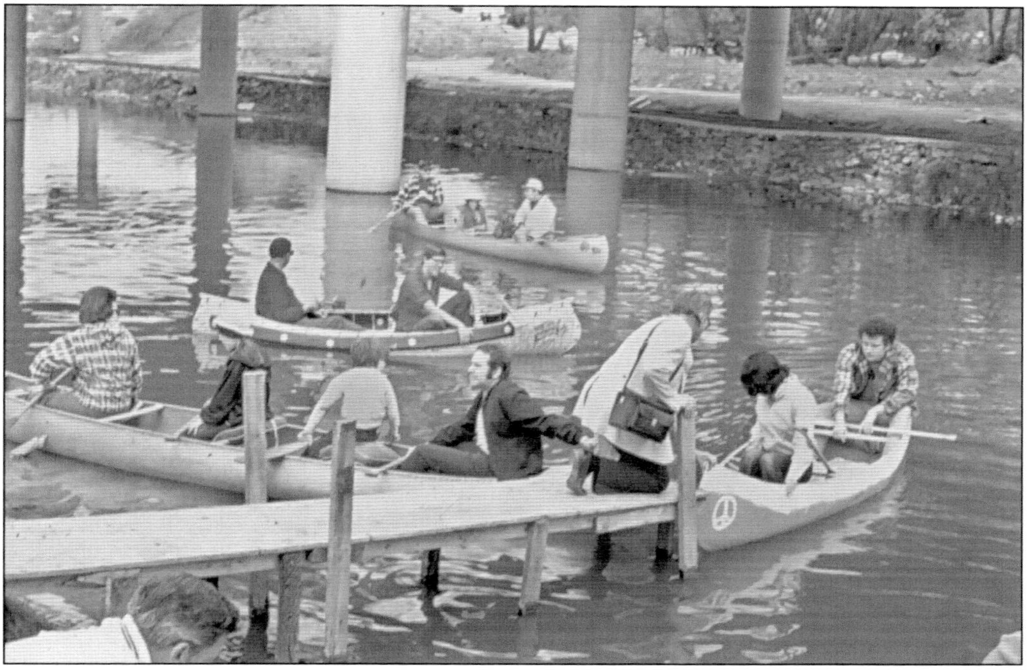

Canoers depart from the dock at the end of Cherry Tree Lane at the start of Canoe the Canal Day in May 1973. Bob Immordino initiated the event in the early 1970s as a way to raise awareness of the Delaware and Raritan Canal and its rich history. The event was held each June until 2011.

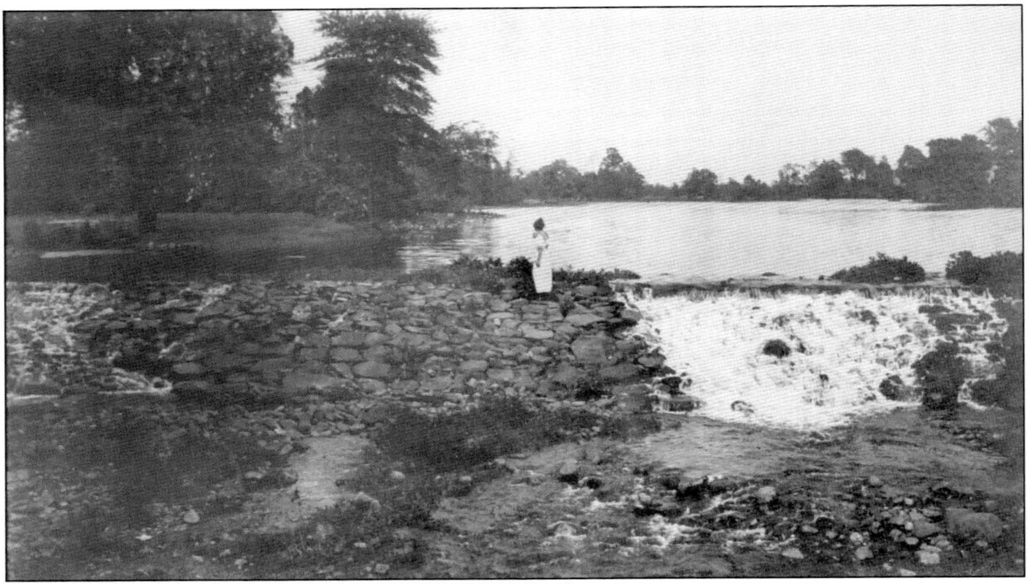

An unidentified woman stands on the stone bank of the dam at the Whitehead Pond falls, around 1920. The pond is located behind Cherry Tree Lane and was once connected to the mill near Lawrence Station Road by a sluiceway. The falls are on the Whitehead Road side of the pond. Both the pond and sluiceway were popular recreation spots during the early 20th century, frequented by both canoers and swimmers during the summer months. Two canoes, below, navigate the sluiceway, around 1920. The low concrete sides of the sluiceway, seen on both sides of the canoes, made it easy for boaters to launch, since they could enter their boats from solid ground.

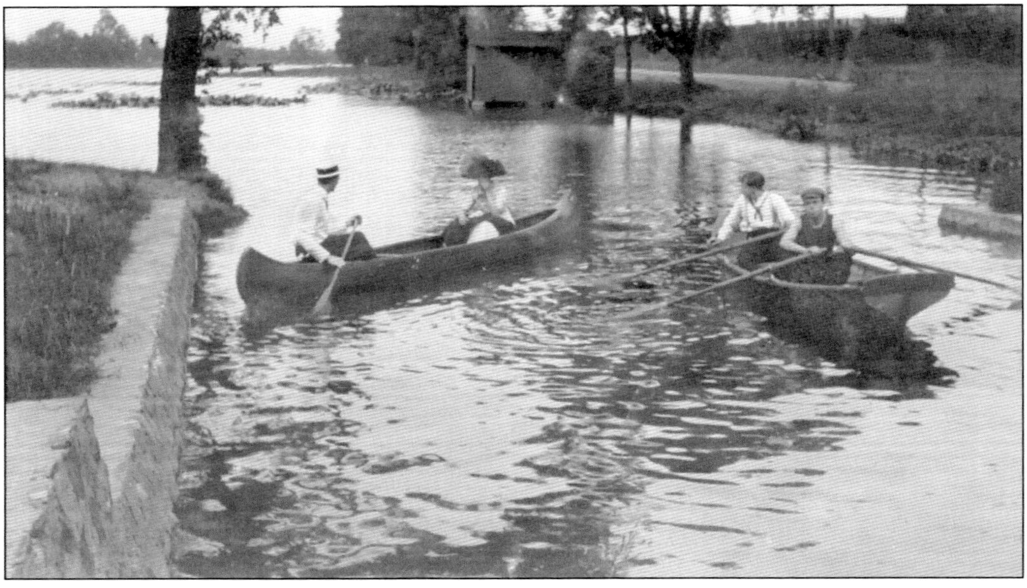

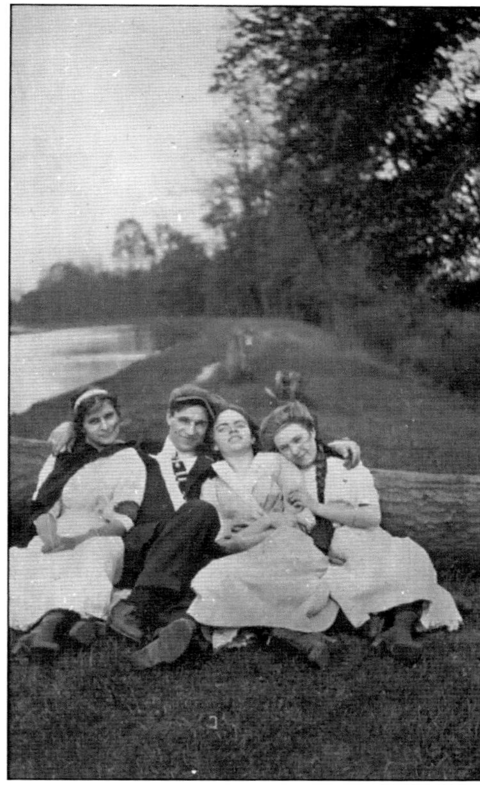

The Delaware and Raritan Canal was officially designated as a New Jersey State Park in 1974, but was a popular recreation site long before. The wide, well-maintained towpath was often the scene of picnics, long walks, or just relaxation (as demonstrated by the 1908 foursome pictured right). Others took to the water to swim or boat. A pleasure yacht cruising along the canal, like the one in the c. 1908 photograph below, was not an unusual sight. In addition to serving as recreational crafts, yachts were also used to transport passengers from town to town along the canal.

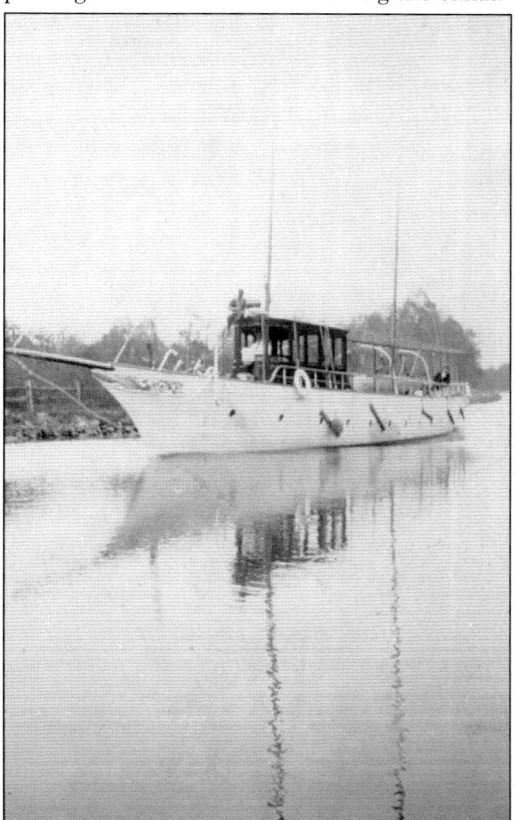

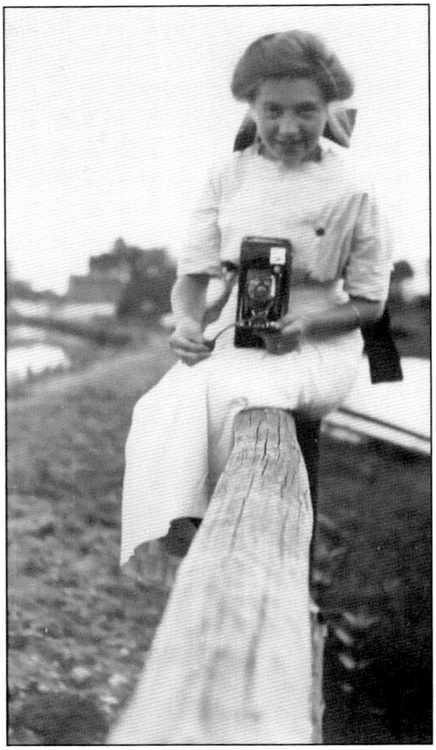

Mary Nash (left) and an unidentified male companion (below) test out their new cameras at the marsh on Shabakunk Creek, around 1910. The pair sit on a wooden railing that ran next to the marsh, which was converted into Colonial Lake in 1923. The pastoral scene was much different a decade later, when Colonial Land Company held a series of "gold rushes" to lure potential homeowners to their new development, Colonial Lakelands. The developer tucked gold pieces in the wooded area near the marsh, where the houses were to be built. During the "hunts," salesmen would pitch the area as a quiet, secluded neighborhood away from the busy city. One key selling point was easy access to the new bus routes that connected the suburbs to Trenton, the busses being cheaper than the trolley that served other parts of Lawrence.

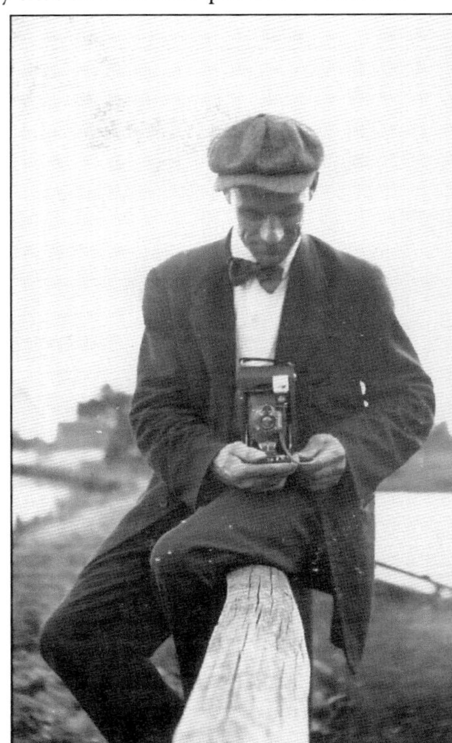

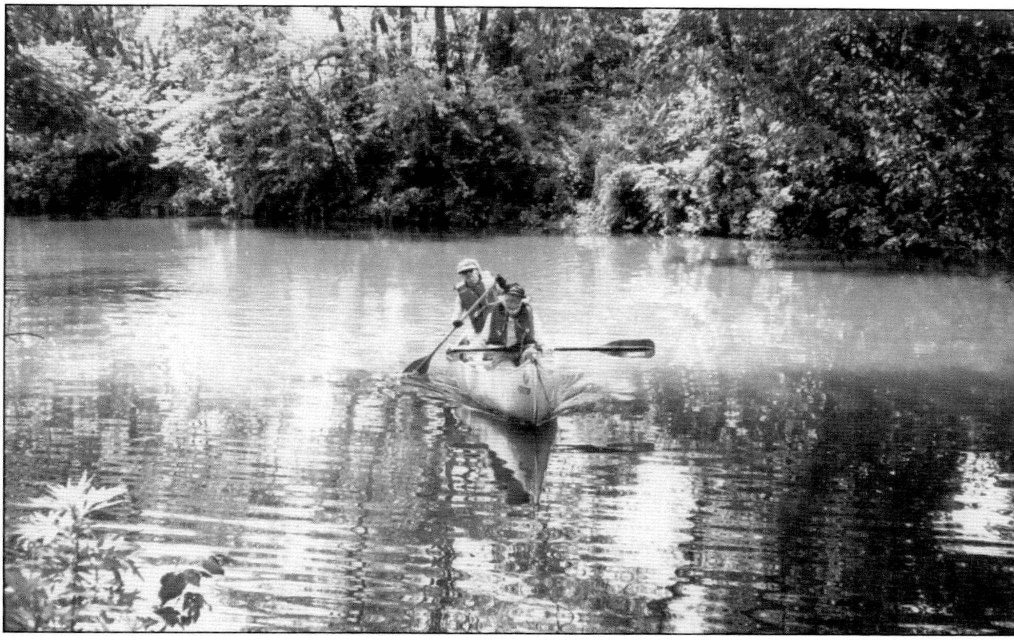

Canoe the Canal Day was an annual event for many years, with canoers paddling from Cherry Tree Lane to the Port Mercer Canal House. Mary Tanner is seen navigating a canoe toward the banks near Port Mercer in June 1993. Tanner was active in town government and historic preservation for several decades.

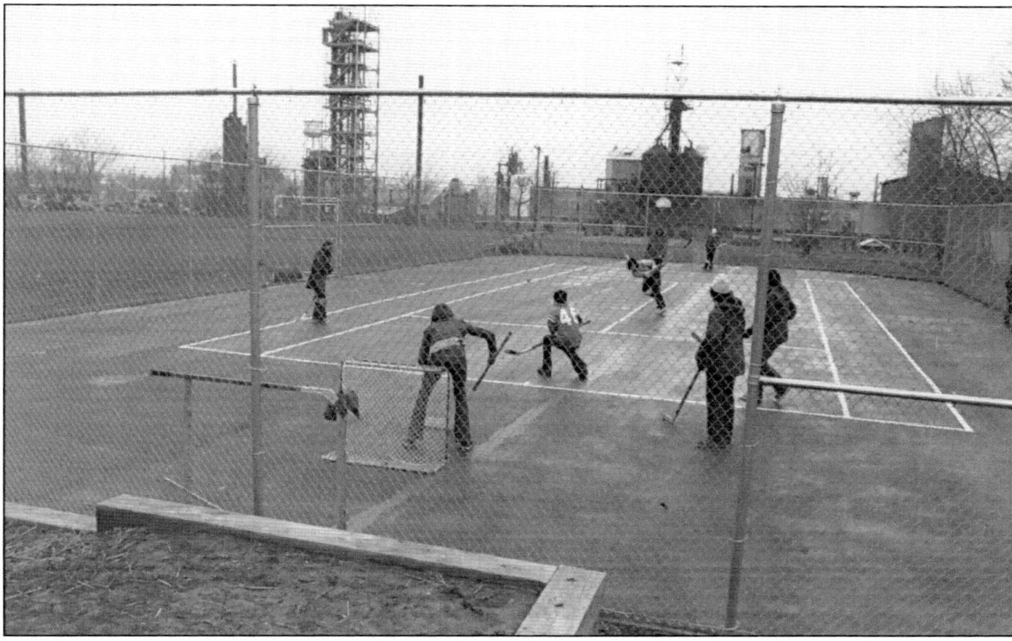

The neighborhoods of south Lawrence are now mostly residential, but reminders of the area's industrial past still remain. Old towers and buildings from the Trenton Fiber Drum Company provided the backdrop for this hockey game in Tom Hamnett Memorial Park on Ohio Avenue, around 1980.

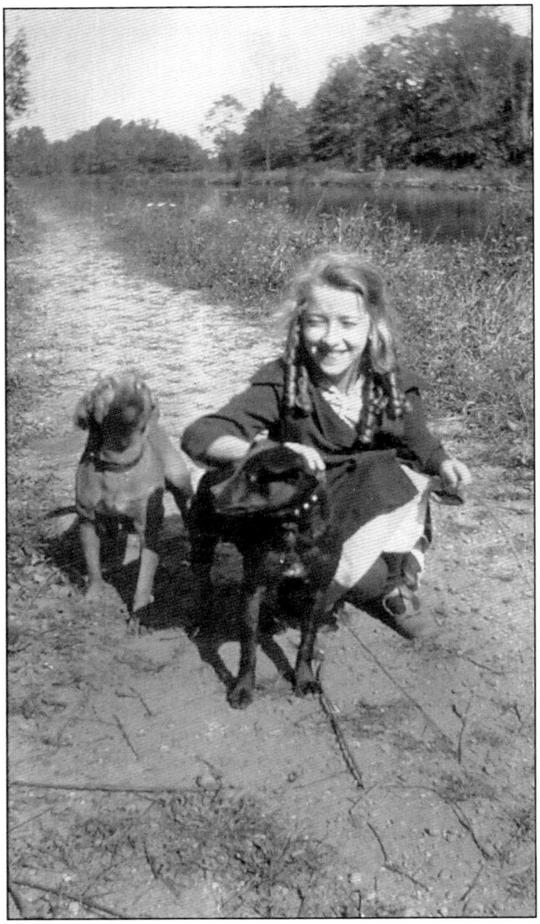

The Delaware and Raritan Canal was more than just a route for shipping and transportation, it was also a popular place for recreation and social gatherings. Many residents had their pictures snapped with the canal in the background. Left, Marjorie Astbury takes time out for a photograph while walking the family dogs on the towpath, around 1920. Below, Elsie Nash, Hazel Nash and Olive Pillsbury take a walk on the towpath, also around 1920. The canal has remained a consistently popular recreation spot, as residents continued to use the towpath even after the canal closed in 1933. In the 1940s, the State of New Jersey began converting the canal to a residential water supply system. In 1973, the canal was added to the National Register of Historic Places; it became a state park the following year.

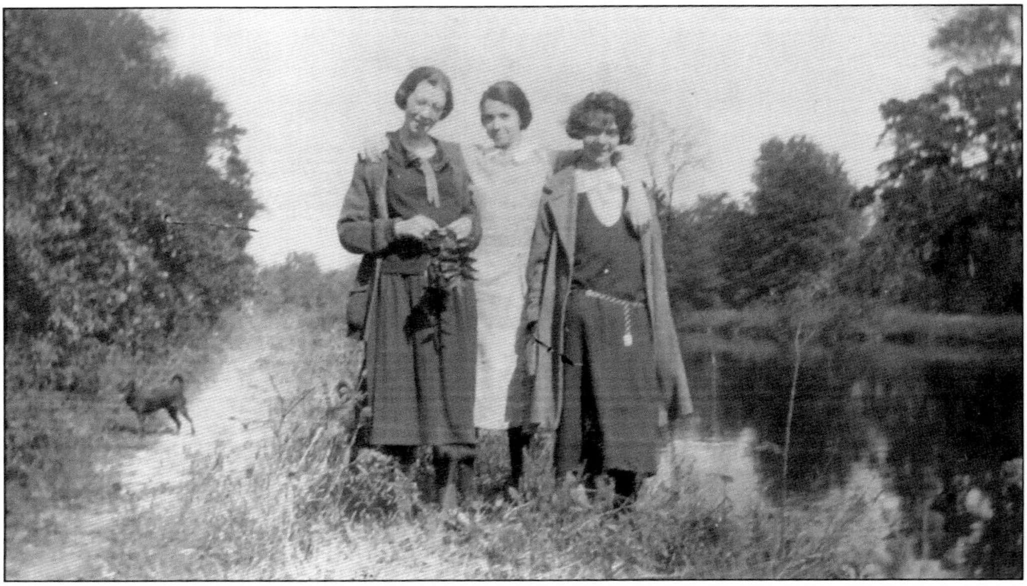

Seven

PEOPLE AND FAMILIES

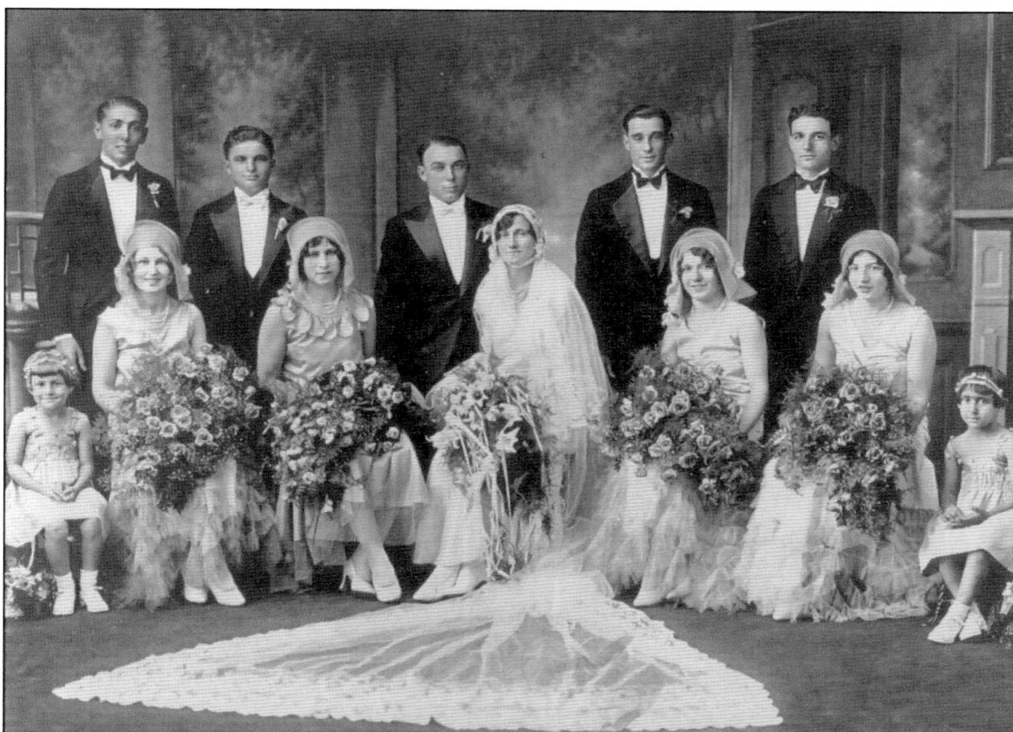

Pictured from left to right at the wedding of Joseph Colavita and Anna Perna, on June 28, 1930, are (first row) Grace DiAntonio (flower girl and niece of the bride), Gertrude Feddy, Rose Perna, Anna Perna (bride), Frances Colavita, Angeline Colavita, and Florence Russo (flower girl and niece of the bride); (second row) Tony DiTilleo, James Colavita, Joseph Colavita (groom), Andrew Cermele, and Ed Colavita. The Colavitas have been active in the community and politics of Lawrence for over a century.

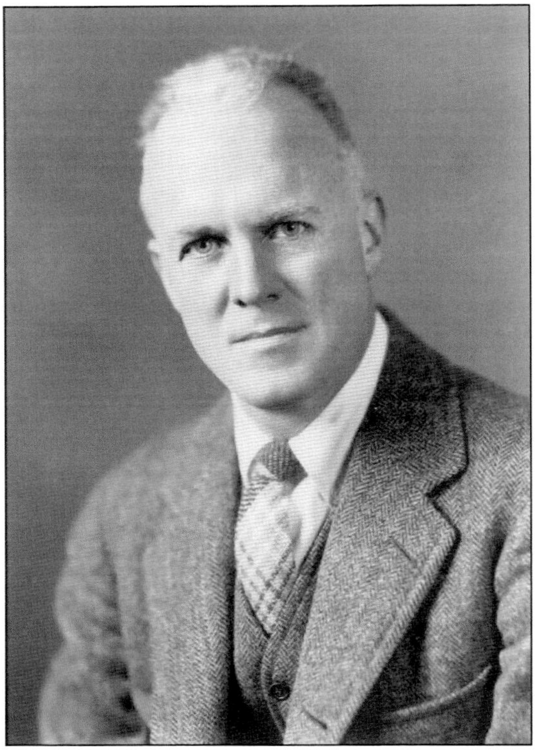

Donald Homer Tyler's book *Old Lawrenceville: Early Houses and Homes* was published in 1965. Tyler based his work primarily on oral history accounts and family legends about life in Lawrence. The first comprehensive book on the township, it has endured as one of the cornerstone works about Lawrence history.

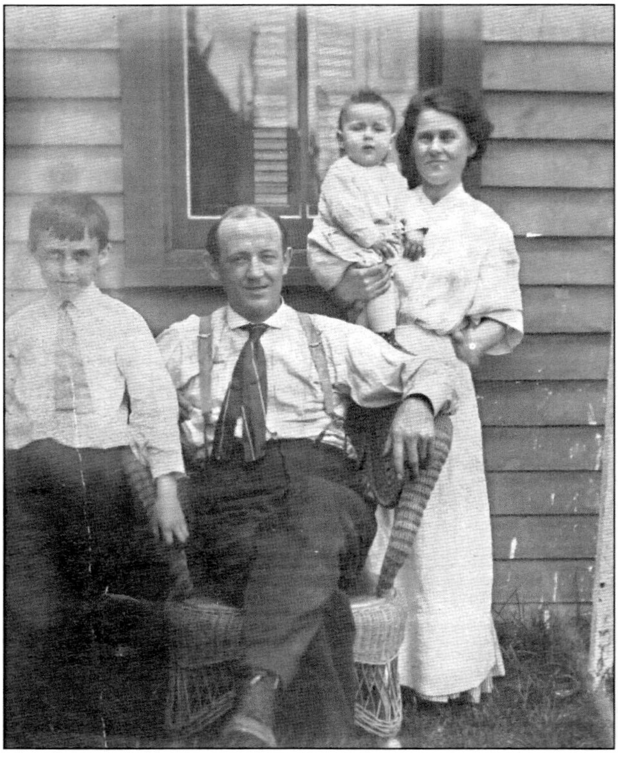

The Hulse family, seen around 1909 on the porch of their Lawrence Road home, are, from left to right, Bill, John, Ronald, and Catherine. The Lawrence Road area was one of the first to develop in the township, and the Hulse family was one of the first to move into the new homes that were replacing the farms along the growing highway during the first decade of the 20th century.

Della (Pierson) Nash, former town clerk, is shown just before her 100th birthday in July 1995. A lifelong resident, Nash was a descendent of the Mershon family. She became one of Lawrence's first female elected officials when she was selected by voters as clerk in 1938, and served until she retired in 1956. Nash passed away in 2001 at the age of 106.

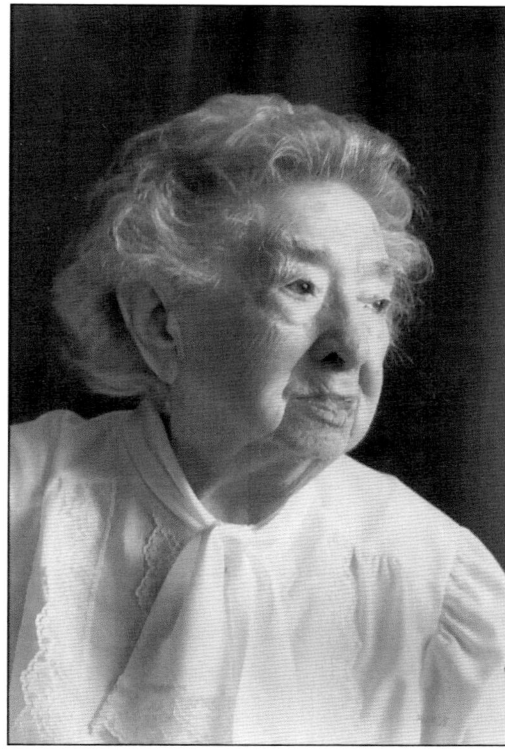

On September 19, 1925, members of the Mershon family gathered at the gravesite of Henry Mershon to dedicate a large grave marker. Mershon died in 1738, and was buried in an unmarked grave, possibly next to his wife, Ann. One of the town's early settlers, Mershon was the patriarch of what became a large, influential family in Maidenhead. Descendents still come to Lawrence for a family reunion each summer. (Courtesy of the Mershon Family Association.)

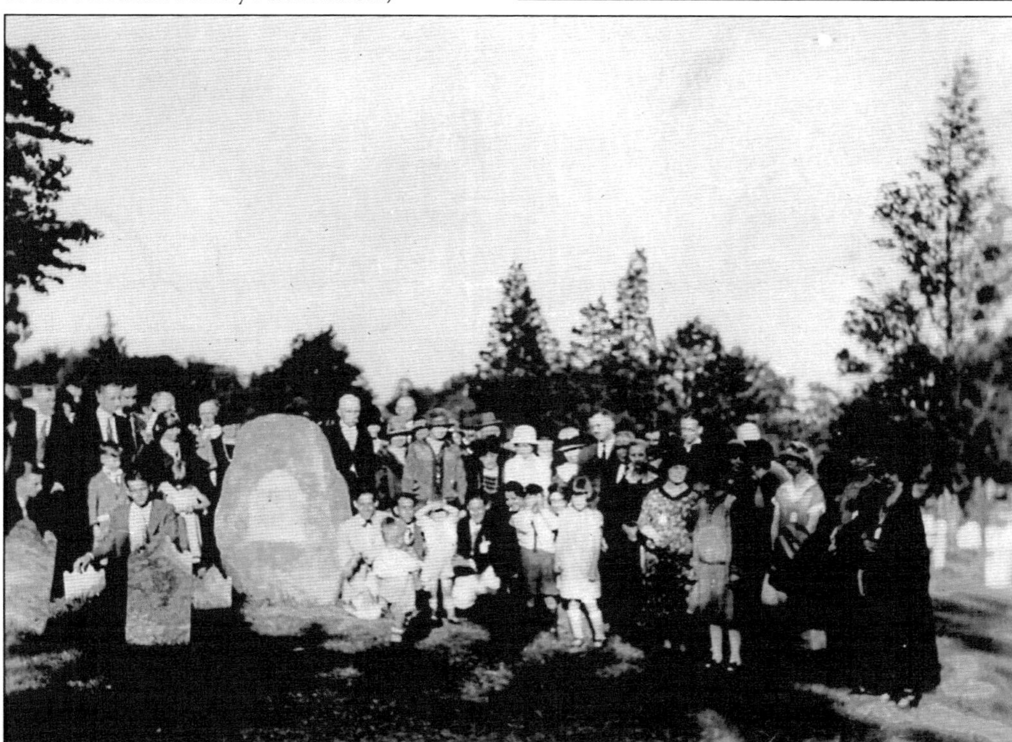

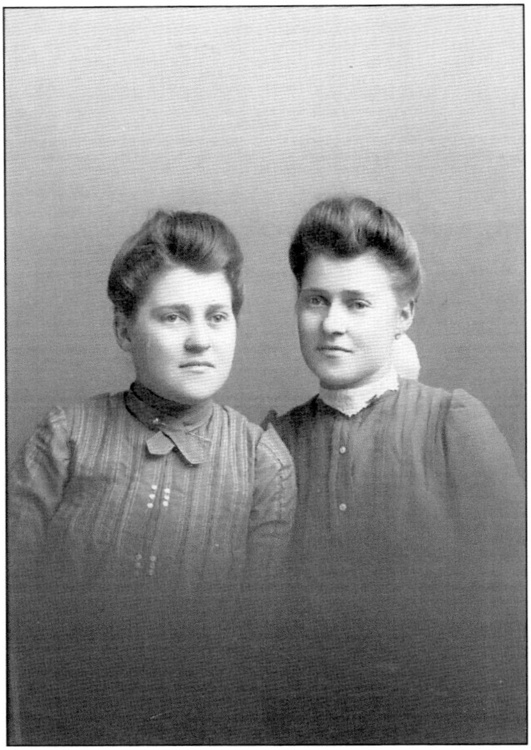

Left, identical twins Gertrude Kearns Lee (left) and Catherine Kearns Hulse (right) pose together as teens. Below, Catherine (left) and Gertrude (right) are photographed as they near their ninetieth birthday. Gertrude died at the age of 92 in 1972, and Catherine passed away in 1975 at the age of 95. Born to English immigrants in Ohio, the twins moved to the township as children and remained lifelong residents of the area. They often hosted Republican Party Ladies Auxiliary events, and Catherine was also active as a committeewoman for the party. After their husbands passed away, the sisters spent their later years living together in the Hulse family home on Lawrence Road.

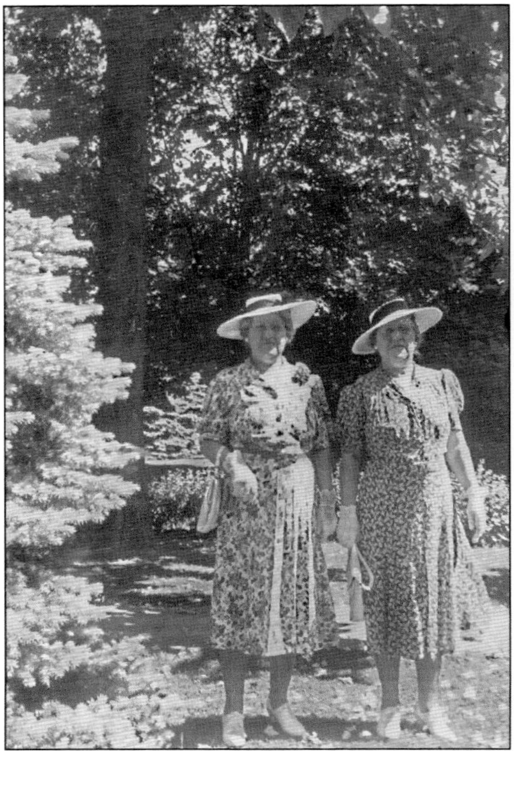

Albanus Goulding was the owner of Trenton Brick and Tile Company, which had locations on Mulberry Street and Princeton Avenue. The Goulding family was involved in several businesses in the early 20th century, including cattle sales, steam heating, and construction. Albanus moved to Texas following his wife's death in 1941.

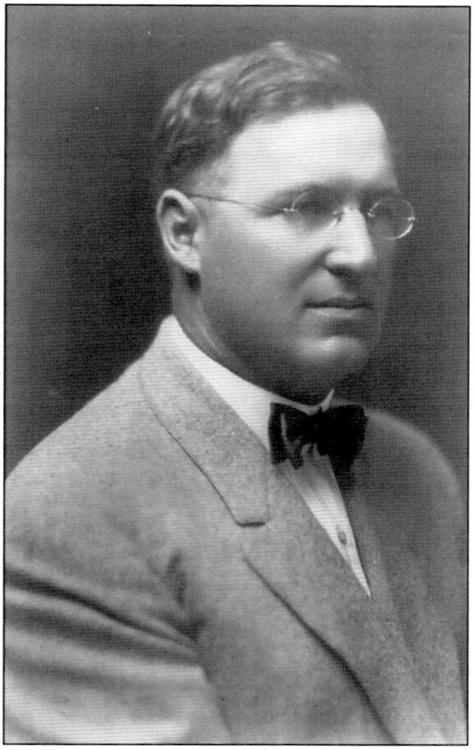

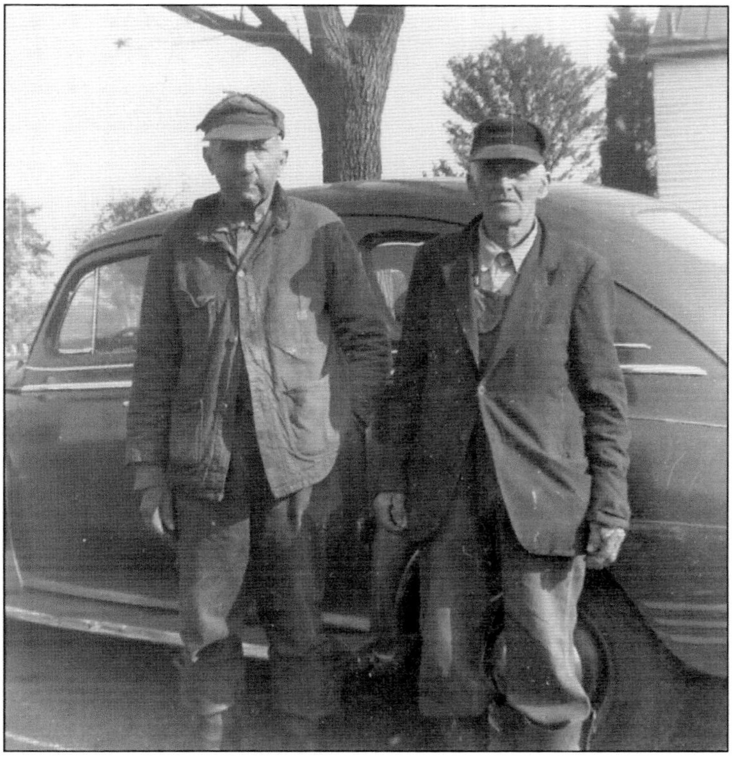

Harry Baldwin (left) and Howard A. Fackler (right) pose together, around 1959. The Fackler family owned a large plot of land on Princeton Pike. Baldwin lived on the Fackler family farm and was known to area residents as "Harry the Trapper" for his hunting and trapping skills. According to Donald Tyler's book *Old Lawrenceville: Early Houses and Homes*, Baldwin trapped muskrat, skunk, raccoon, and other small animals, selling the skins for 50¢ to $3.

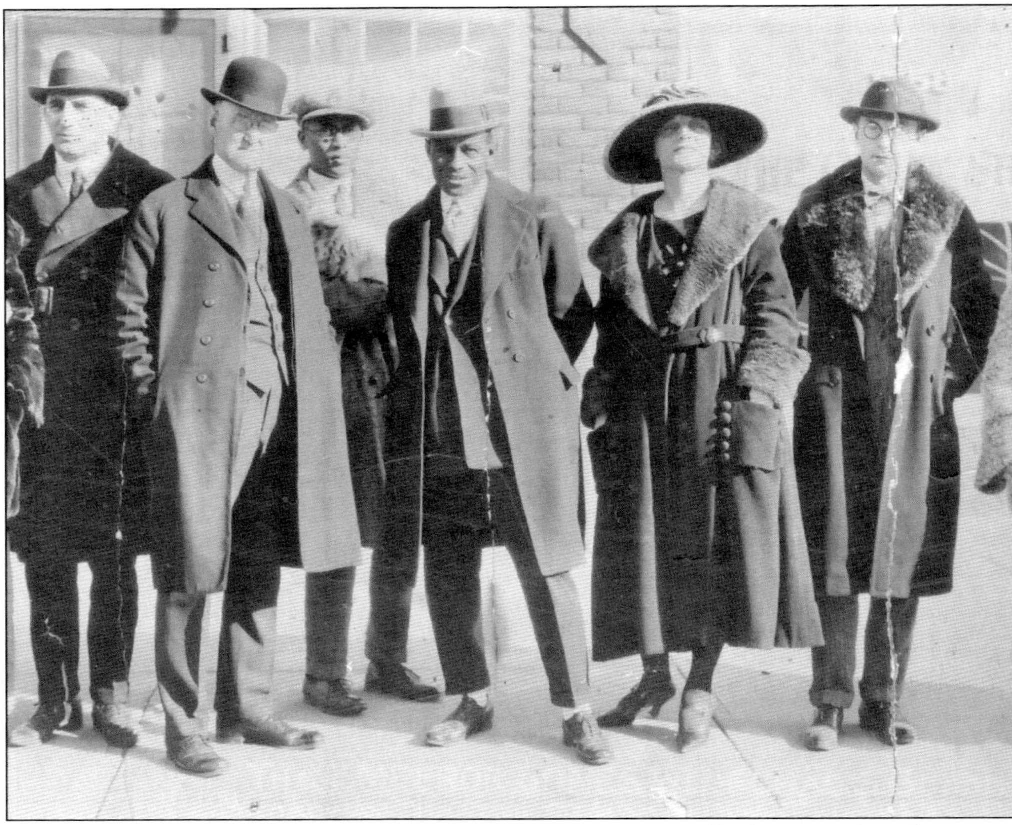

Charles S. Gilpin (center) starred in the lead role of Eugene O'Neill's dramatic play *The Emperor Jones*. Gilpin was recognized by the Drama League as one of the top 10 contributors to theater in 1920. After his run as Jones and the loss of his voice, he was unable to find any work in leading roles and moved to the Eggerts Crossing area of the township. Gilpin passed away in 1930.

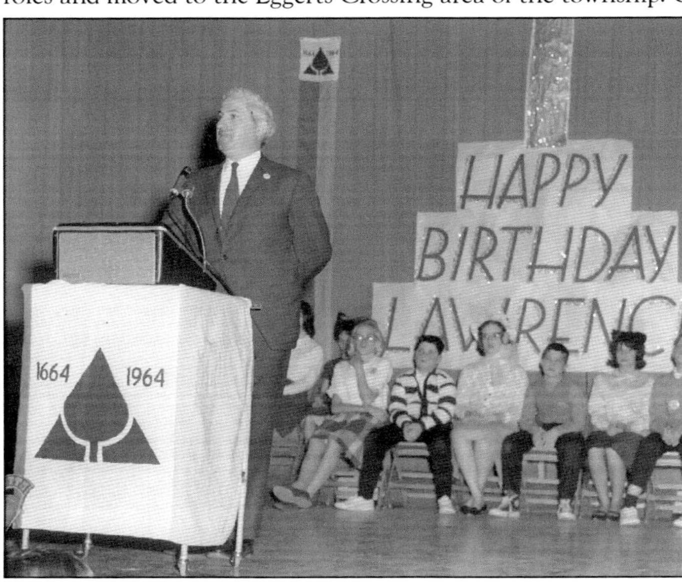

Bob Immordino speaks at a program celebrating Lawrence Township's 267th birthday in 1964. Immordino served two terms as township historian and was active in collecting memorabilia for the town's archives. A former township tax assessor, Immordino was also active in the Italian American community and hosted an annual event marking the birthday of William Albertus, a Lawrence resident who was the first Italian American to settle in New Jersey.

J. Roscoe Howell was perhaps Lawrence's first historian. Born in 1881 to a family of millers in Baker's Basin, Howell wrote extensively about the industrial area around Lawrence Station. Howell's work detailed every building's location and included a blueprint that was used to create a large diorama of the area as part of the township's 275th birthday celebration in 1972. Howell also served on the school board.

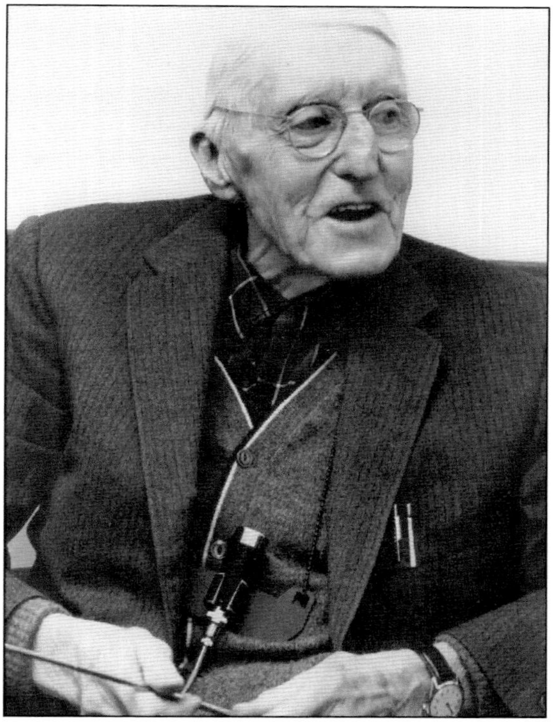

Rotary Club president Jack Frost (right) presents Dorothy Bayless (left) with a lifetime service award in 1982. Bayless was active in the community, serving on the board of education and championing environmental causes as a member of several non-profit groups and government committees. A longtime member of the Township Conservation Advisory Committee, Bayless helped create the community gardens and outdoor education programs in Lawrence.

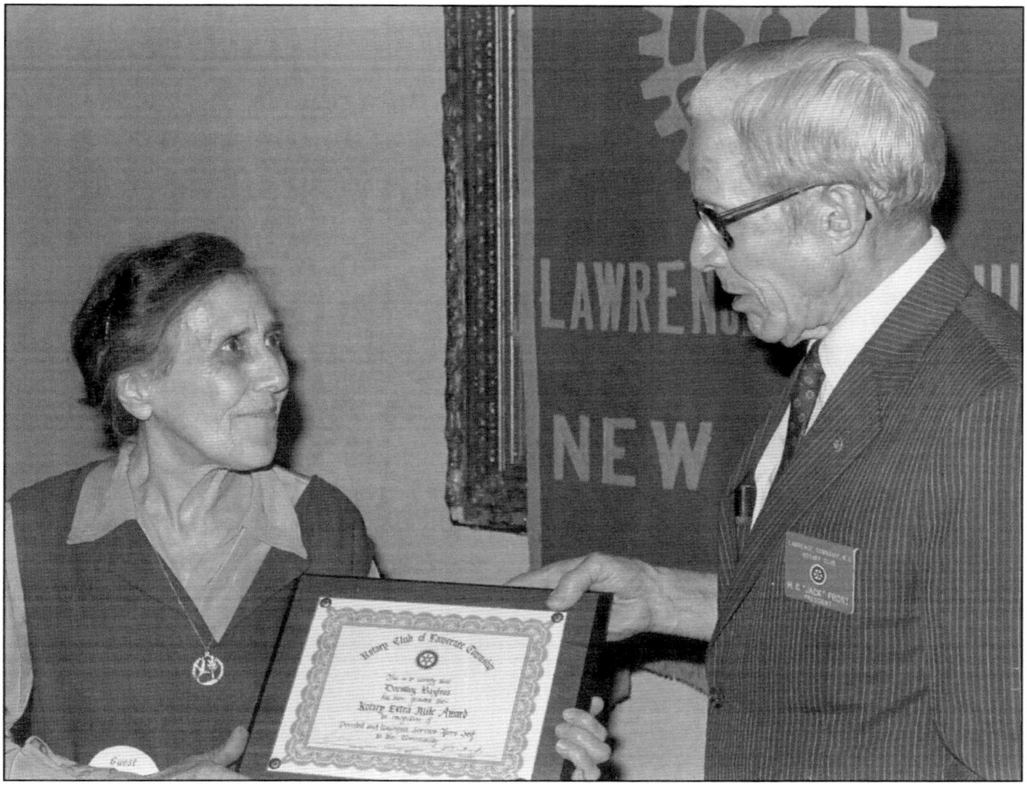

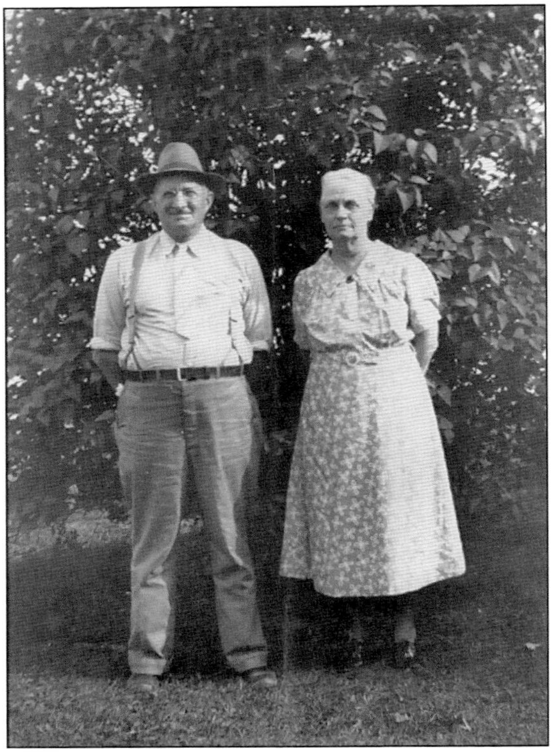

Standing together in this c. 1940 photograph are Thomas Smith Stevens (left) and Emma Jane Green Stevens (right). The Stevens family home is located just before the Whitehead Road jug-handle on the southbound side of Brunswick Pike. The area south of the Lawrence Shopping Center known as Stevens Meadow is named for the family, who once owned the land. Stevens Avenue runs behind the property, off of Bunker Hill Road.

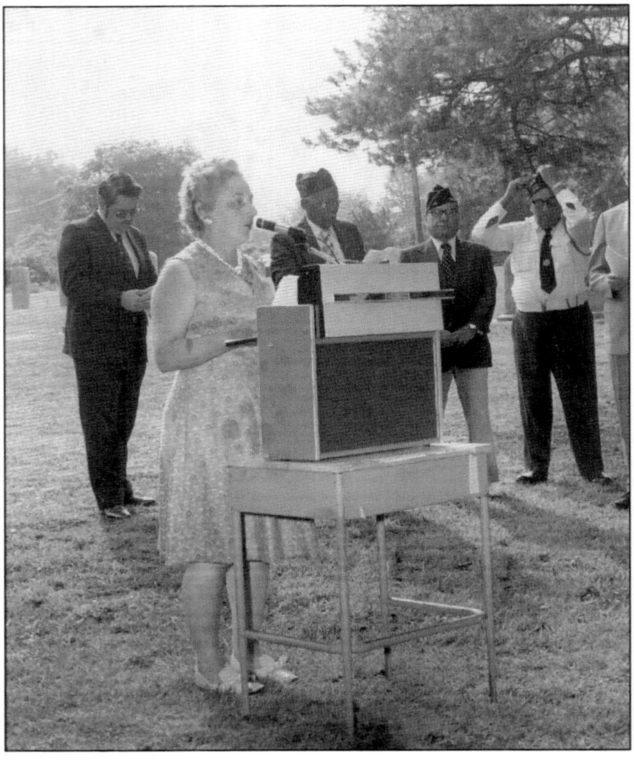

Winona D. Nash, chairman of the Historic and Aesthetic Committee, speaks at the Princessville Cemetery Bicentennial Dedication on July 4, 1976. The dedication celebrated the rehabilitation of the cemetery, one of many projects Nash was involved in as a member of the committee and, later, as township historian. In addition to cultivating a lifelong interest in history, Nash served on a variety of government committees and was active in the Slackwood Fire Department's Ladies Auxiliary.

Eight

SCHOOLS

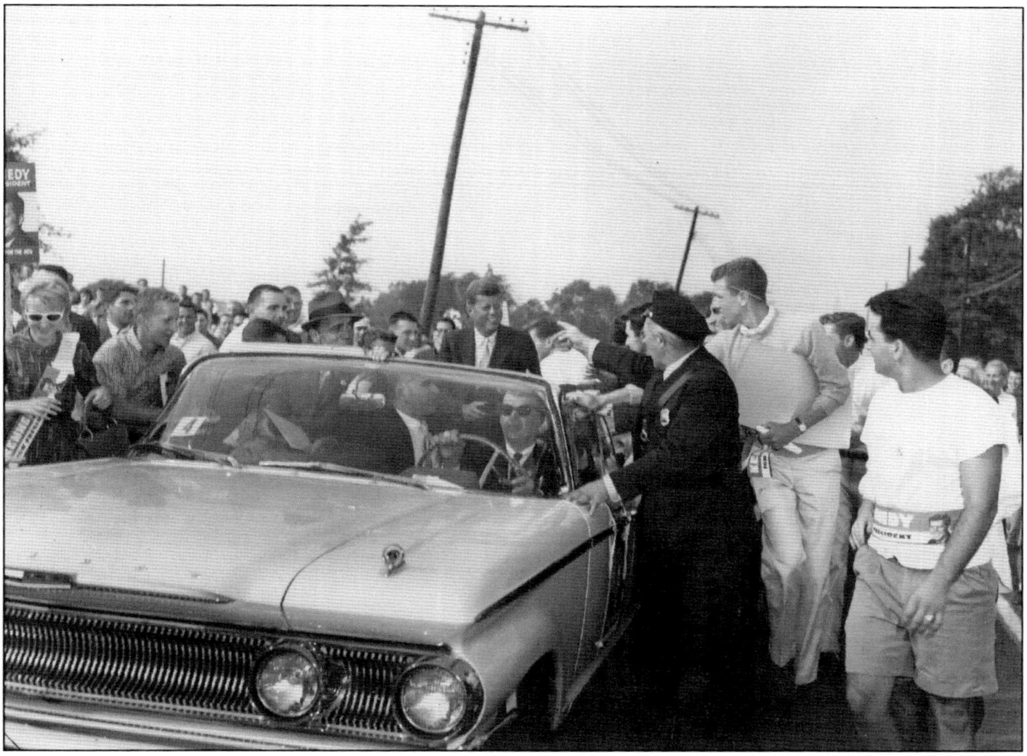

On September 15, 1960, Sen. John F. Kennedy made a whirlwind tour of New Jersey. After a speech in Princeton, the future president took a motorcade down Route 206 to the State House in Trenton. Students at Rider College gave the candidate an enthusiastic welcome as he passed by their campus. (Courtesy of Rider University, Moore Library Special Collections and University Archives.)

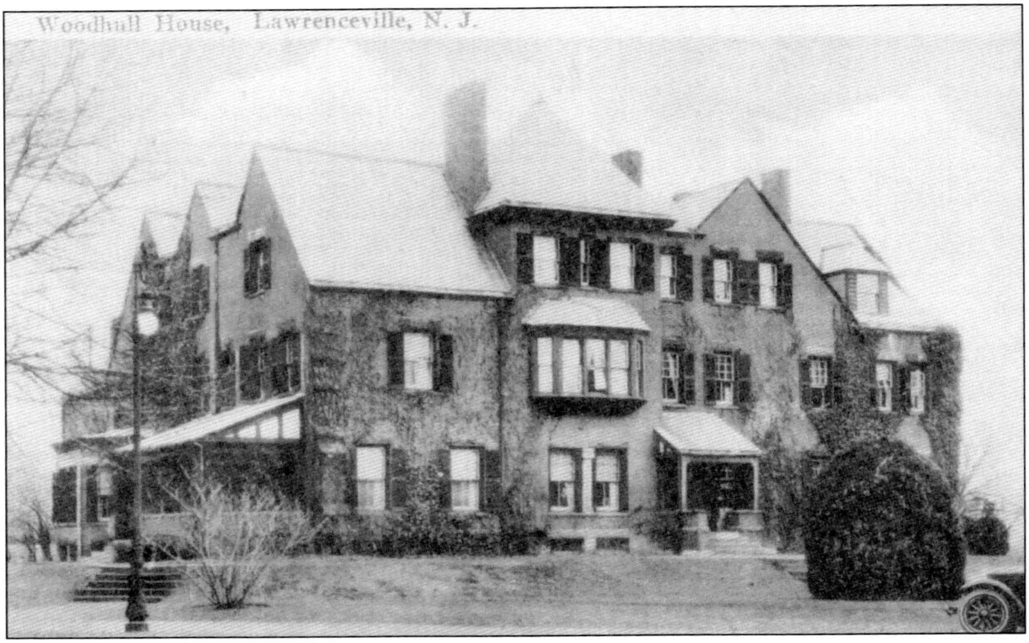

Woodhull House (depicted on a c. 1920 postcard, above) and Griswold House (depicted on a 1908 postcard, below) served as residence halls on the campus of The Lawrenceville School. Both buildings were constructed around 1885. Woodhull burned down and had to be reconstructed in 1892. The houses were built with funds donated by John Cleve Green, a Lawrence resident who had been a member of the school's first class. Green made his fortune in tea and textile trading in China. Later in life, he became a well-known philanthropist, donating to The Lawrenceville School, Princeton Theological Seminary, and Princeton University, among others.

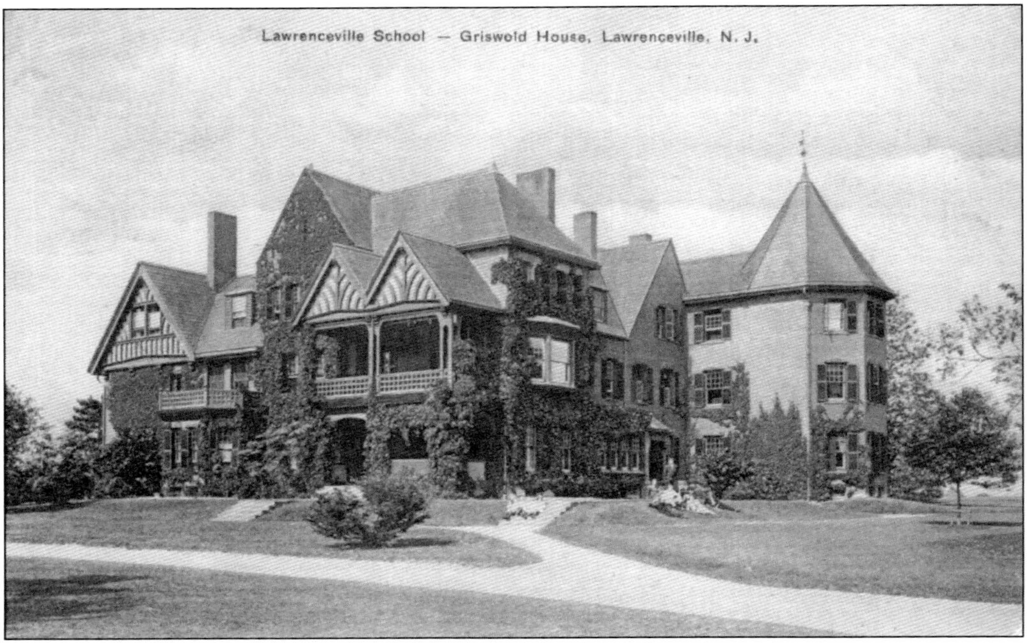

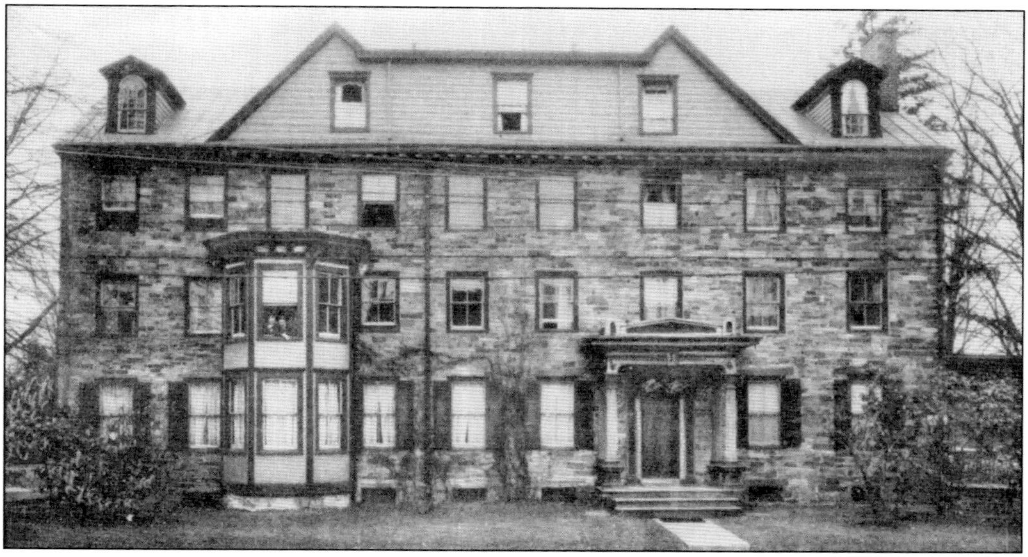

Hamill House, pictured around 1920, was opened in 1814 as a residence hall for the newly started Maidenhead Academy and was originally called the Hamilton House. The structure was built by Rev. Isaac Brown, who founded the school in 1810. The house was later renamed in honor of the school's third headmaster, Samuel McClintock Hamill, and has been in continuous service as a residence hall since its construction.

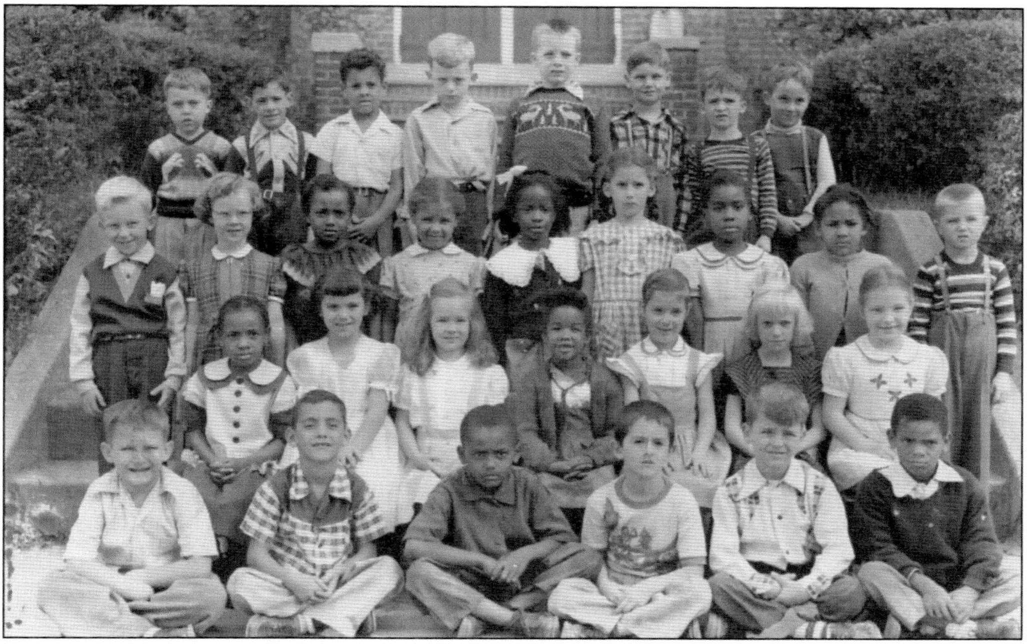

Pictured at Elridge Park School in 1953, from left to right, are (first row) Mark Cermele, Don Lombardo, unidentified, Tom Radlinsky, Joe Picarello, and Dennis Perkins; (second row) Sandy Joyner, Janice Scalzo, Ginger ?, Pamela Marrow, Roseanne Kraus, Maryann Ziegler, and Joan Cornell; (third row) Ricky Sarvat, Kathy Clark, unidentified, Linda Bullock, Jaqueline Bethea, Linda Wilson, Elsie Vereen, Lennie Lennon, and Ted Clemen; (fourth row) Sam Lombardo, Frank Toleno, Eric Walker, Robert Lamb, Jack Walters, unidentified, Bobby Salt, and unknown.

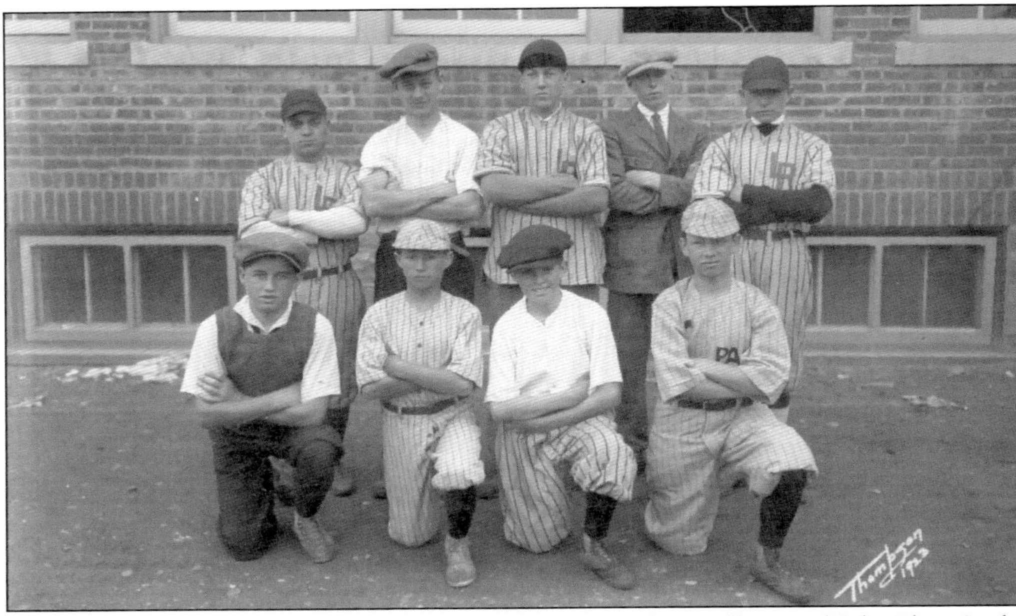

The 1923 Eldridge Park School baseball team, from left to right, are (front row) John Plant, Leslie ?, Leo Balam, and unidentified; (second row) Bill Rich, Joe King, Ron Hulse, Walter Hutchins, and Bill Baker. Before little league and other organized sports, schools would sometimes sponsor teams and put ads in the paper seeking games against other school or neighborhood teams.

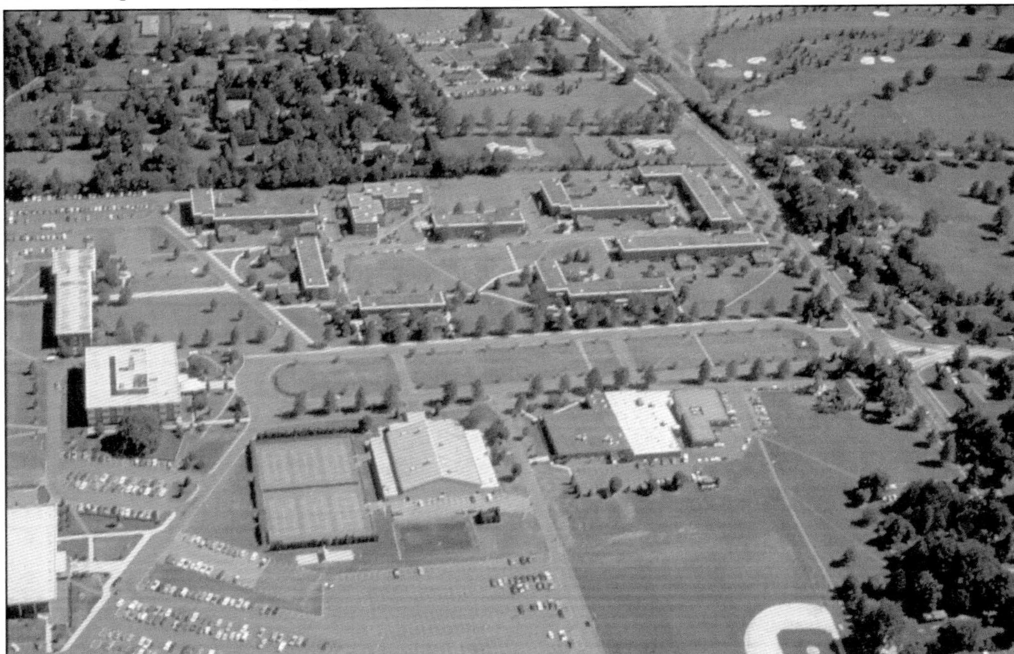

The footprint of Rider College in 1974 was much smaller than it is today. New residence halls, as well as academic, arts, and athletic buildings have been added behind the student center (left), many since the school achieved university status in 1994. Rider moved from downtown Trenton to Lawrence in the late 1950s.

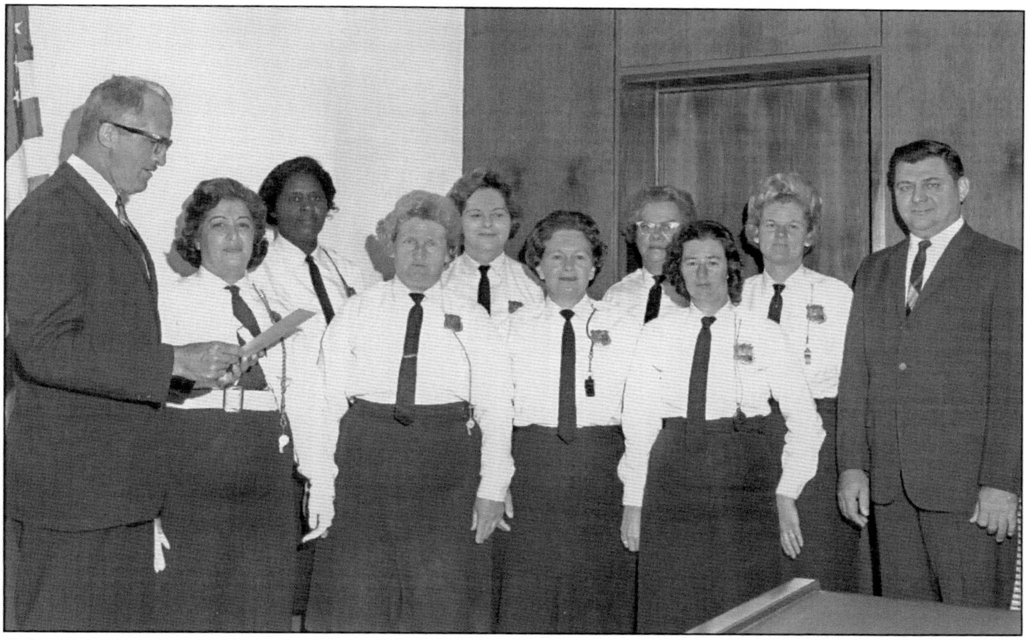

School crossing guards were honored for their service at a town council meeting in May 1966. Pictured from left to right are Mayor Joseph M. Mahan (reading a letter thanking the guards), Emma Williamson, Audrey Kauffman, Helen N. Albertson, Shirley Katona, Audrey J. Maher, Helen LeCompte, Vivian Huber, Kathleen Gulden, and police chief William F. Seabridge.

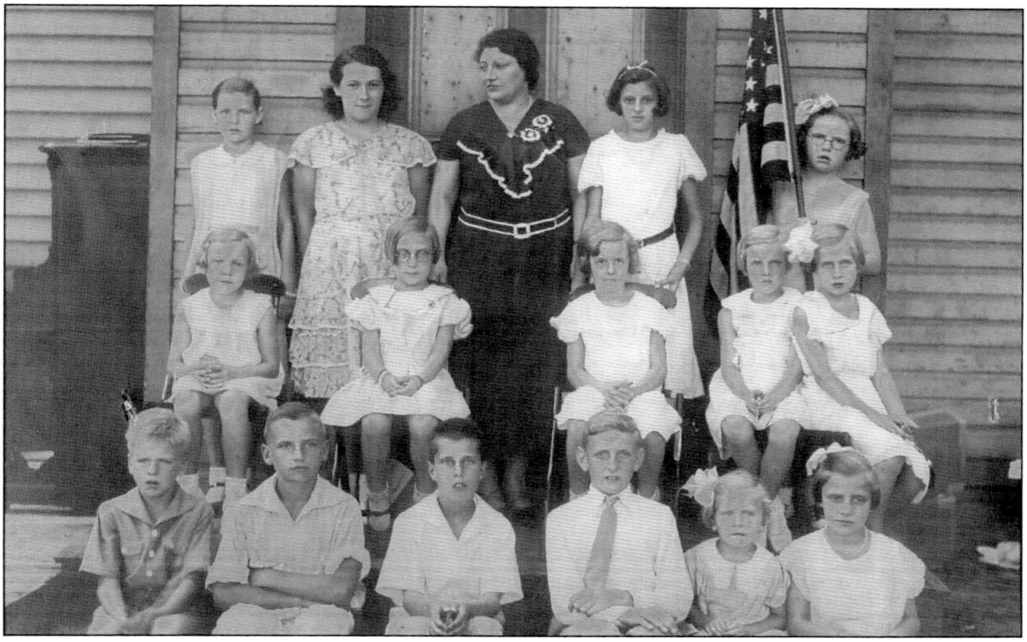

This Rosedale School class picture was taken at the beginning of the school year in August 1933. The 1933–1934 class was one of the last to attend the one-room school. The elementary school typically had fewer than 20 students across all grade levels. After the school closed in 1937, the students were transferred to the Lawrenceville Elementary School.

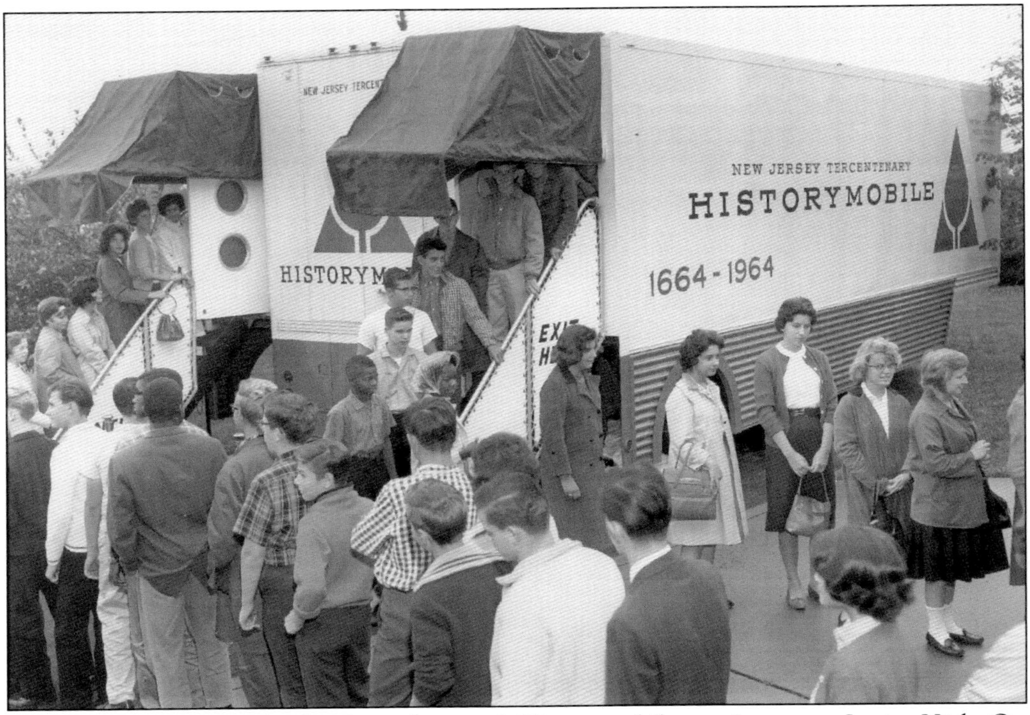

The first New Jersey school to host the state's Historymobile was Lawrence Junior High. On October 3, 1961, the traveling museum opened in the school's parking lot. The 16-ton truck brought artifacts and educational displays to towns across the state as part of a five-year program celebrating the 300th anniversary of New Jersey's founding. The Historymobile also made stops around the country, including one in Washington for the Seattle World's Fair in 1962.

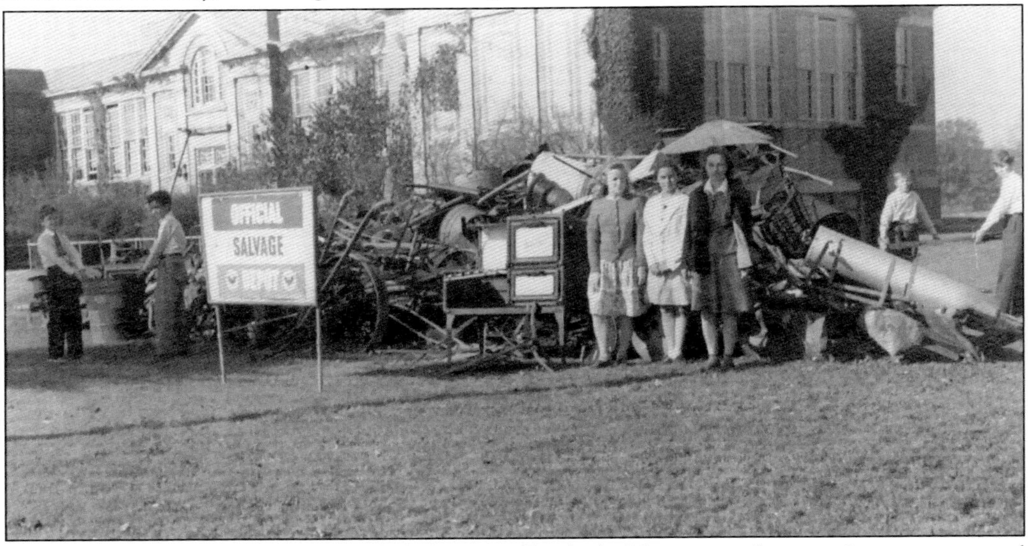

During World War II, Lawrence aided the war effort by holding scrap drives at locations around town. Residents were invited to drop off used metal goods that could be melted down to produce vehicles and munitions. The fall 1943 drive was held at School Number 4 on Route 1 and yielded about 15 tons of scrap metal.

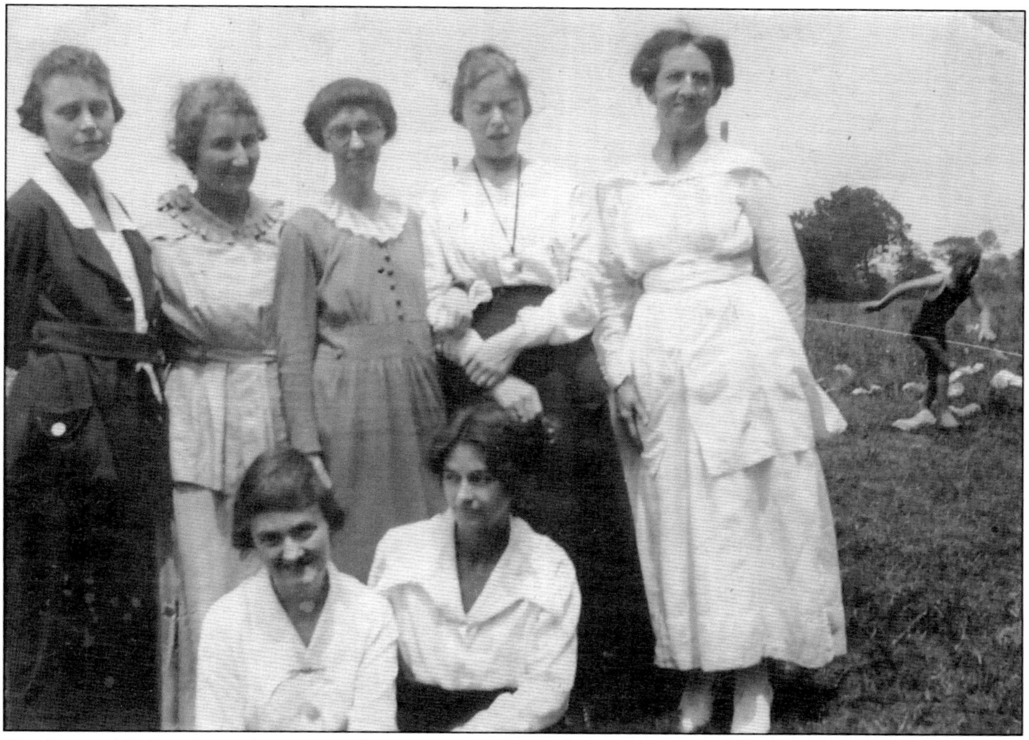

Slackwood School teachers pose for a picture, around 1910. Pictured from left to right are (front row) Allie Bechtel and Arlene Keephart; (second row) Gladys Skillman, Mabel Updegrove, Mabel Sterling, Alice Nash, and Mary Nash (not a teacher, but Alice's mother). Mabel Updegrove taught in Lawrence schools for 48 years; the first five were spent at Rosedale, and the rest at Slackwood, where she retired as the principal in 1951.

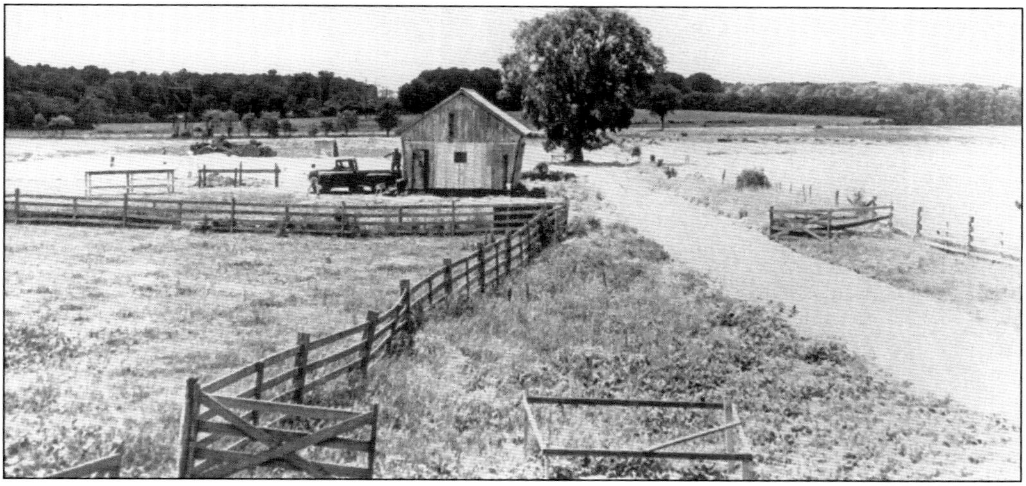

This late 1940s image of the Pate Farm (Parsonage Farm) shows an access road, a small shed, and a large elm tree. Rider College, now University, purchased the farm in 1956 and held a ground breaking for the Lawrenceville campus on April 27, 1957. Freshmen began using the new campus in 1959, and the entire Trenton campus was moved by the end of 1964. The elm tree, situated between Moore Library and the administration building, became part of the university's logo.

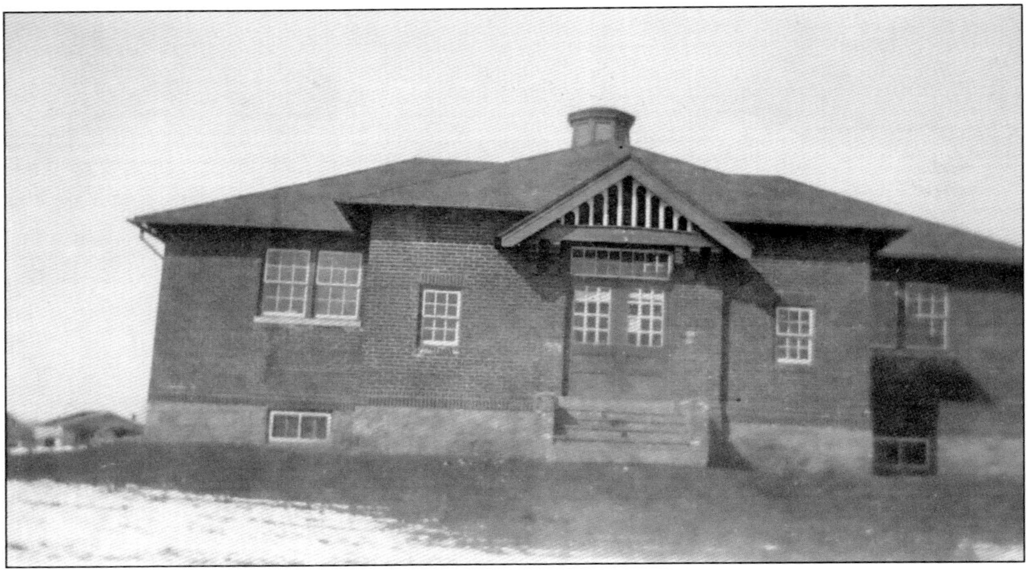

Eldridge Park School (pictured above, about 1914) was, like many early schools, built as a one-level building that eventually became too small to accommodate the number of students in its classes. The township elected to build a second level. A roof raising was held in 1916, and the first addition was completed around 1918 (pictured below). The school underwent further expansion, but ironically was closed in 1979 because of declining enrollment. After a decade of use as a rental property, the school was reopened in 1990 to house the township's fourth-grade students as the school district faced overcrowding.

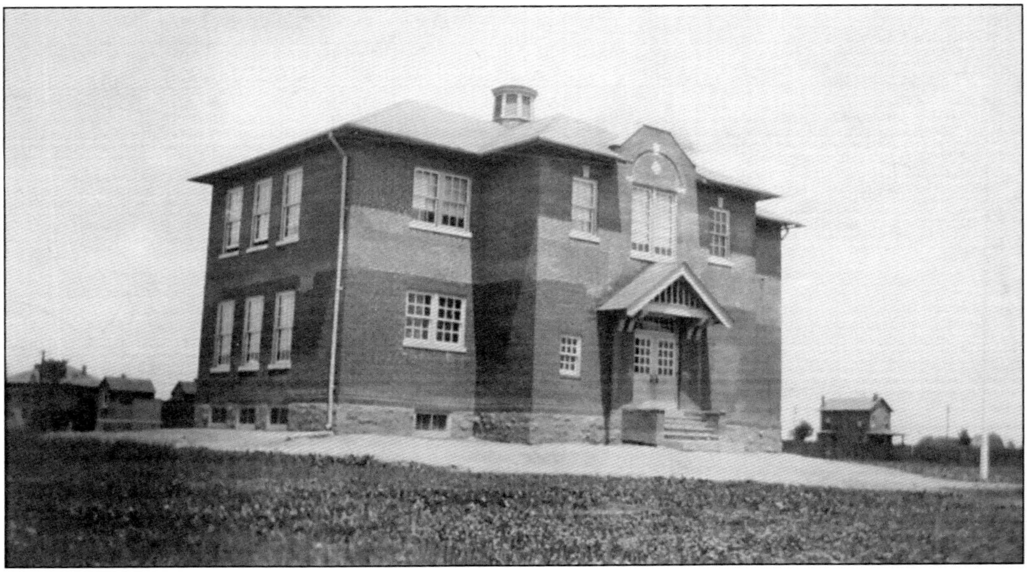

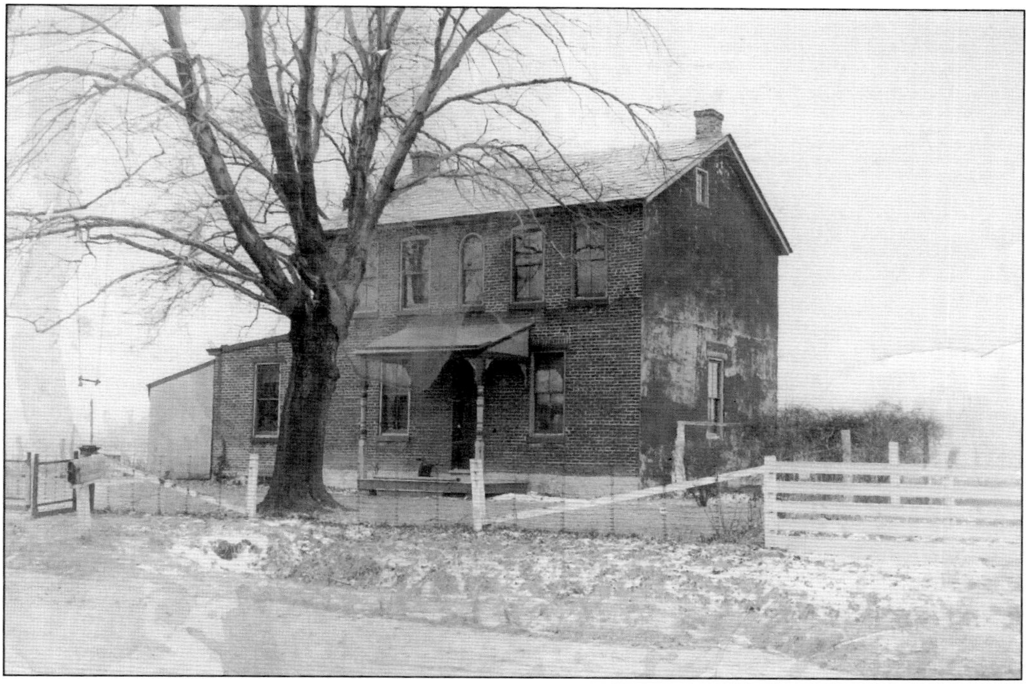

The Valley School (or "Red Brick School") at the corner of Princeton Pike and Smithfield Avenue was built in 1832 as a one-level school. A second story was added in the early 1900s. The building served as a school until the early 1900s, when it was sold as a private residence. It is the only 19th-century school building left in Lawrence, as all the other early buildings were demolished after they were closed. The c. 1910 photograph above shows the school after the second-floor construction was completed. Below, a c. 1975 view shows that very little has changed, aside from an addition to complete the second floor and another in the rear of the house.

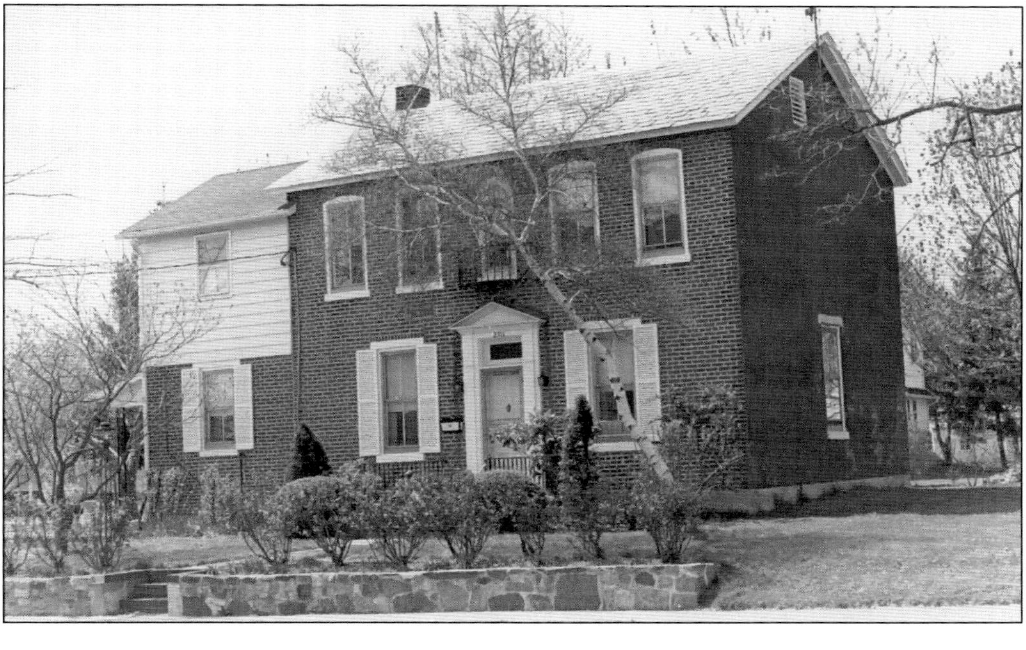

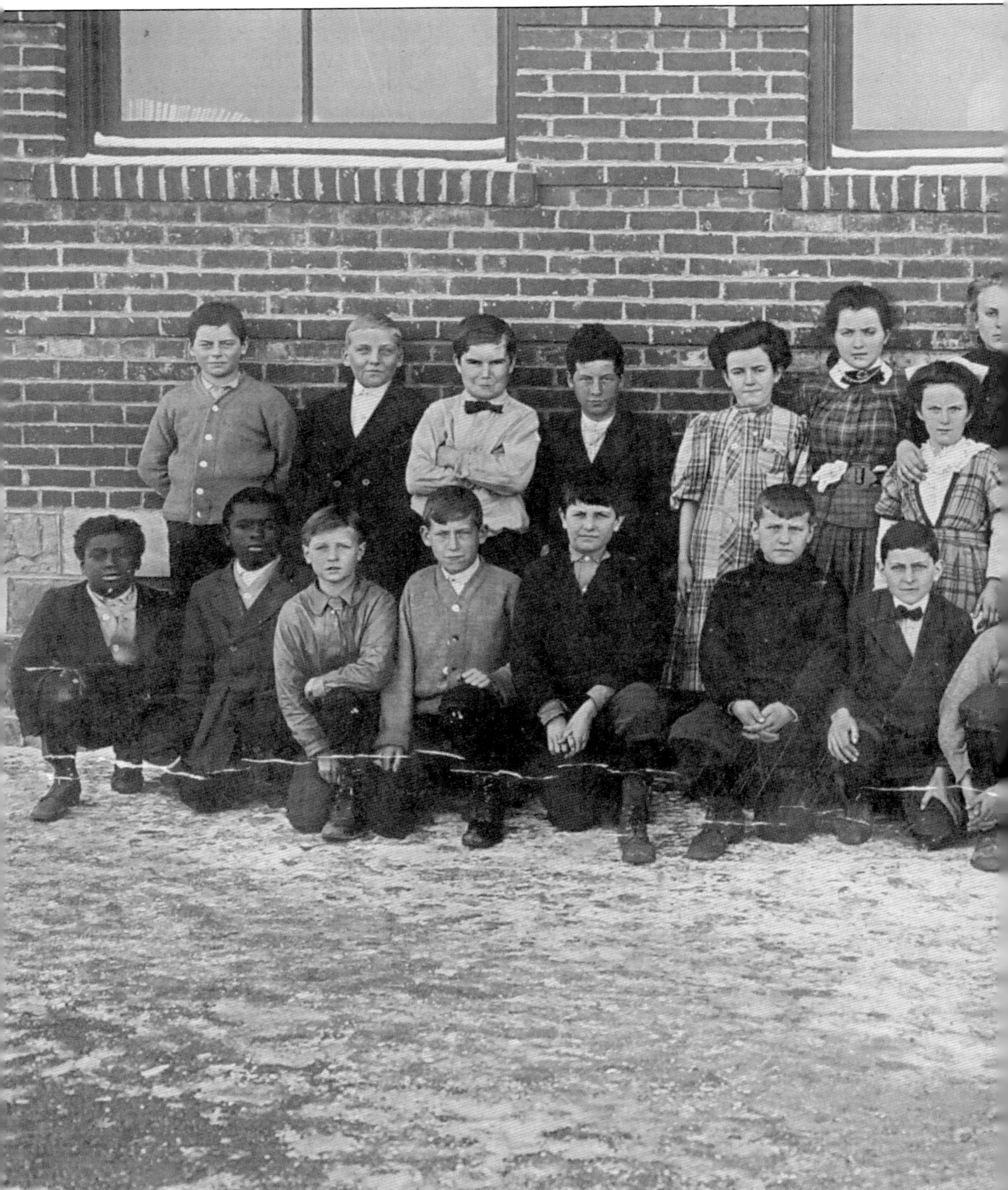

This Slackwood School class picture was taken in 1911. The school was constructed in 1904 on Princeton Pike and Carr Avenue. The name *Slackwood* was derived from the names of the two landowners of the property the school was built on: Joseph Slack and William Wood. The original building was only two rooms, but was expanded in 1909 when a two-room brick addition

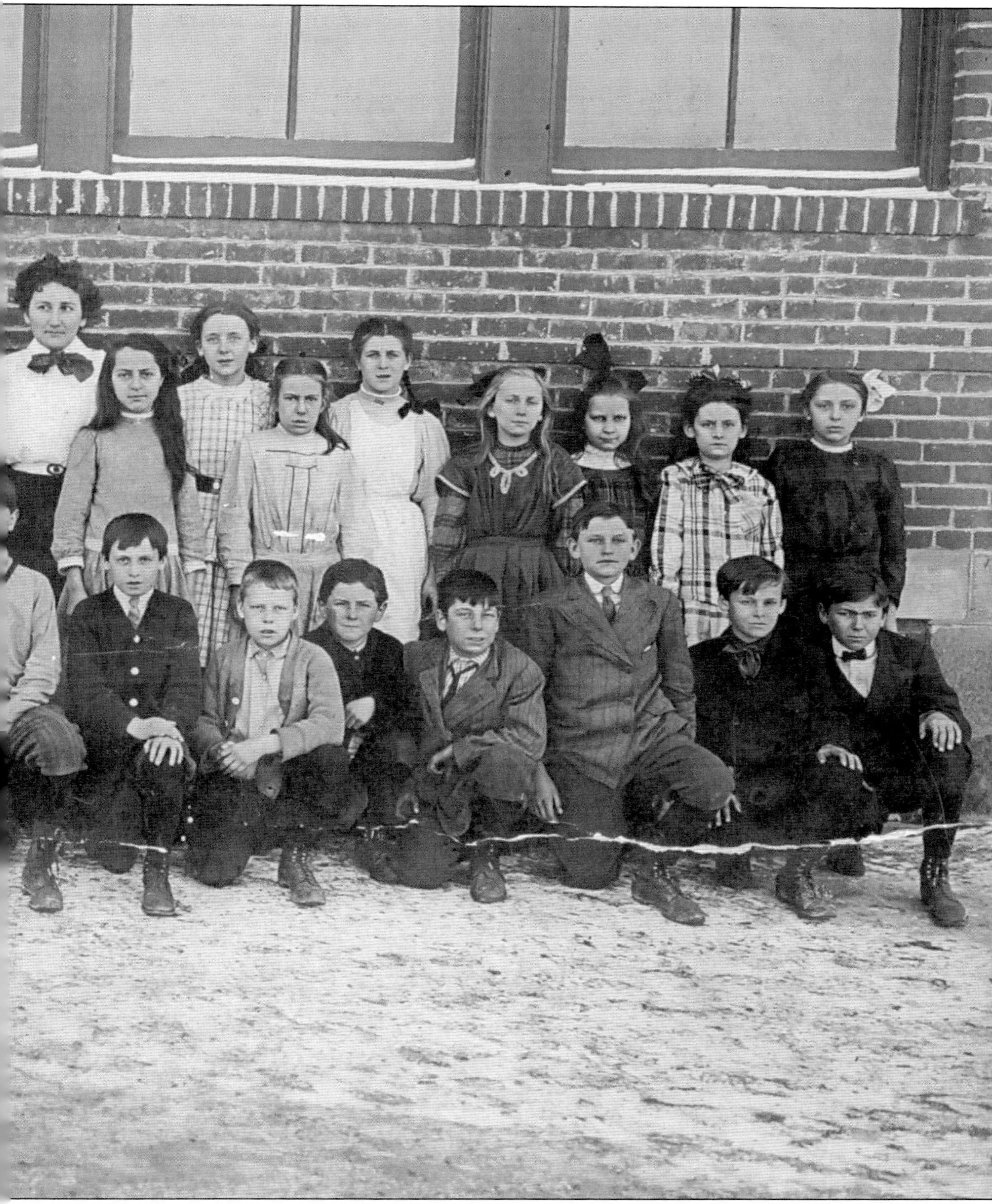

was added underneath the original structure (which was raised). In 1930, the school was able to purchase more land and expand to accommodate all of the new students. The school housed kindergarten to eighth grade until 1952, when the upper grades moved to the newly constructed Lawrence Junior High.

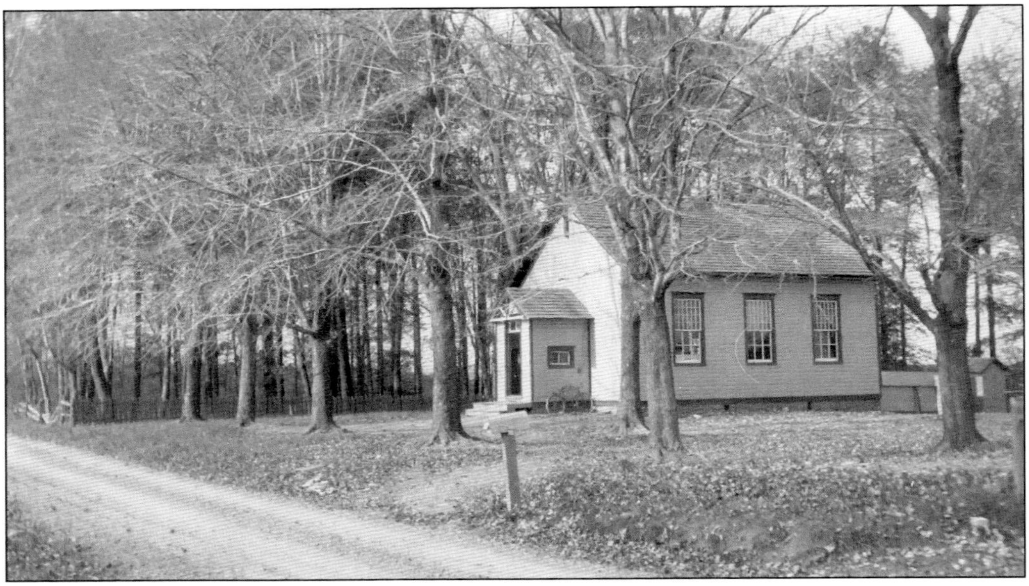

The Rosedale School on Cold Soil Road was the last one-room schoolhouse in operation in Mercer County, closing in 1936. The school was built in the late 1800s to replace an old log-cabin school that had burned down. The township maintained the school until it was sold in 1947. During the decade between the closing and the sale, reunions were held at the school each year.

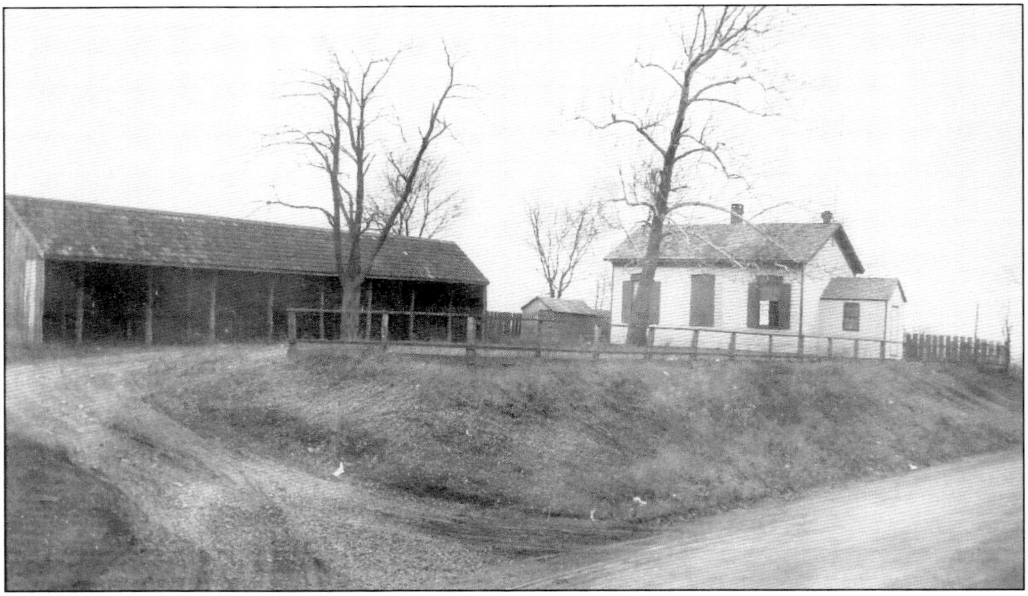

The Clarksville School was located on Quakerbridge Road, across from Clarksville Road on land that is now used as an access road to Quaker Bridge Mall. The school was built on the Berrien family farmland, and many of the farm buildings, including the farmhouse, were near the school. Horse stalls are seen to the left of the school in this photograph, and Quakerbridge Road can be seen in the lower right-hand corner.

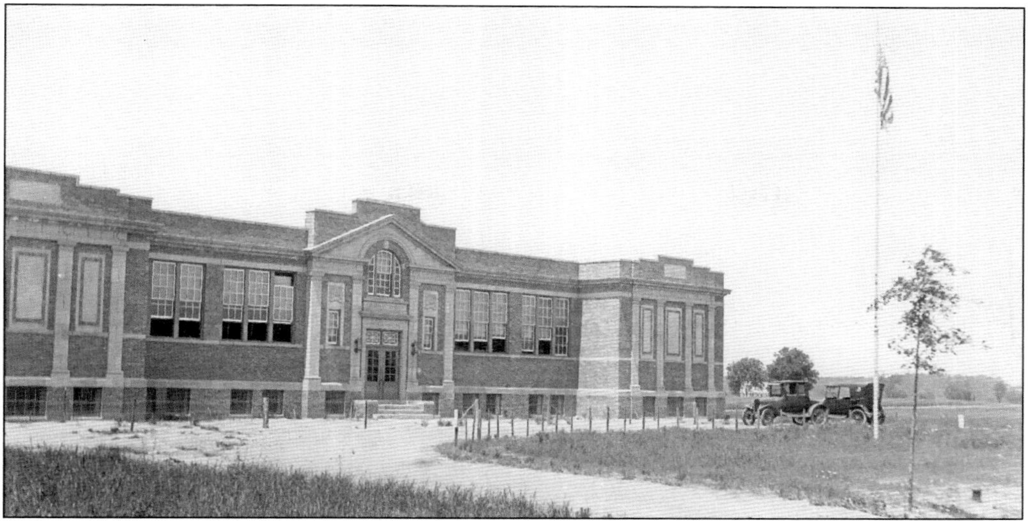

Public School Number 4, sometimes called Baker's Basin Public School, was built in 1925. The school was located on the southbound side of Brunswick Pike, just north of Allen Lane. In 1961, the Benjamin Franklin Elementary School was built as a replacement, but the school district continued to use the older building to combat the overcrowding of classrooms. The school was sold and demolished in 1972.

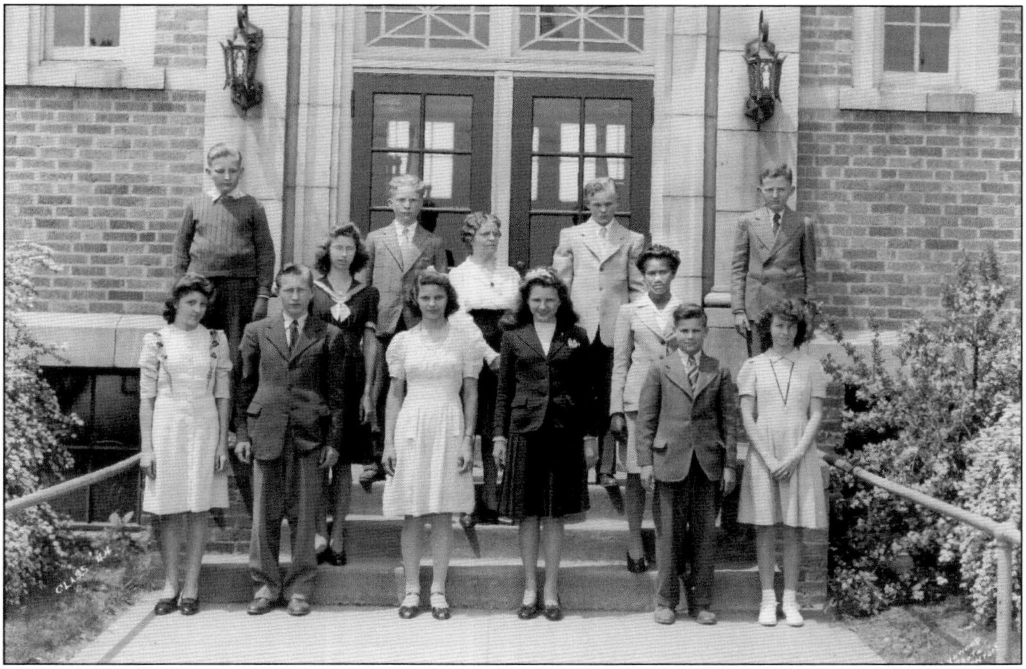

Members of the Public School Number 4 class of 1944, identified in an alphabetized list, are Dorothy Breedon, William Bowen, Joseph Cebulski, Helen Dumont, Peggy Falls, Robert Gilton, Robert Hafner, John Hood, Clifford Jones, Lorraine Jones, Marjorie Lewis, and Patricia Shoemaker. Principal Alice Sailey stands in the center of the photograph (second row, second from the left). Sailey lived her entire life in Lawrence Township and was hired in September 1913 as a kindergarten teacher at Slackwood School.

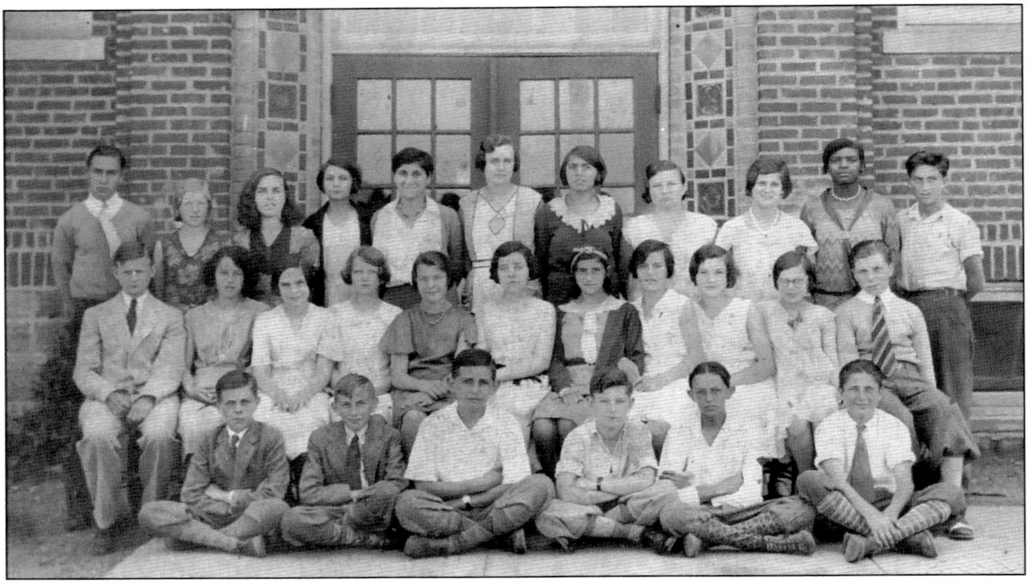

Members of the Eldridge Park School class of 1931, pictured from left to right, are (first row) George Wood, Tom Fischer, Paul Parker, Howard Louderback, Francis Mendry, and Eugene Sneth; (second row) Ronald Willinger, Dorothy White, Jean Titsworth, Ellen Cartlidge, Pearl Udy, Doris Guhl, Madeline Cermele, Joyce Lownie, June Lownie, Eleanor Carson, and Rudy Gronert; (third row) John Jabel, Mary Mularczyk, Dorothy Peacock, Virginia Boyle, Anna Pilla, Harriet Bayless, Alvera Di Tullio, Dorothy Hutchinson, Advena Chesner, Eleanor Justice, and Mark Cermele.

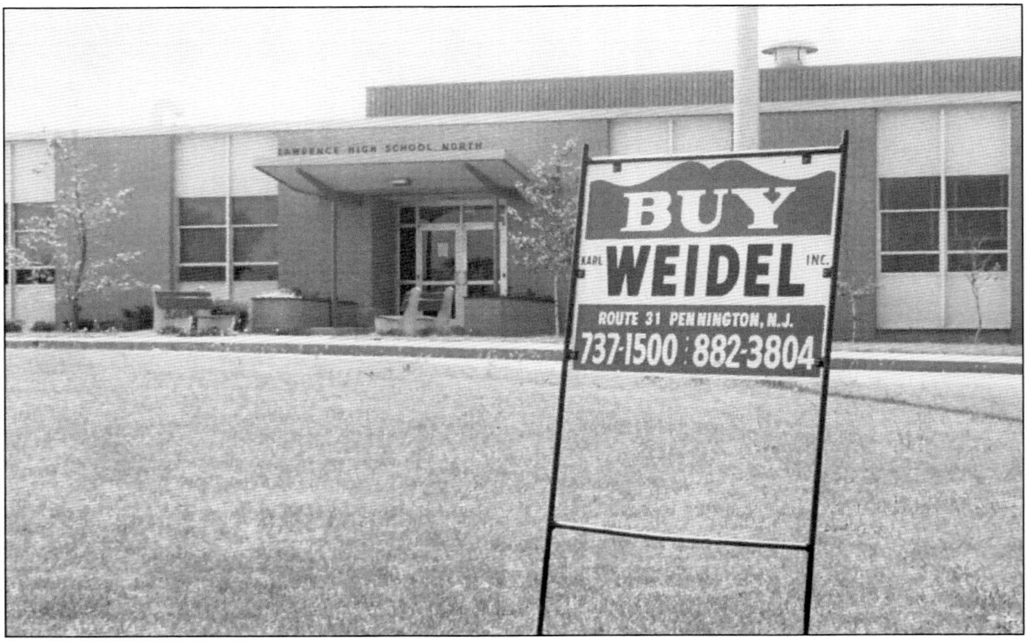

Lawrence High School on Princeton Pike sports a for-sale sign on the lawn as part of a senior-class prank, around 1980. The school was completed in 1966, with the first class graduating in 1968. Previously, Lawrence students had attended either Trenton Central High School or Princeton High School. (Courtesy of the Lawrence Ledger.)

Nine

Transportation

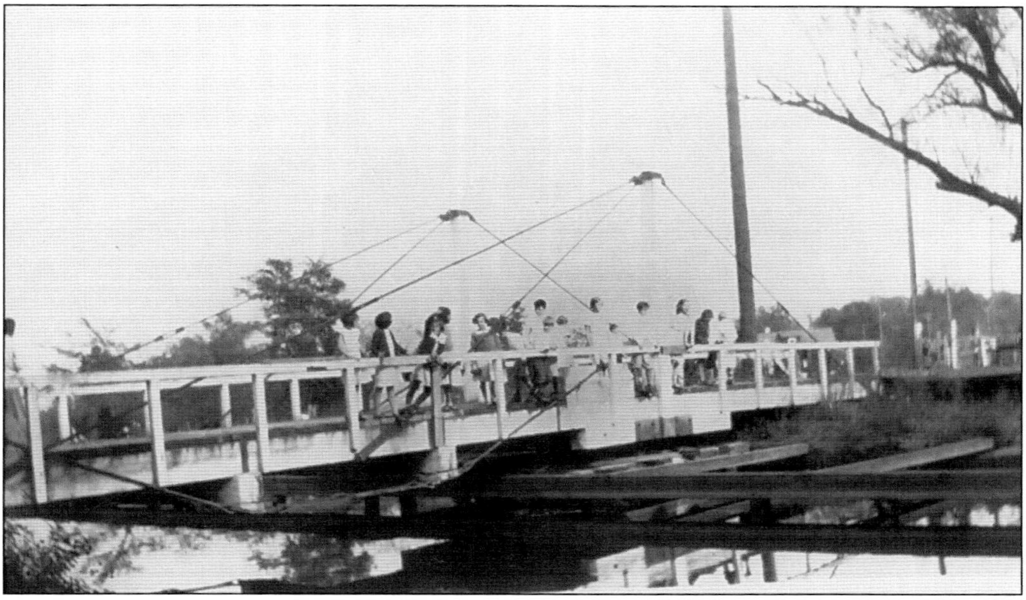

The bridge at Baker's Basin on the Delaware and Raritan Canal, photographed in the early 1900s, was next to the bridge tender's house. The bridge bore pedestrian and vehicular traffic over the canal, and the tender was responsible for opening the bridge to allow canal boats and other vessels to pass. The king-post bridge shown here could be swung open like a gate.

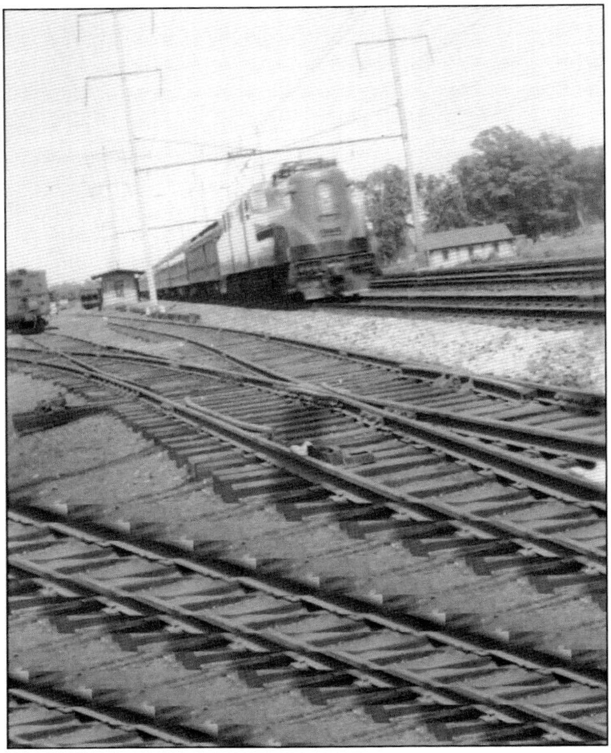

The main line of the Pennsylvania Railroad and freight siding at Lawrence Station in August 1935 (left) and around 1920 (below) was a busy depot for both passengers and freight traffic. The station once housed a post office and shops. The tracks were notoriously dangerous where they crossed Quakerbridge Road. Following the deaths of several people and animals at the crossing, area residents successfully petitioned the county freeholders to allow the railroad to build a bridge over the tracks. While the station is now gone, support buildings have been reused, now housing businesses; the main line is still used by Amtrak and New Jersey Transit as part of the Northeast Corridor line.

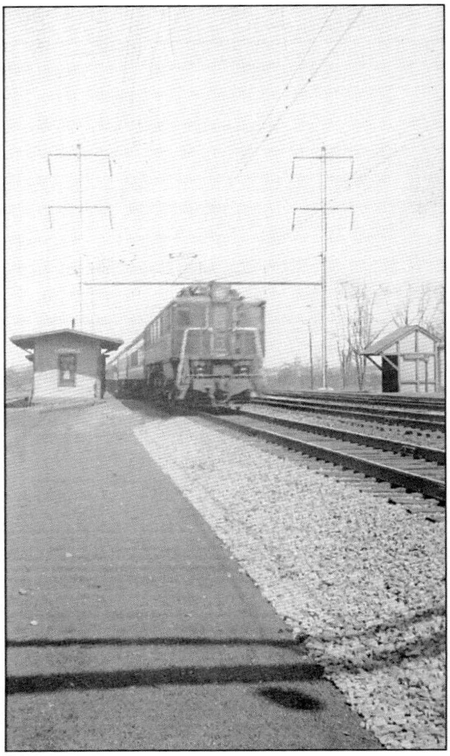

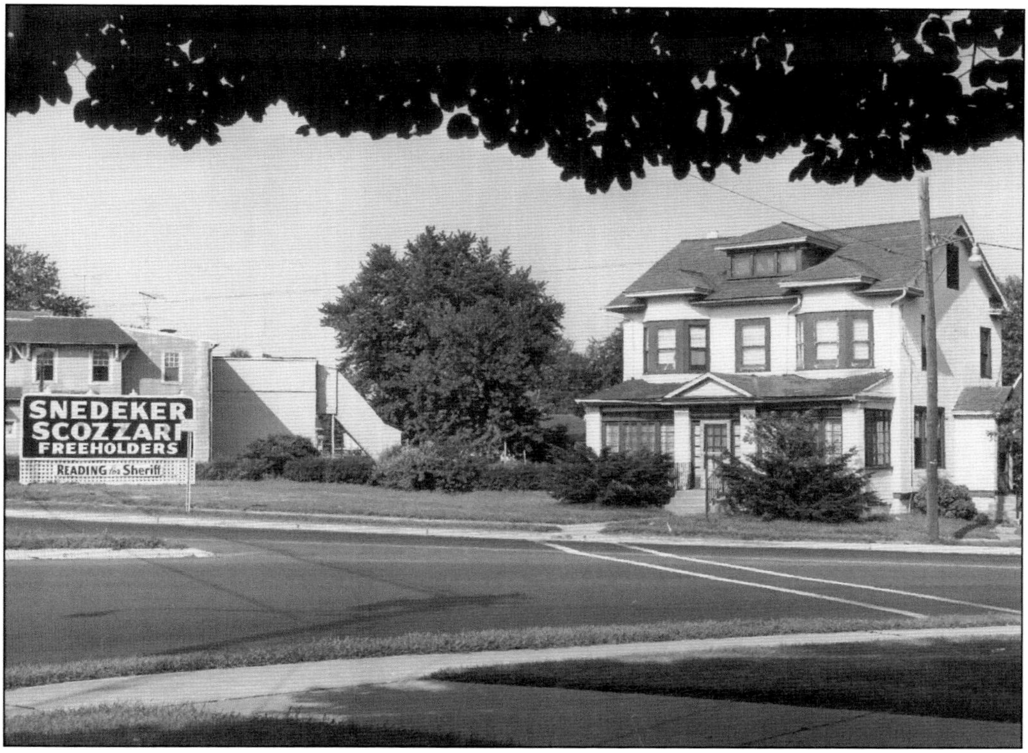

As the population of Mercer County grew, so did the need for roads. The Trenton Freeway (Route 1) project required the demolition of several structures near the Trenton border. The freeway project was approved in 1947, and the Lawrence portion was completed in 1955. Nobody's property was safe, including the house seen above, which was owned by George Page (onetime mayor of Trenton). The freeway was formally renamed Route 1 in 1973, when the portion from Whitehead Road to Carnegie Road was completed by the state. At the same time, an improvement plan for the Brunswick Circle Extension called for widening and realigning the road, which meant the demolition of more buildings near the circle (including businesses like Lafayette Radio, seen right).

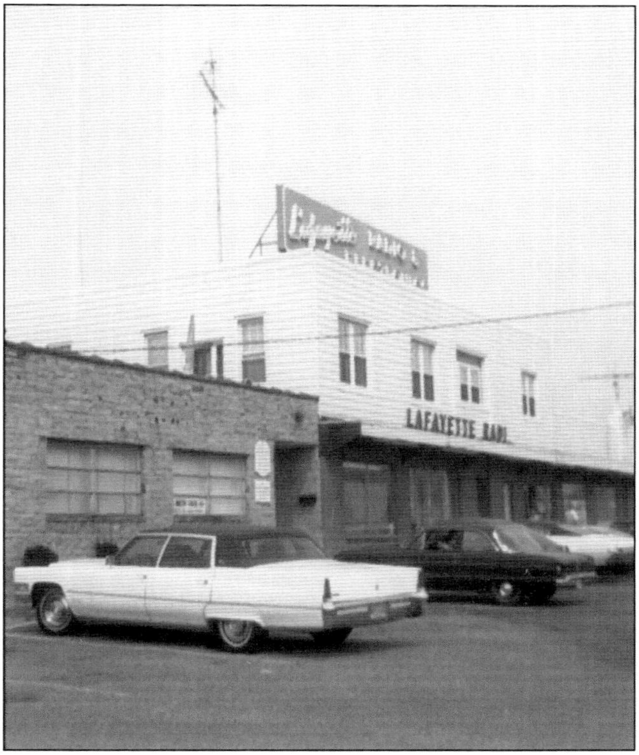

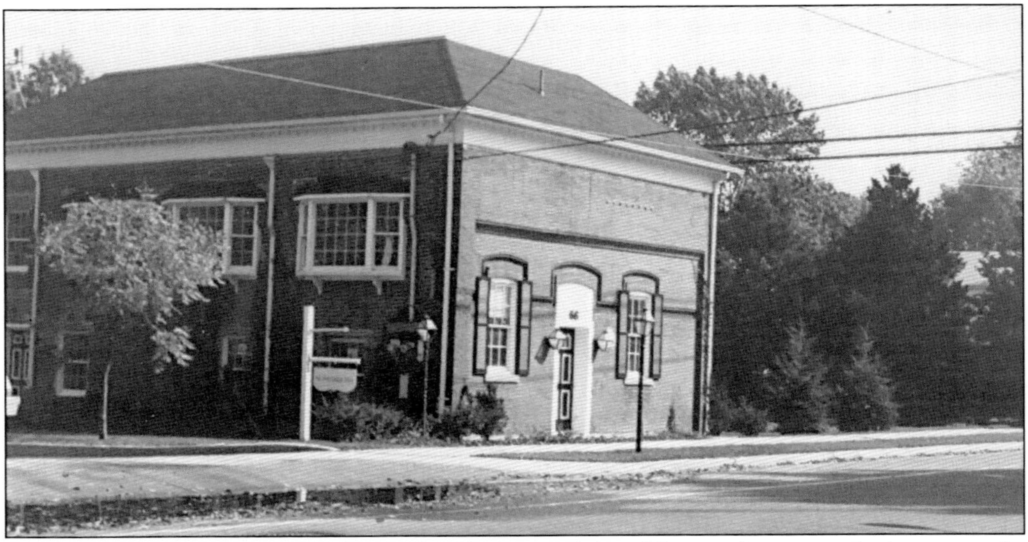

Aside from the replacement of the window frames and the addition of a storage shed on one side, the exterior of the old Johnson Trolley substation (seen around 1980) looks the same as it did when built in 1909. The station carried a 13,000-volt power-line, which connected to the main plant in Yardley. The station did not serve passengers, but the trolley did make a stop in front of the building.

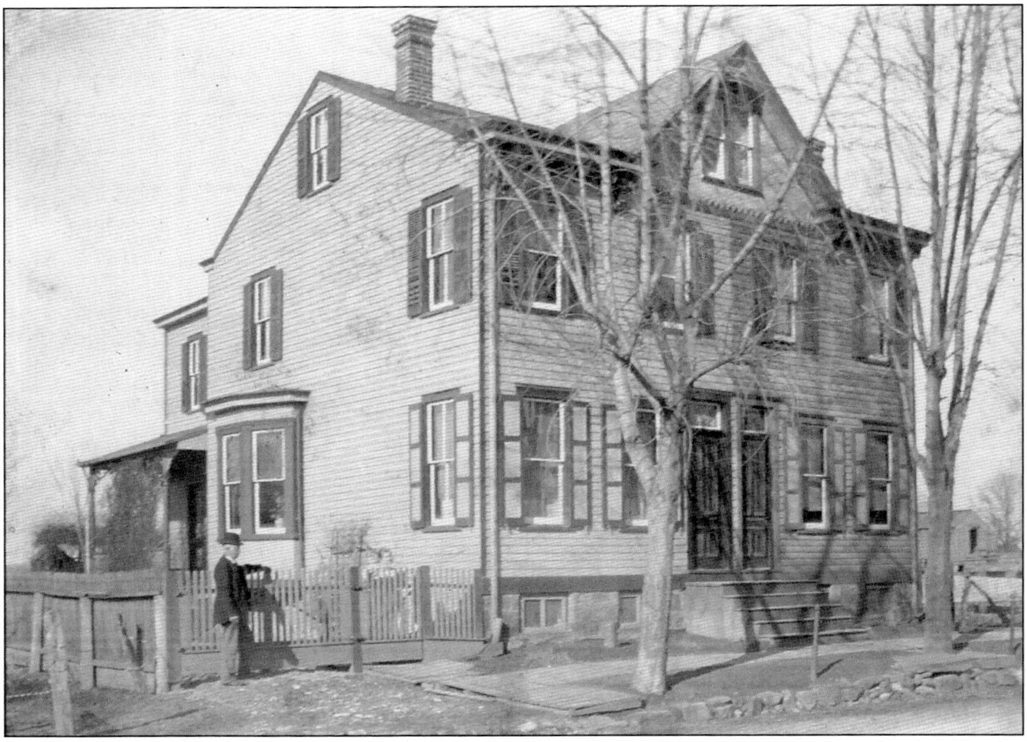

The Hulse family home on Brunswick Avenue, photographed in 1920, was torn down to make way for the construction of the Brunswick Avenue traffic circle. The circle was built in 1929 as a means to divert traffic away from downtown Trenton by redirecting it to Calhoun Street.

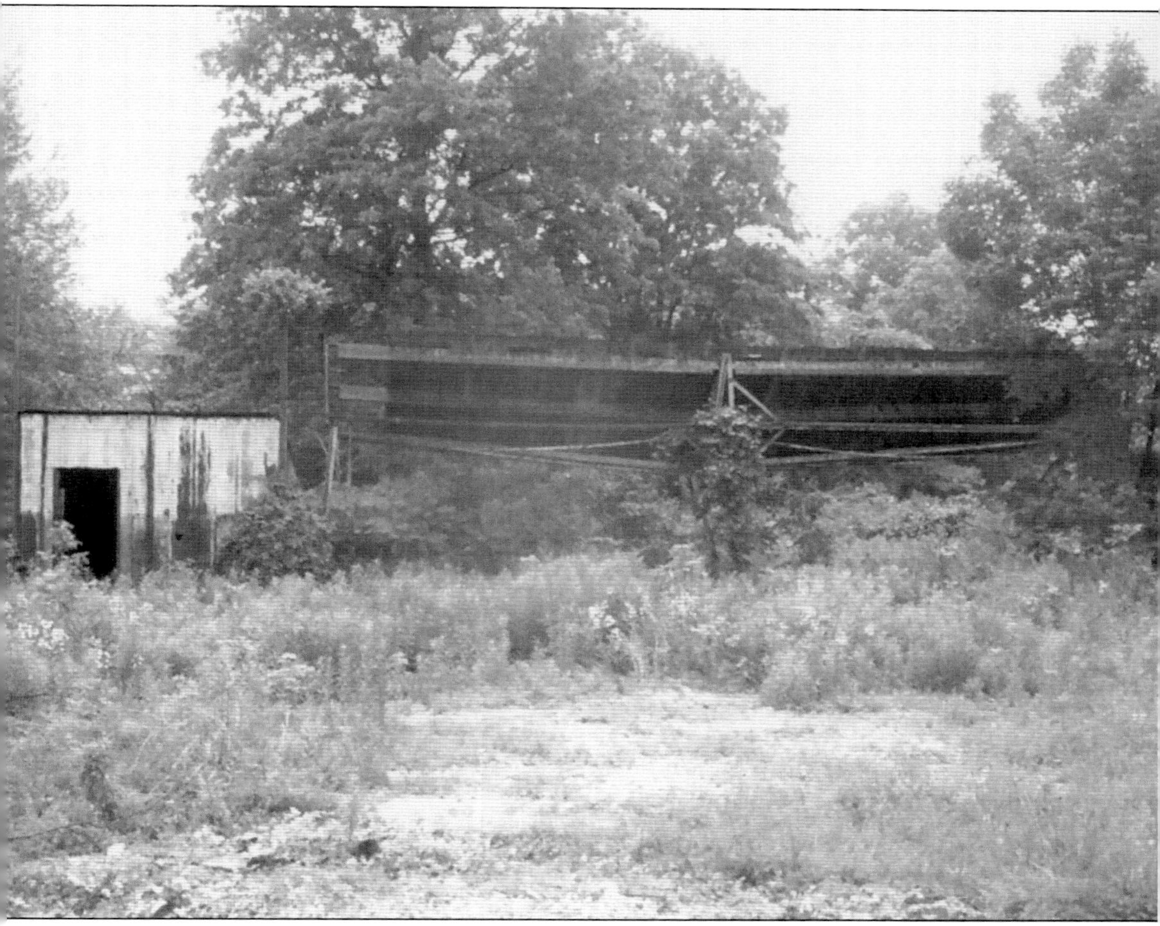

The remnants of airport buildings, photographed in June 1973, stand off of Route 1. The New Jersey State Forest Fire Service operated an airport on state-owned land between Route 1 and Baker's Basin through at least the 1950s. Planes stationed at the airport would have been responsible for doing surveillance flights over the forests of southern New Jersey to detect and assist in the suppression of forest fires. The airport was closed in either the late 1950s or early 1960s, but the state retained the property. Eventually, the State of New Jersey built a Department of Motor Vehicles inspection facility and a television/radio transmission tower for New Jersey Network on the property, both of which are still in use. It is unknown when the airport was originally built, but it is evident from maps of the area that some type of airport existed on the property as early as the 1920s. There is no indication on the earlier maps as to the proprietorship of the facility, so it is unclear whether it was a state-owned at that time.

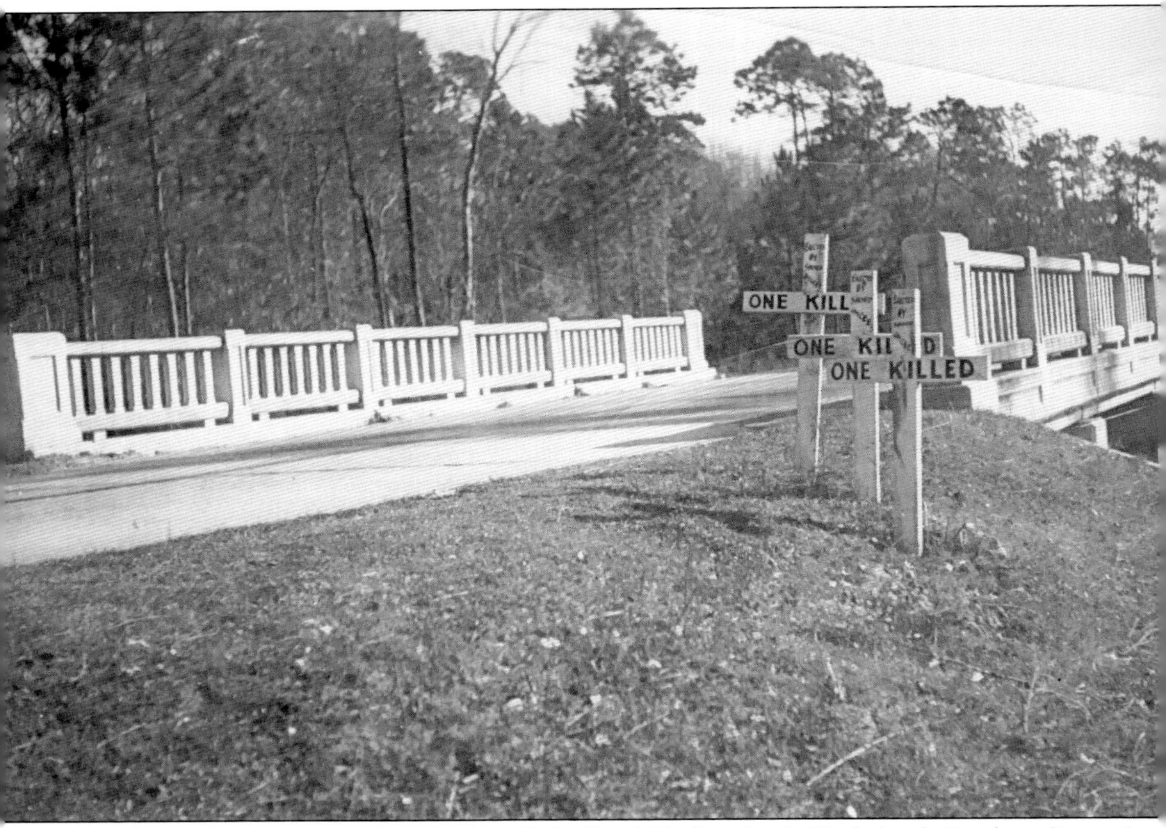

This bridge, seen around 1948, crossed the Five Mile Run/Little Shabakunk Creek on Route 1 near Allen Lane. The crosses marked the deaths of three travelers killed in an accident. Route 1, then called Brunswick Pike, started out as a dirt road through a wooded lot and grew to a two-lane, macadam road in the early 20th century. In 1930, it was paved with cement and expanded to four lanes. As traffic and speed increased, a series of horrific accidents occurred on the road, particularly between Allen Lane and Bakers Basin. Several truck and bus accidents with a high casualty-rate led to citizen concerns about the safety of the road. One newspaper report counted the fatalities at 43, with over 500 injuries in a one-year span. The town responded by setting up speed traps and creating a traffic safety committee.

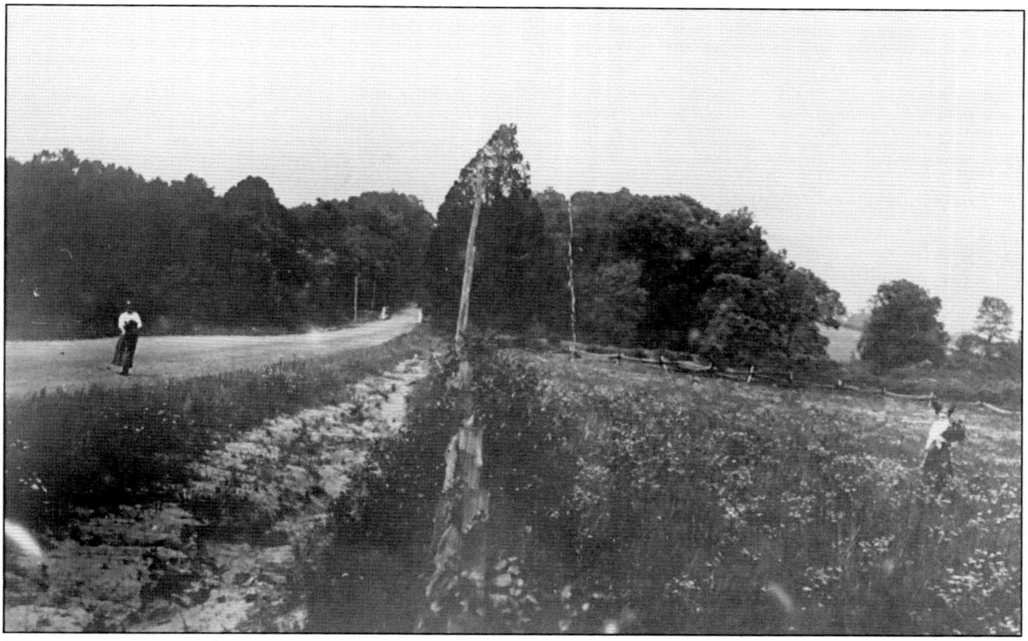

This c. 1910 view of Stevens' Meadow shows Brunswick Pike to the left with the bridge over the Shabakunk Creek in the distance. Brunswick Pike was once nothing more than a dirt lane through some farms and wooded areas. At the time of this picture, the one-lane road was macadamized, surfaced with a mixture of stone and binding agent. The road was expanded to two lanes when it was paved in cement during the 1930s.

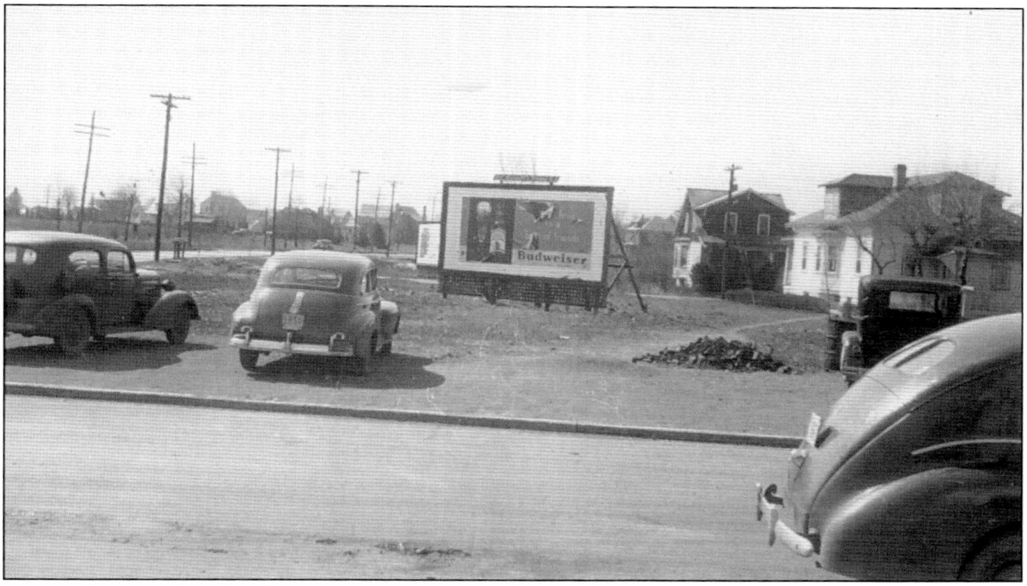

Pictured around 1940, the intersection on Eldridge Avenue and Lawrence Road (Route 206) features a billboard, which stood on the empty lot for nearly 70 years. The billboard originally stood further north, but was moved to the lot when St. Ann's Church was built in 1937. Houses and shopping centers were built around the billboard, and the surrounding empty lot served as a parking area.

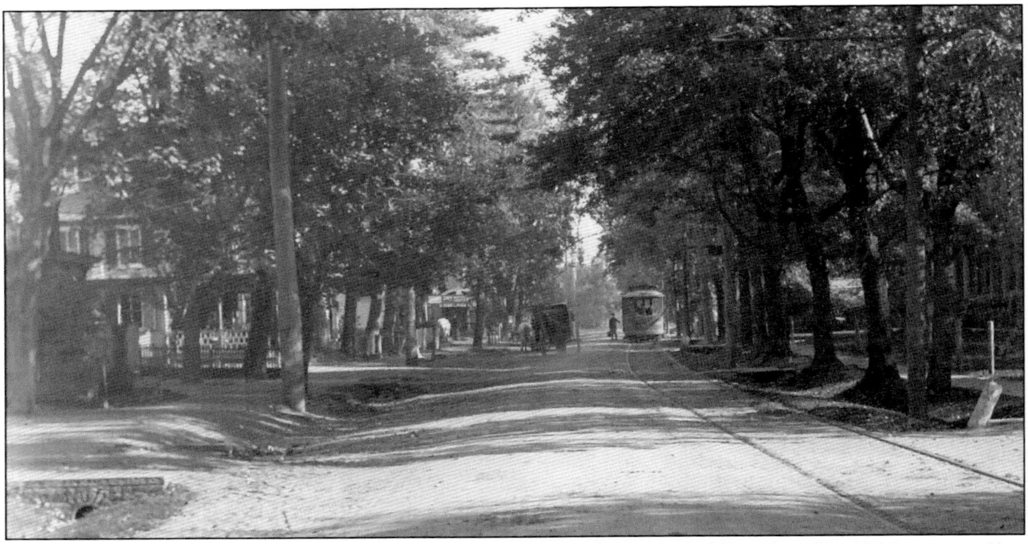

Two forms of transportation passed each other on the afternoon of October 22, 1902, as a trolley and a horse-drawn carriage both stopped to pick up passengers in front of Furman's Dry Goods Store on Main Street. Main Street, also known as Route 206 (and by many other names), has been the main roadway through town since the founding of Maidenhead in the 1600s.

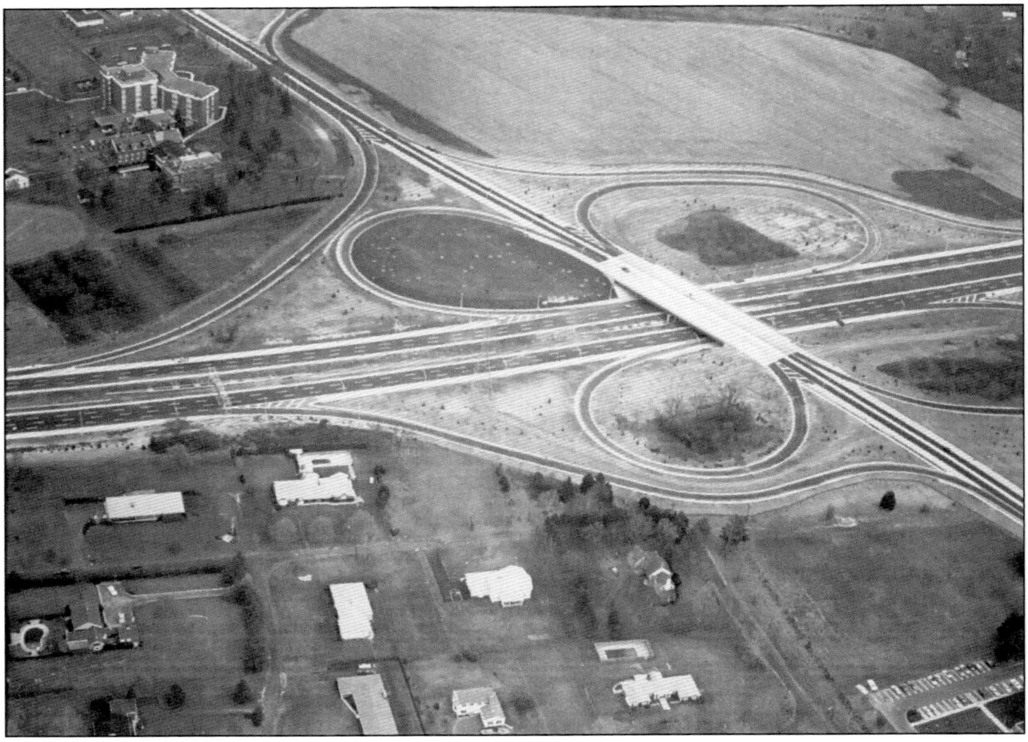

The Interstate 295 and Route 206 interchange, shortly after construction was completed, on November 27, 1974. Construction of Interstate 295 began in 1972 and was finished in 1974. In the upper left-hand corner stand Morris Hall and St. Lawrence Rehabilitation Center. Just below those buildings and the new highway are houses in the Long Acres neighborhood.

Ten

WEATHER, ETC.

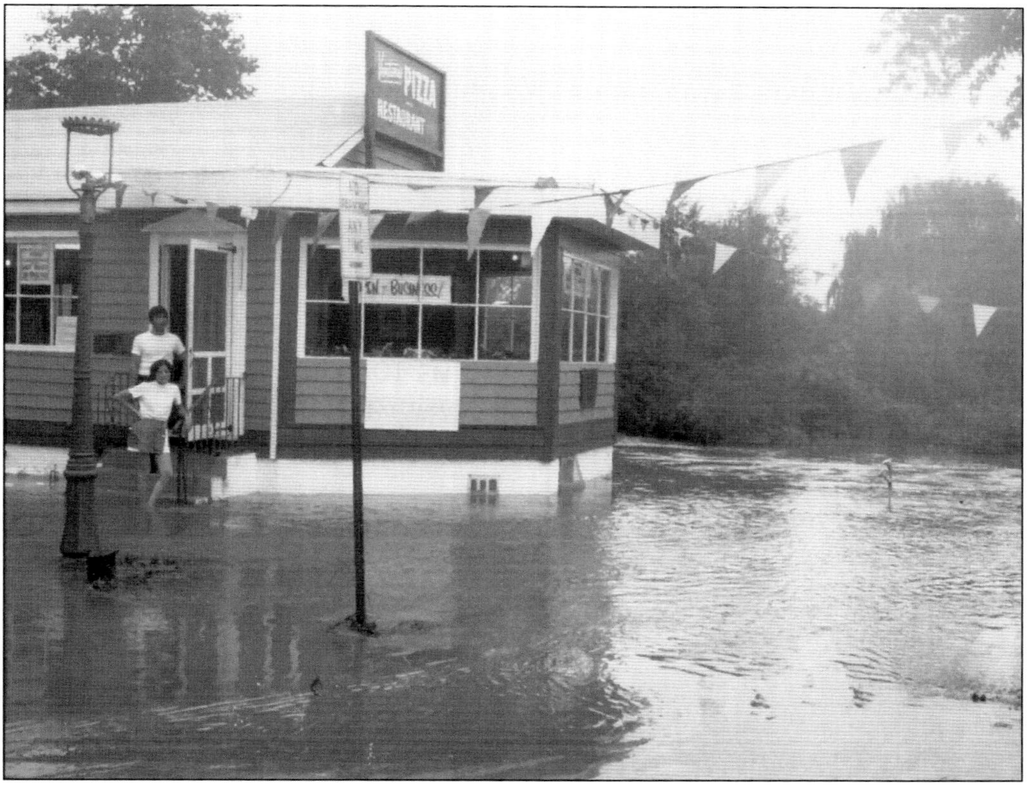

Despite flooding in their parking lot, brought on by Hurricane Doria, Ventura Pizza Restaurant stayed open for business. The pizzeria was located at the corner of Allen Lane and Brunswick Pike. The little stand-alone restaurant survived a rough beginning when its owners failed to obtain the proper permits prior to opening in the summer of 1971. The building succumbed to a fire in August 1974.

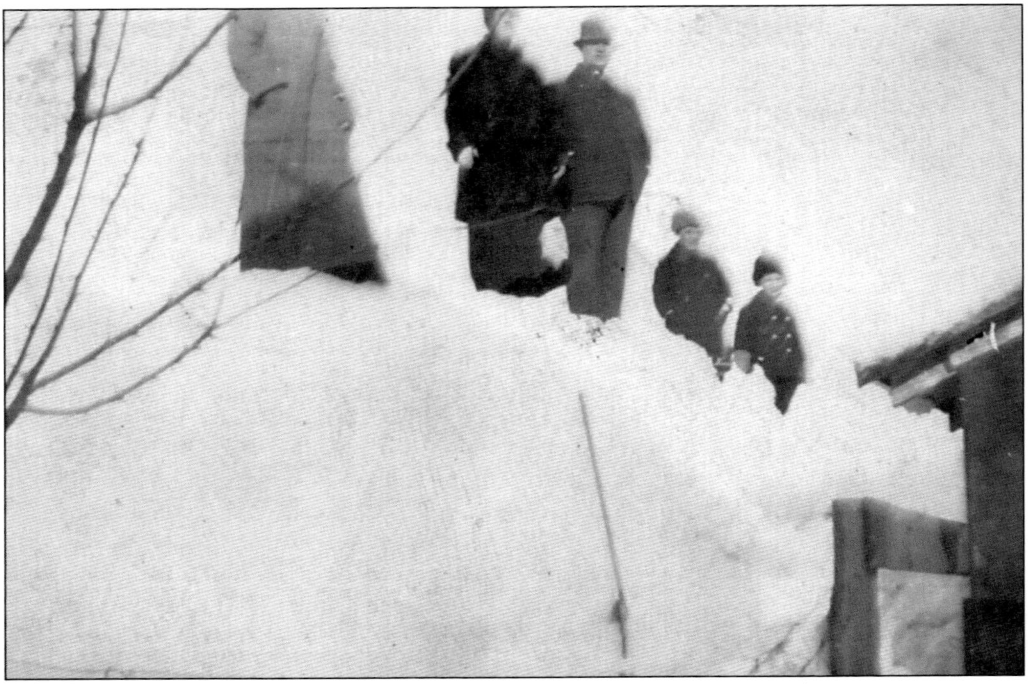

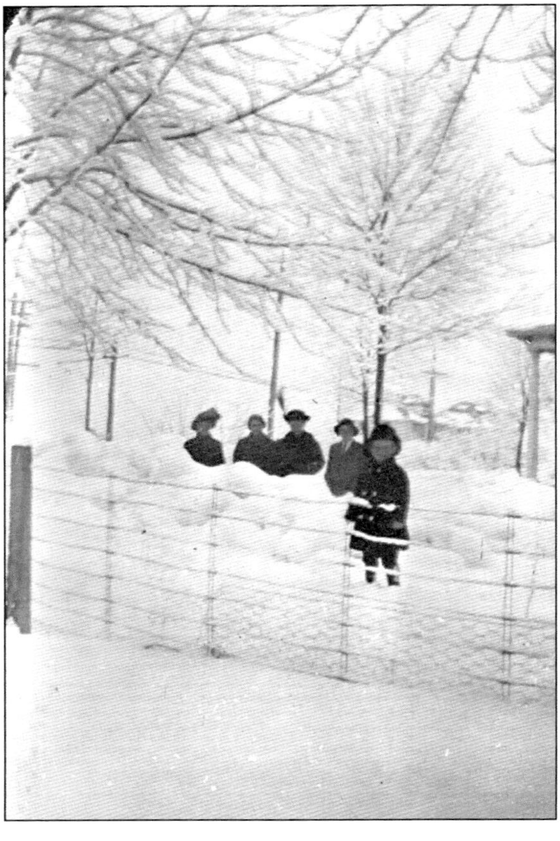

A blizzard blanketed Mercer County with up to 20 inches of snow on February 13th and 14th, 1914, causing traffic delays, particularly on the trolley lines. Most Lawrence residents could not go into the city for work or shopping. The storm's high winds produced very tall drifts, such as this one on Lawrence Road, which grew to the height of the garage roof. Residents are seen on top of the garage roof (above) while neighborhood children make snow forts in a nearby yard (left). The initial storm was followed by bitter cold and two smaller storms the same week, making it difficult to clear the streets and rails.

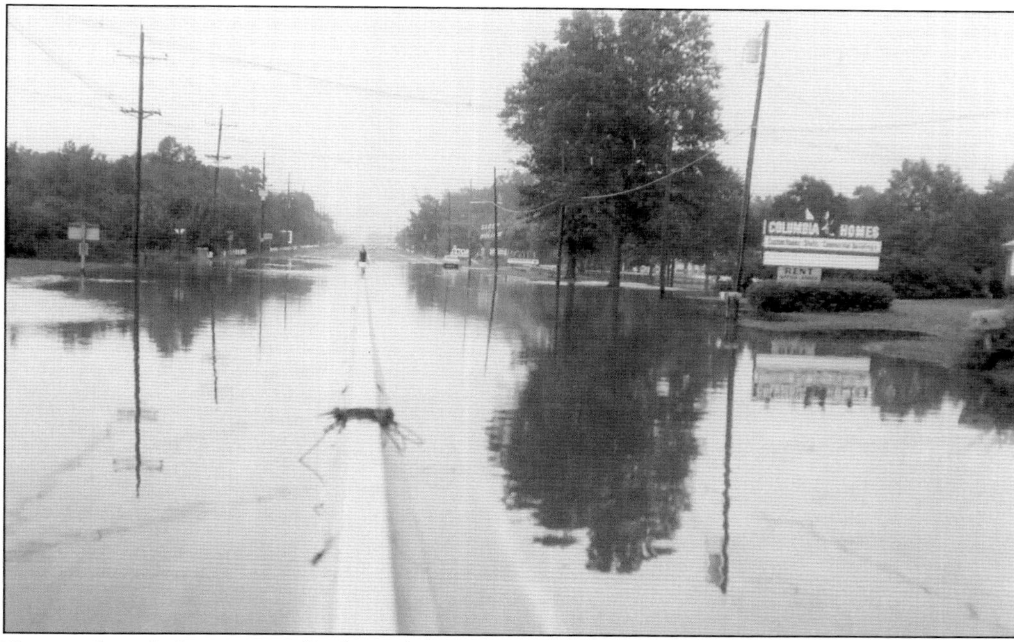

Two unidentified women walk along the concrete divider on Route 1 on the afternoon of August 28, 1971. Heavy rain from Hurricane Doria flooded the low-lying area, including the Sleep-E-Hollow Motel, seen to the right. The Sleep-E-Hollow has been flooded by three hurricanes in the last 40 years: Doria (1971), Floyd (1999), and Irene (2011).

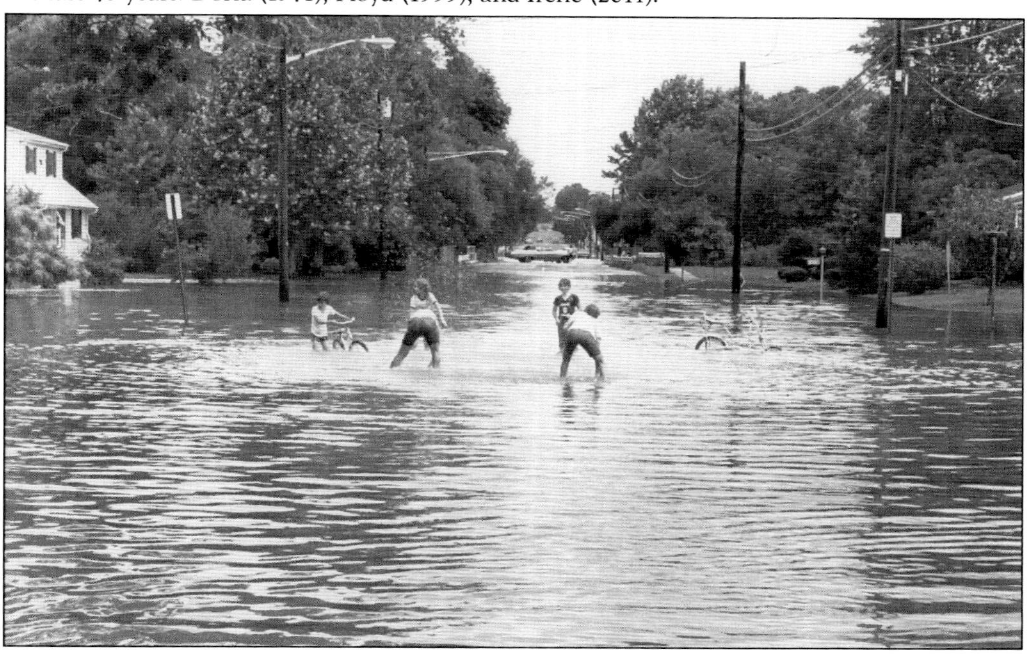

The southern part of the township also saw heavy flooding from Hurricane Doria. Children splashed in the deep floodwaters from the Shabakunk Creek, which reached the intersection of Graf Avenue and Princeton Pike. The Shabakunk used to flood frequently near Lawrence Shopping Center, and one July 1975 flood left up to three feet of water in the center's stores.

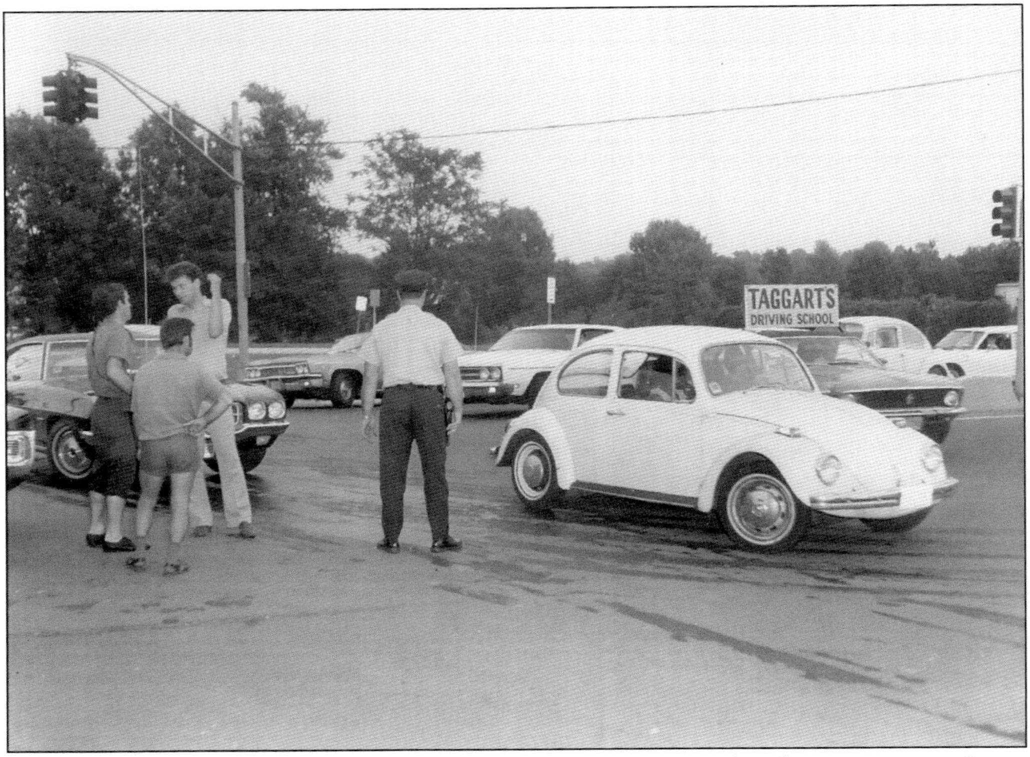

Traffic became congested at the intersection of Route 1 and Baker's Basin Road after Hurricane Doria hit Mercer County on August 28, 1971. Water overflowed from the nearby Delaware and Raritan Canal, which was flooded by water running into it from the Stony Brook. A police officer is seen directing drivers to make a U-turn at the intersection, sending cars back down the southbound side of Route 1.

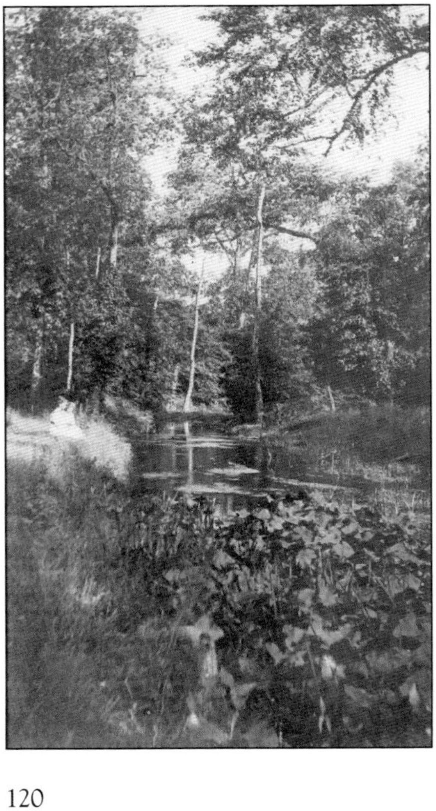

Before the man-made lake was created in 1923, the area now known as Colonial Lakelands was a wooded plot of land with a large marsh. Lawrence residents used the area for walking, bird watching, and fishing in the Shabakunk Creek. Two women are seen sitting by the creek, around 1910. The Colonial Land Company converted the area into a housing development and transformed the marsh into a lake.

Stone roadside-markers, such as this one, were once used to denote historic locations in New Jersey. This particular one marks the "route of Washington's march by night from Trenton to Princeton and victory January 5, 1777." The markers were installed in the early 1900s.

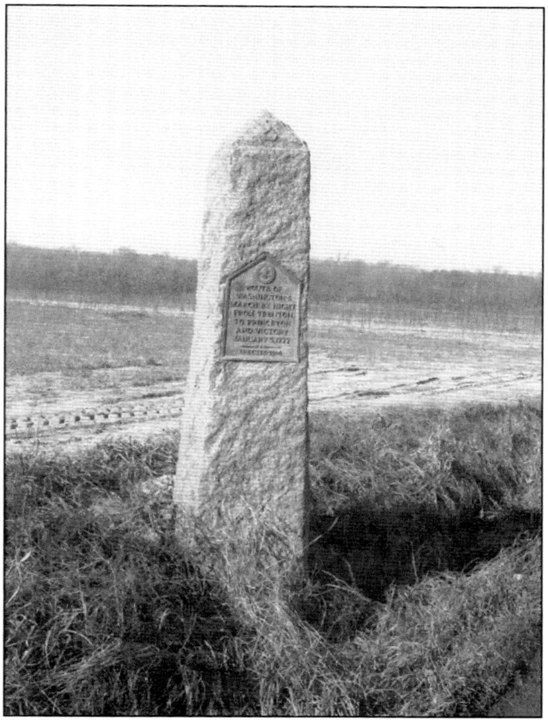

George Phillips was a farmer who lived in Lawrenceville in the 1800s. His diary, which holds entries from about 1835 to 1865, is housed in the township archives. It contains details about weather and farming, descriptions of church services, brief records of business, and other observations about daily life in the town.

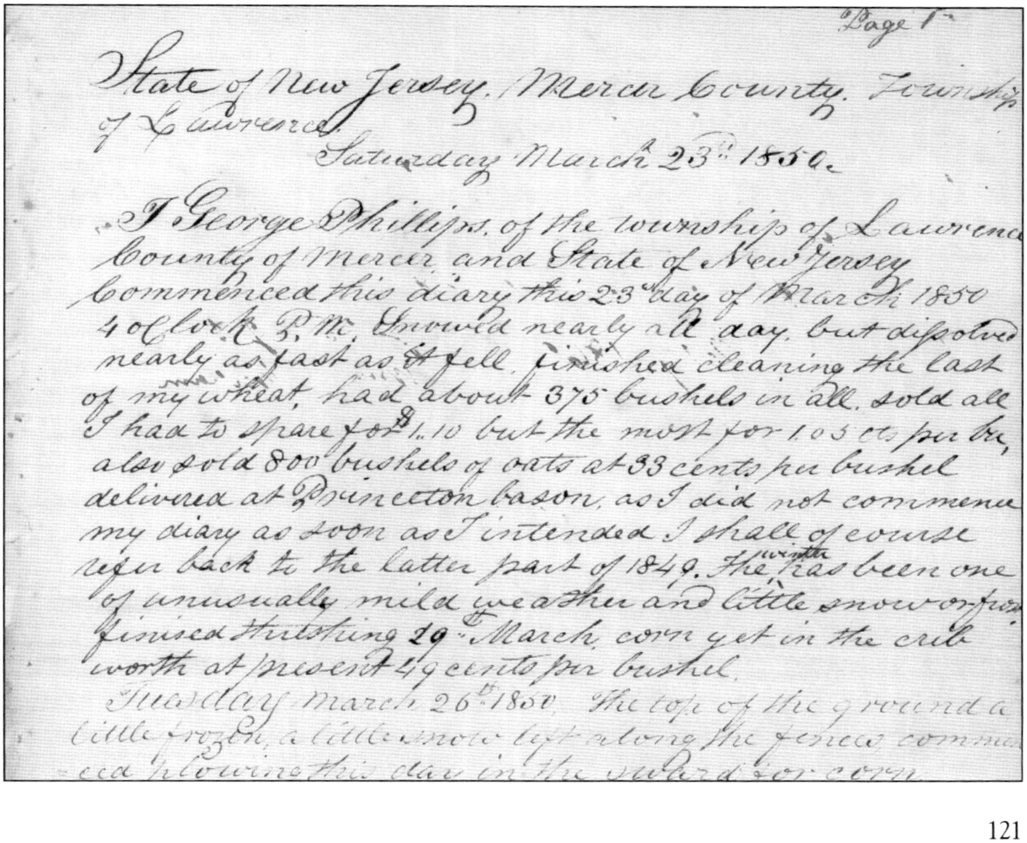

Page 1

State of New Jersey. Mercer County. Township of Lawrence.

Saturday March 23rd 1850.

I George Phillips, of the township of Lawrence County of Mercer and State of New Jersey Commenced this diary this 23rd day of March 1850 4 o'clock P.M. Snowed nearly all day, but dissolved nearly as fast as it fell, finished cleaning the last of my wheat, had about 375 bushels in all, sold all I had to spare for $1.10 but the most for 1.05 cts per bu, also sold 800 bushels of oats at 33 cents per bushel delivered at Princeton bason, as I did not commence my diary as soon as I intended I shall of course refer back to the latter part of 1849. The winter has been one of unusually mild weather and little snow or frost finised threshing 29th March, corn yet in the crib worth at present 49 cents per bushel.

Tuesday march 26th 1850. The top of the ground a little frozen, a little snow left along the fences commenced plowing this day in the sward for corn.

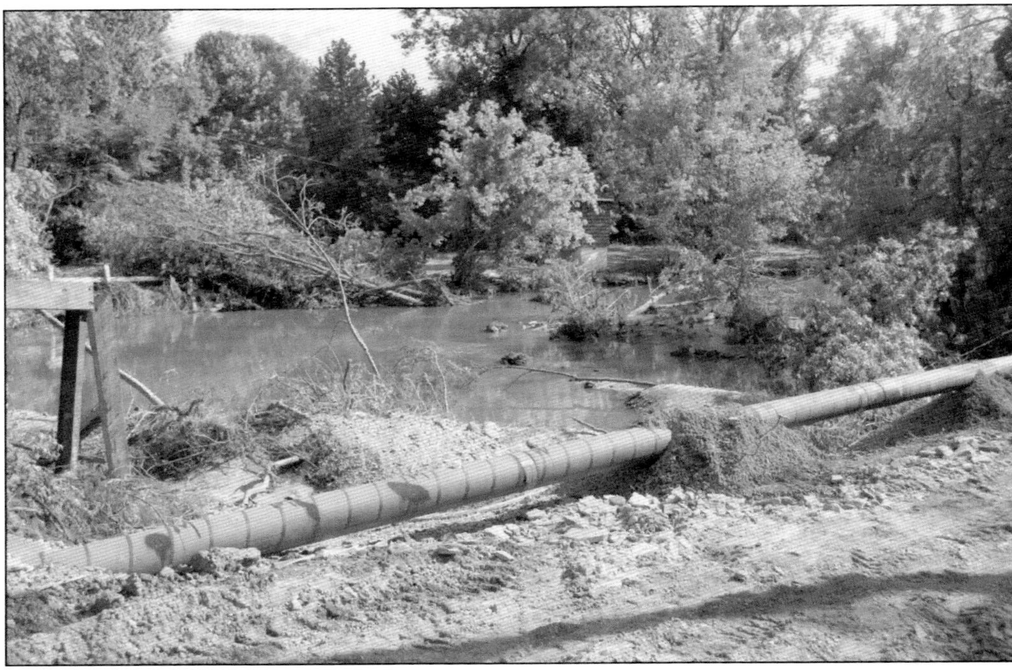

Hurricane Irene hit Lawrence Township with heavy rain and wind on August 28, 2011, and left flooding and debris in her wake. Above, flooding from Stony Brook caused a breach of the Delaware and Raritan Canal at Port Mercer, exposing a high-pressure gas line and leaving toppled trees lying in the canal. Below, excess water from the canal spilled onto Route 1, between Bakers Basin and Quaker Bridge Roads. An abandoned car floated under the high tension tower near the I-95 interchange. (Courtesy of Laura Nawrocik.)

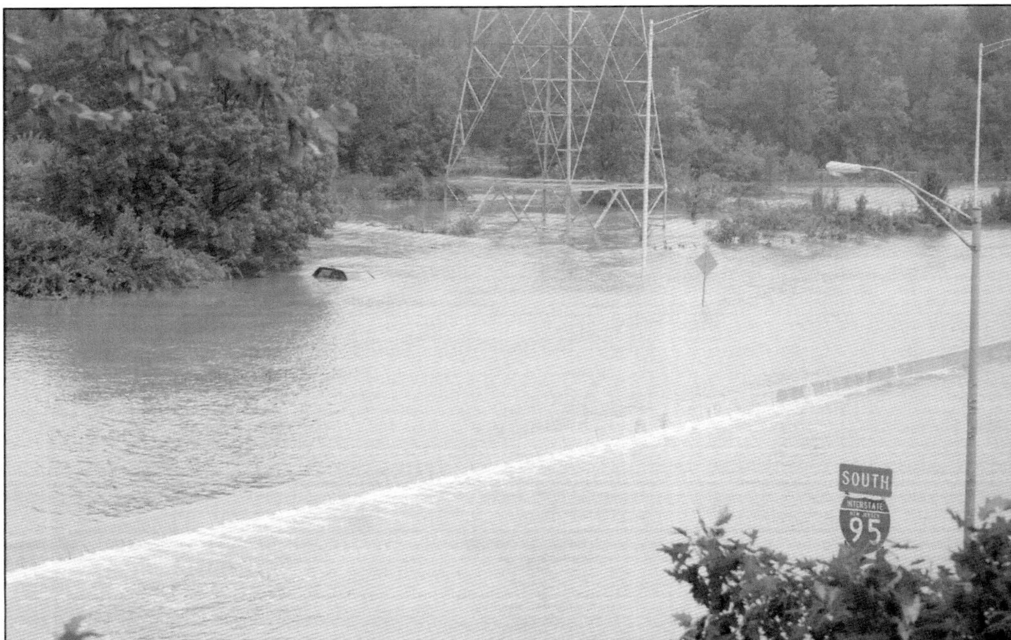

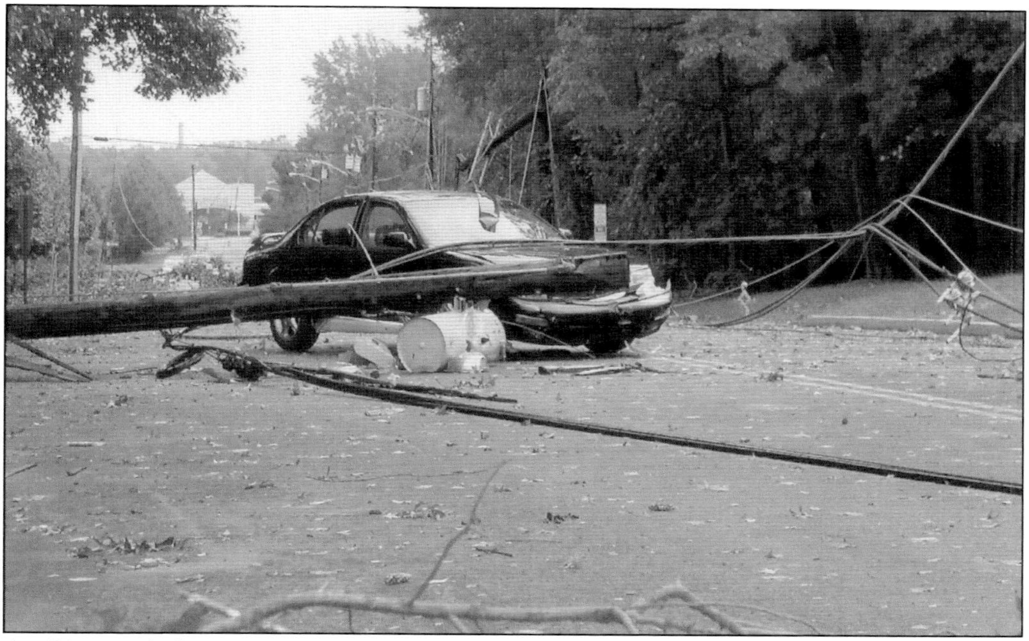

An F0 tornado hit Lawrence in September 2003, cutting a swath of destruction through the Nassau and Norgate neighborhoods. Damage to structures was minimal, but many mature trees in the neighborhood were toppled by the high winds. A car on the corner of Darrah Lane East and Glenn Avenue was caught in the path of a falling utility pole. (Courtesy of Laura Nawrocik.)

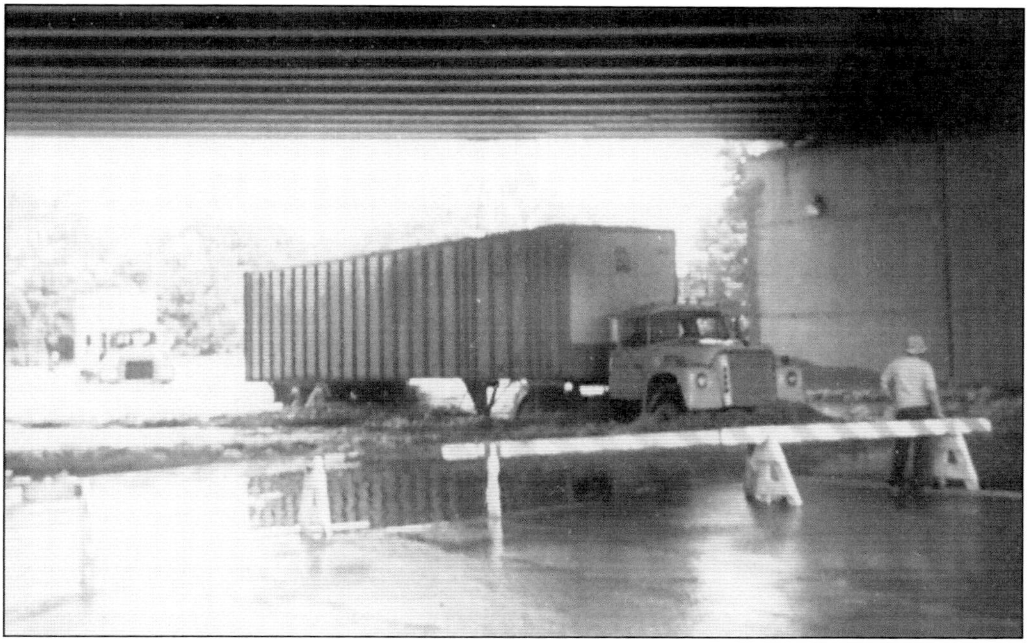

These Mack trucks tried to make their way under the Route 1 overpass on Whitehead Road near the Assunpink Creek on July 14, 1975. Due to intense rainfall during a storm, the Assunpink Creek basin had flooded during the night. No lives were lost, but there was immense damage to the surrounding buildings, houses, and water supply systems.

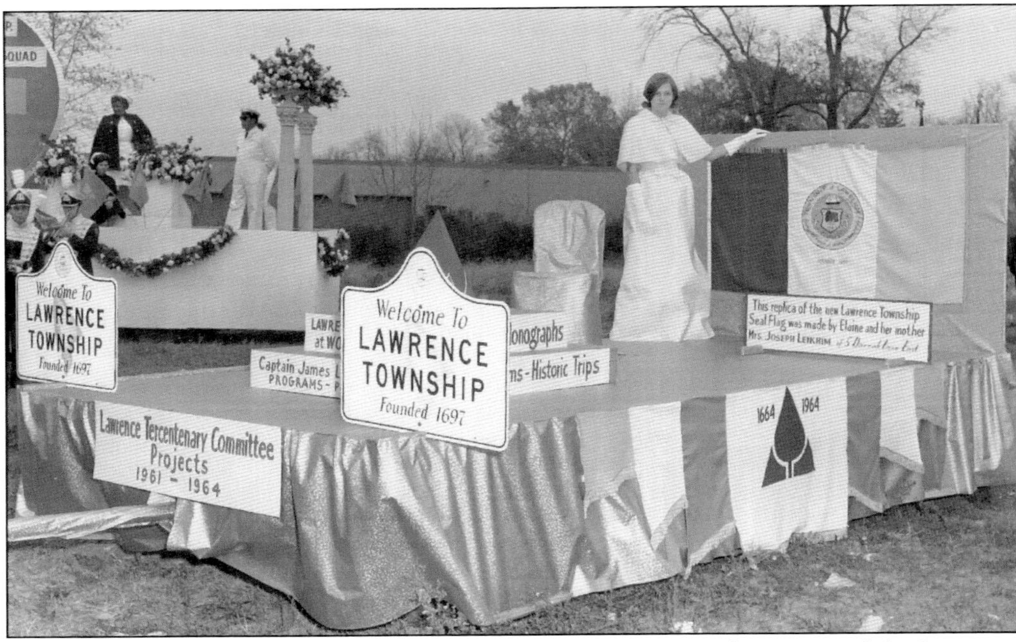

The township flag was on display during a November 1964 parade, as part of the Lawrence Tercentenary Committee float. The flag was presented to the township by the Lions Club in December, 1963. There had previously been no official flag. A replica was made for the float by Elaine Leikhim and her mother.

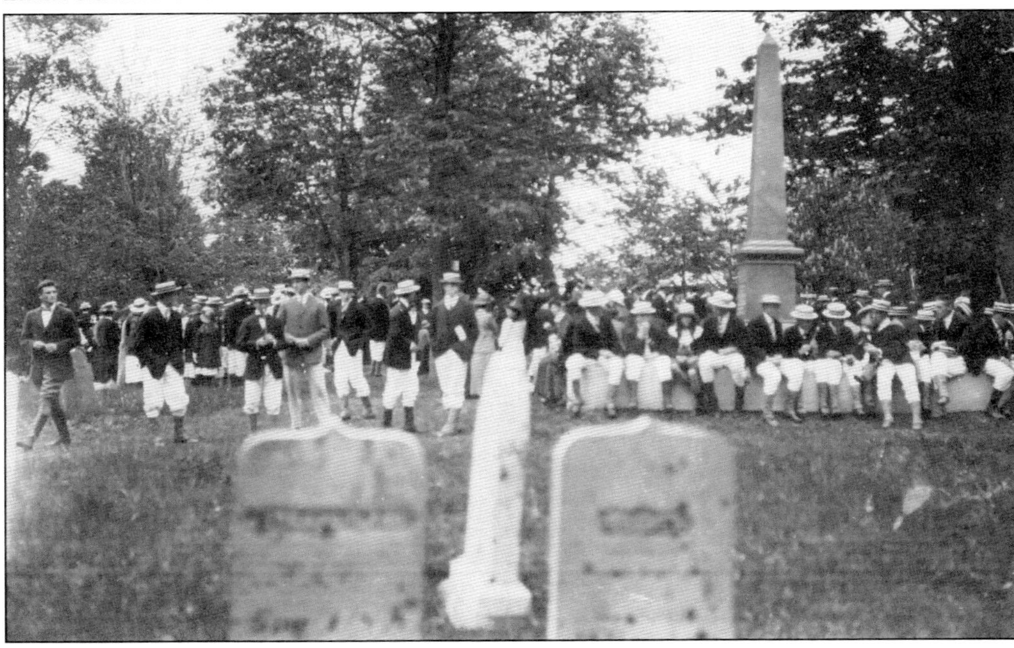

A group of young men gather around a stone monument in the Upper Cemetery, around 1900, possibly as part of a Memorial Day ceremony. The cemetery dates to 1857 and sits adjacent to the Upper Burial Ground on Route 206. As of 1997, it was the only cemetery in the township that still received burials.

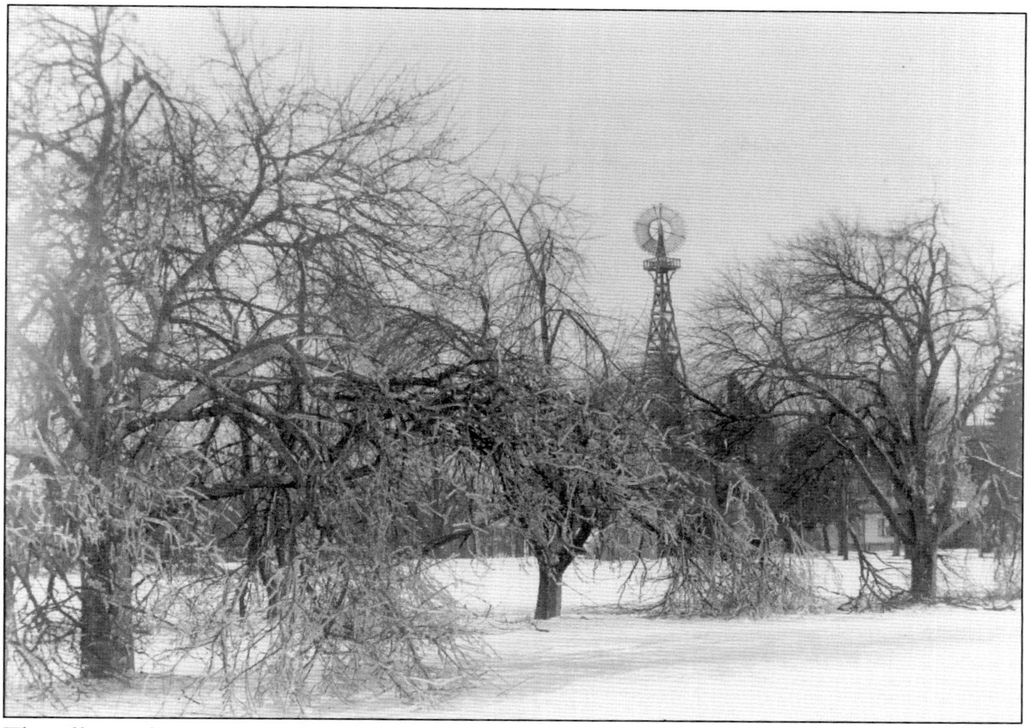

The effects of a severe wind- and rainstorm that took place on the night of February 23, 1902, can be seen in the Green orchard (above) and next to the Brearley home on Main Street (below). Rain and cold temperatures led to icing conditions and, when paired with the high winds, caused downed trees and telegraph wires.

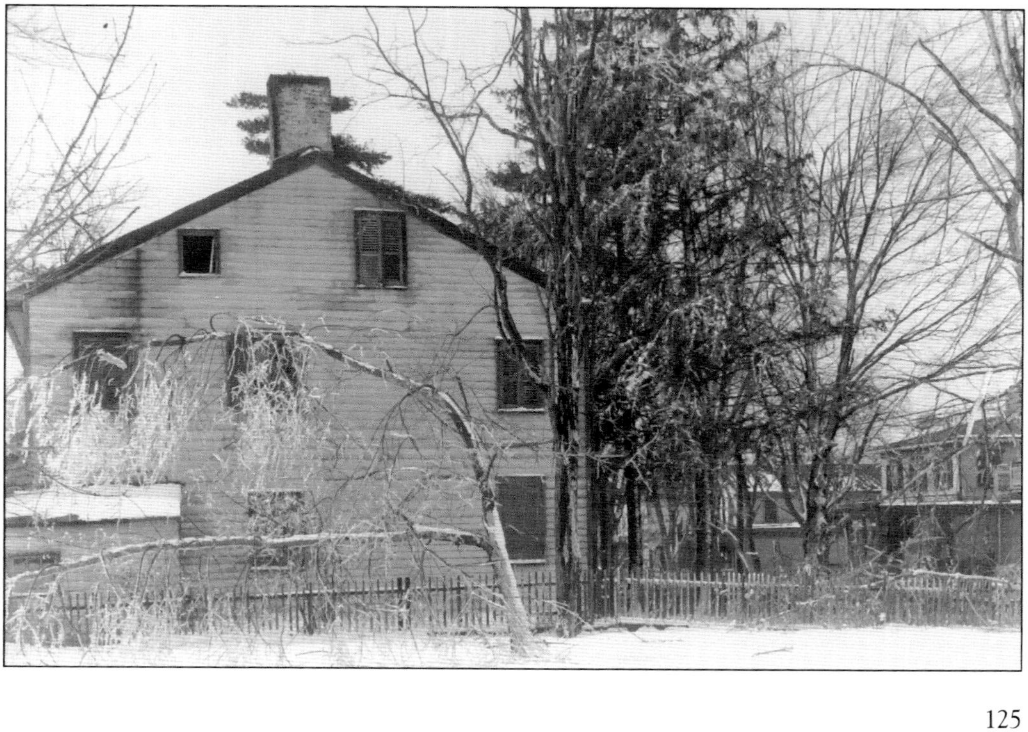

BIBLIOGRAPHY

Barth, Linda. *The Delaware and Raritan Canal.* Charleston, SC: Arcadia Publishing, 2002.
Brower, Walter. *Full of Promise: The Story of Rider College, 1865–1994.* Private, 1997.
Celebrating 300 Years. Succasunna, NJ: Jostens, 1997.
Lawrence Township. *A Guide to Lawrenceville's Historic Landmarks, 2nd ed.* Lawrence, NJ: Three Bears Publishing, 2009.
Middleton, Kathleen. *Lawrence Township.* Augusta, ME: Alan Sutton, 1994.
Mulford, Roland J. *History of The Lawrenceville School.* Princeton, NJ: Princeton University Press, 1935.
Tyler, Donald H. *Old Lawrenceville: Early Houses and People.* Private, 1965.

About the Organization

Lawrence Historical Society was founded in 1975 as a non-profit group dedicated to the preservation and promotion of Lawrence Township history. The society is the designated caretaker of two historic houses in the township, the 1761 Brearley House and the Port Mercer Canal House. In addition to offering house tours and the popular New Year's Eve Hogmanay Bonfire, the society hosts several educational events each year, including the Annual Meeting each winter and the Mary Tanner Lecture in the fall. The society also sponsors a scholarship for a deserving high school senior each spring and offers internship opportunities for college students.

For more information about Lawrence Historical Society, contact us:

www.thelhs.org
Lawrence Historical Society
PO Box 6025
Lawrenceville, NJ 08648